The Women Who
Saved Catholic England

The Women Who Saved Catholic England

Risking All to Protect Tudor and Stuart Priests

Martyn Beardsley

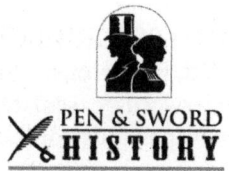

First published in Great Britain in 2024 by
Pen & Sword History
An imprint of Pen & Sword Books Limited
Yorkshire – Philadelphia

Copyright © Martyn Beardsley 2024

ISBN 978 1 39904 230 7

The right of Martyn Beardsley to be identified as
Author of this Work has been asserted by him in accordance
with the Copyright, Designs and Patents Act 1988.

A CIP catalogue record for this book is
available from the British Library

All rights reserved. No part of this book may be reproduced or transmitted in any form or by any means, electronic or mechanical including photocopying, recording or by any information storage and retrieval system, without permission from the Publisher in writing.

Typeset by Mac Style
Printed in the UK by CPI Group (UK) Ltd, Croydon, CR0 4YY.

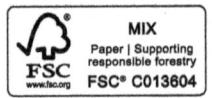

Pen & Sword Books Limited incorporates the imprints of After the Battle, Atlas, Archaeology, Aviation, Discovery, Family History, Fiction, History, Maritime, Military, Military Classics, Politics, Select, Transport, True Crime, Air World, Frontline Publishing, Leo Cooper, Remember When, Seaforth Publishing, The Praetorian Press, Wharncliffe Local History, Wharncliffe Transport, Wharncliffe True Crime and White Owl.

For a complete list of Pen & Sword titles please contact

PEN & SWORD BOOKS LIMITED
47 Church Street, Barnsley, South Yorkshire, S70 2AS, England
E-mail: enquiries@pen-and-sword.co.uk
Website: www.pen-and-sword.co.uk
or
PEN AND SWORD BOOKS
1950 Lawrence Rd, Havertown, PA 19083, USA
E-mail: uspen-and-sword@casematepublishers.com
Website: www.penandswordbooks.com

'It is primarily to the great Catholic families that the survival of Catholicism is due. Without their heroic zeal, their wealth, and their great houses, the work of the priests would have been impossible. Few amongst the wealthy families were as prominent as the Vaux.'

Godfrey Anstruther
The Vaux of Harrowden

Contents

Introduction		viii
Chapter 1	The Pearl of York	1
Chapter 2	Mother of all the Good Wives in York	8
Chapter 3	Consider Well What You Do	15
Chapter 4	An Innocent Lamb	36
Chapter 5	Growing Greatly in Debt	42
Chapter 6	Illustrious by Birth	57
Chapter 7	To Die for Christ	64
Chapter 8	Graceful Comeliness	77
Chapter 9	A Man of Cruelty	85
Chapter 10	A Wise Woman	102
Chapter 11	These Wild Heads Had Something in Hand	110
Chapter 12	Why Then, Lady, You Must Die	123
Chapter 13	Where is Mrs Ann?	131
Chapter 14	The Jesuit Has Not Had Fair Play	139
Chapter 15	Never Had a Priest Been Taken Under her Roof	147
Appendix I: Brief Overview of Catholicism in England After the Vaux Sisters		160
Appendix II: The Featured Priests and Associates		162
Appendix III: Locations Mentioned in the Book		178
Bibliography		192

Introduction

During the course of researching and writing a book about the Gunpowder Plot (*The Gunpowder Plot Deceit*, Pen & Sword), I was struck by the courageous and absolutely vital role played by women in protecting the priests from whom the Catholic plotters received their spiritual guidance and ministrations. The priests themselves had nothing to do with the Plot; in fact they condemned it, partly on moral grounds, but also because they knew there would be devastating repercussions for Catholics in general, and them in particular. The Protestant government, with its highly effective spy network and propaganda machine, was keen to use any means – fair or foul – to blacken the reputations of the priests in order to justify their capture, torture and execution. This applied especially to the Jesuits, who feature strongly in this story.

The work of the women whose lives we shall be examining has been likened to that of the French Resistance, particularly the way they provided a network of 'safe houses' and how they were able to move priests from imminent danger to a place of safety in the way that soldiers and downed Allied pilots were helped by the French during the Second World War.

There are some important differences, of course. The Resistance was formed because the country was occupied by a foreign power, and it specialized not just in sheltering the vulnerable but attacking the enemy. England, on the other hand, was not invaded – not even by the Spanish – but was simply in a state of religious turmoil. And the Catholic Resistance was for the most part a private affair consisting of people merely trying to practise their faith in peace, and never really engaged in aggressive action. (I'm classing things like the Gunpowder Plot – in many ways an anomaly – the Northern and Essex rebellions and the Babington Plot as being more to do with power and politics, despite religion being a prominent factor.)

Thus, the major difference between the people who will feature in this story and the work of the wartime Resistance was that the primary role of the latter organization was to attack, whereas the sole desire of the Elizabethan and Jacobean Catholic Underground was to defend and protect. The only lives at risk were their own.

One strong similarity between the two movements is that many of those who fell into 'enemy' hands and were tortured, and sometimes died, did so because they had been betrayed by traitors, sometimes for religious reasons but often for money.

In addition to the priests and their protectors, there was a third category of person in the Underground movement, the collateral victims caught in the net because of their association with the main targets: occasionally friends and associates, but mostly the servants and children of the principal actors. Once they had them, the authorities knew just how to apply the right sort of pressure, not hesitating to use lies and threats as a means of extracting information.

The life of the priest and the helper was one of uncertainty and anxiety, never sure who to trust, constantly having to move from one compromised location to another. The Elizabethan and early Jacobean spy network was probably as good as any that ever existed, and better than most. To be fair to Queen Elizabeth and her ministers, this was a time of justified fears about Spanish interference and even possible invasion, and of internal plotting against the queen and the government. The Spanish Armada, along with the Babington and Gunpowder plots mentioned above (and there were others), demonstrate this perfectly, and show that it was not mere paranoia or authoritarianism that lay behind the prevailing atmosphere. The problem was that the government could not, or chose not to, separate the Catholic desire for tolerance of their religion from the threat to the Crown and State. The vast majority of Catholics, and all of the main players in this story, were patriotic and loyal to their monarch. They just wanted to be able to worship, baptize, marry and bury according to their tradition – which had been the whole nation's tradition until relatively recently.

* * *

I began by mentioning the Gunpowder Plot, but the period we are interested in begins well before that foolhardy enterprise was ever dreamt up.

In many ways, the heroine of this story is Anne Vaux, but we shall begin by looking at the life of Margaret Clitherow of York. The stories of these two very different but equally brave women will help to illustrate the part played by class and status in the way such people – male and female – were treated in this era. Margaret Clitherow wasn't a peasant – her husband was a successful tradesman and leading citizen of York – but she wasn't noble-born like Anne. Margaret Clitherow's ultimate fate has become famous in a notorious sort of way, but no English noblewoman was ever tortured or martyred in the Catholic cause; indeed, there was a reluctance to even commit them to prison (although eventually some were). It just didn't sit right with the authorities that people of noble birth should be thrown among the lower orders in stinking, disease-ridden jails – and perhaps it is reasonable to say that in doing so, they would have been inflicting a greater punishment on the person involved.

But this is with the benefit of hindsight. Even the daughter of a baron like Anne Vaux could never be sure that they wouldn't end up on the rack or the gallows, and some were threatened with it. For the Margaret Clitherows of this world, it was more of a personal affair – them against the authorities. What makes Anne Vaux and others like her different is that because of their wealth, their large homes and their ability to rent other properties around the country, they were able to keep alive the whole Catholic Underground movement. Their husbands and fathers were generally in London most of the time, and it was they who were left to manage and partially finance the secret Catholic networks, and who bore the brunt of the harassment by the authorities. Without them, there could have been few, if any, priests in circulation, and without the priests, Catholicism in England may even have withered and died.

* * *

A couple of points about some of the terminology used in the book.

For simplicity's sake, I have tended to call Anne and Eleanor Vaux 'the Vaux sisters', even after Eleanor married and became a Brooksby. A single woman like Anne Vaux was sometimes referred to as 'Mrs' Vaux, which can be a little confusing since as an abbreviation of 'mistress' it is the root word of both the modern 'Miss' *and* 'Mrs'. At this time, 'mistress' was just as likely to indicate that a woman was the mistress of her house, in the same way that a man could be termed the master of the house, regardless of marital status.

Anne and Eleanor had a step-sister, Elizabeth, after their father's remarriage. They already had a sister called Elizabeth, not to mention a mother and grandmother bearing the same name, so to avoid confusion, as this step-sister signed her letters as 'Eliza' and was probably known to her family and friends by that name (perhaps for the same reasons I am citing here), that is how she will be referred to in this book. (She is also commonly called 'the Dowager Lady Vaux'.)

The Cecils William and Robert, father and son, both held senior posts under Queen Elizabeth, and Robert also under James I, including responsibility for intelligence work. William became Lord Burghley during the time covered by this story, and Robert the Earl of Salisbury. They are sometimes referred to by their noble titles, but more often as one or the other 'Cecil', and I have opted to go down that route. To make things easier, unless otherwise stated, all mentions of 'Cecil' refer to Robert, who was trained in spycraft by the renowned Francis Walsingham.

Finally, the pronunciation of the Vaux family surname. It should rhyme with 'hawks' rather than 'go'. This seems so counterintuitive that even having worked on this book for two years, and even now as I write this, in my head it still rhymes with 'go'. Perhaps the reader will have better luck!

* * *

I would like to thank Martin Dodwell for letting me use his pictures of Braddocks, and, as ever, the brilliant team at Pen and Sword.

Chapter 1

The Pearl of York

Margaret Clitherow

On 25 March 1586, an execution took place in York, the gruesome details of which reverberated around not just that city but all of England and further afield. Even in a Europe used to religious persecution, torture and grizzly executions, the circumstances, method and victim of the judicial killing still had the capacity to shock.

How had it come to this? It's easy to forget that Britain had been a Catholic country in belief, practice and culture ever since Christianity had reached the British Isles. The term 'Catholic' can be, and sometimes is, applied to Protestant Christianity, since its literal meaning is merely 'universal' (which explains why I was always puzzled that my Protestant christening certificate referred to the Catholic Church!). But I am using it here in the way that it is understood by most people, i.e. as a shorthand form of 'Roman Catholic'. Alfred the Great himself visited Rome and was introduced to the Pope, and the Roman form of Christianity was ingrained in people's lives, informed the way they worshipped, celebrated birth, death and marriage, and what they believed about the afterlife. There is a debate about how much Celtic Christianity differed from the religion as prescribed by Rome, but that is as nothing when compared with the cataclysmic effect of the growth of what came to be called Protestantism. Although the conversion of the country didn't happen overnight, it is hard to underestimate what a profound change it eventually wrought and how profoundly it affected the lives of ordinary people at a time when religious belief and conformity had a far more central place in their lives than today. It was perhaps culturally the most fundamental shift ever to take place in this country; arguably even more profound, albeit not so sudden, than the Norman conquest.

2 The Women Who Saved Catholic England

The Protestant Reformation itself can be traced back to Martin Luther, but the person associated with the religious revolution as far as England is concerned, in the minds of most people, is obviously Luther's contemporary, Henry VIII. This is part of the truth, but not the whole picture. Relatively few people are probably aware that for the rest of his life after his split with Rome, Henry remained as committed a Catholic (hearing up to five Masses a day) as any of the Sisters of Mercy in this story. His main point of contention was with the authority of Rome over the Church in England, not with the tenets of Catholicism themselves, but his actions paved the way for the bigger eventual change. His marriage to Catherine of Aragon providing him with no male heir, and his desire to have the marriage annulled so that he could marry Anne Boleyn, is a story which has been told many times. It was the first link in a chain of events which would go way beyond that one self-centred issue and lead to the creation of a form of Christianity inimically and vehemently opposed to papal authority and the Roman Catholic religion itself. Centuries of division, fear, persecution and slaughter were to follow.

As Margaret Monro points out in *Blessed Margaret Clitherow* (1947), 'Margaret Clitherow belongs to the first thirty years of Elizabeth's reign, when all but the youngest could remember an all-Catholic England.' How rapidly and to what extent ordinary people were truly won over by this Anglican form of Christianity is hard to judge, since these were days when the state dictated how church services were conducted, and ordinary people had no choice but to conform. But for several generations it must surely have been the case that they paid lip service to the new religion while privately continuing following the original one, at least in their hearts. And it varied from region to region: the North and the Midlands remained bastions of the 'Old Way' long after most of London and south-east England converted, as will become clear when we look at the lives of the women and their families who feature in this story.

Fines were levied for not attending Anglican services at the parish church, and it would have been impossible for poorer folk to continue paying for their absences. Dynasties like the Vaux, though, could take the financial hit (although even then, not indefinitely, as we shall see). But before we acquaint ourselves more fully with the family which will play a central role in both this story and in the survival of Catholicism in England, it is to the north we must look, for it is there that we will find one of England's earliest and most famous female Catholic martyrs.

* * *

Much of what we know about Margaret Clitherow comes from the priest John Mush, who was Margaret's chaplain for a time. Unless otherwise stated, the facts and quotations which follow are taken from Mush's *The Life and Death of Mistress Margaret Clitherow*, which itself is reproduced in *The Troubles of Our Catholic Forefathers* (Series II) by John Morris. (It must be borne in mind, however, that Mush's account is somewhat hagiographical, and some of the gushing testimonials to Margaret's saintliness must be treated with caution.)

Margaret Clitherow (her name is sometimes spelt Clitheroe, a common modern variation, but she appears as 'Clitherow' in virtually all historical documents) hailed from York, the same city as Guy Fawkes, who will play a significant role in this story in due course. Fawkes was younger than Margaret, but their families may well have known each other. Margaret's family lived on Davygate, near St Martin's Church, which itself was on Coney Gate, where her father was a churchwarden. Fawkes's putative birthplace of Stonegate was just a couple of minutes' walk away. Their respective fathers were both prominent citizens, and it would perhaps be surprising if they weren't at least on nodding acquaintance, and they quite possibly knew each other personally.

Fawkes would have been into his teens by the time Margaret met her barbarous end. It's possible that he was a witness to the event, as very many townsfolk would have been, although he may by then have already moved south to Sussex to take up his position with the First Viscount Montagu. Like Margaret, Fawkes was born into a Protestant family, and although there has never been any suggestion that the horror engendered by Margaret's execution played any part in the youth's change of religious outlook and allegiance, it is almost inconceivable that he did not hear of it. In that sense, it is perfectly possible that Margaret Clitherow's martyrdom had its own small place on the growing list of grievances which was to inspire the Gunpowder Plot.

The story of Margaret's life, handed down by her confessor, Father John Mush, provides us with many insights into her world and her personality – one or two possibly unintended. She was born Margaret Middleton in about 1556. There is no record of her baptism, since these were the earliest days of parish registers and her own parish did not implement the new system until at least a year after the assumed date of her birth. But it's highly likely that the Christening took place in her father's church, and that she was subsequently raised as an Anglican. Margaret was born into a turbulent time in England's religious history. Elizabeth came to the throne when Margaret was about 2, and the tone of what was to come was set from the outset. It had been the tradition for many centuries that on Sundays and feast days, the monarch would make an offering of gold at Mass. When Christmas arrived a few weeks after her ascension, it was noted that Elizabeth took herself off to her privy chamber rather than perpetuate the custom. As Anstruther (*The Vaux of Harrowden*) puts it, 'With this symbolic gesture the young queen turned her back on the religion of all her ancestors and the majority of her subjects.'

The following year, the Act of Supremacy was passed, enshrining in law the principles that England had cut itself off from Rome and that the English monarch was the head of its own Church. An order was issued that all shrines, candlesticks, stained glass windows and the like should be destroyed. This took time to percolate throughout the country, of course, and in some areas there was strong resistance. London had little choice but to conform, but the North in particular dragged its heels.

There was for a time a kind of status quo, during which the world of what might be called 'conforming Catholics' – ordinary people who maintained their old ways but did so privately and discreetly, not rocking the boat – were given plenty of leeway. But unrest was simmering. When Margaret Clitherow was in her early teens, a group of earls rose up in what became known as the Northern Rebellion. It was easily defeated, but the unrest remained and it wasn't long after this that a new type of resistance to the suppression of Catholicism emerged. For some time, families in the upper echelons of society had been sending their sons to places such as Rome, France and the Low Countries to be educated in the Catholic faith. Some of those young men took it one step further and ordained. They were now starting to return as priests, on a mission not just to support existing Catholics, but to convert Protestants to the 'true' faith.

Incumbent English priests who wouldn't – or couldn't – conform to Elizabeth's new dictates had to flee abroad, taking the same routes as the new generation of young Englishmen to whom the Catholic Church was their calling. Getting out of England was in some ways the easy part – usually secreted aboard a small fishing or cargo vessel. Slipping back across the Channel in disguise and ministering to their flock without getting caught was another matter entirely. (There were tight controls at the ports, and it was probably harder to get into England illegally then than it is now, which may or may not surprise the reader!) Once they had returned, these missionaries in their own country could only operate and survive if there was someone to put a roof over their heads, provide food and money, and hide them when searchers came calling – as they inevitably did.

Many male heads of Catholic families played their part in the cause (and paid the price – sometimes the ultimate price), but the day-to-day work and the 'front-line' risks were undertaken by their wives, sisters and daughters. It was a dangerous world that they entered. During Elizabeth's reign and well into that of James I, a spider's web of agents and informants had been established, initially by Francis Walsingham, until Robert Cecil took over the reins. Taking into account the absence of technology and the comparatively slow and laborious methods of communication and record-keeping then available, this network was perhaps more efficient and effective than any intelligence service that had existed before. Arguably, it has never been equalled since. Nationally, the spy chiefs were able to piece together a remarkably good picture of the numbers, movements, descriptions, names and often aliases of priests. Even overseas, there were silent observers keeping track of anyone who had left England or who might be likely to try to return. On a local level, no matter how remote the location, there always seemed to be spies – not necessarily state-employed agents as we think of them now, but including local town and city officials, nosy villagers and the like. It will become clear that a wealthy Catholic might even have spies among their own servants – sometimes motivated by religious reasons, but more often for cold cash.

* * *

Margaret Clitherow's York was one of the country's Catholic strongholds, yet even here it was no longer the faith of the majority. The current view of historians is that by now, after a relatively short era of Catholic suppression and of people being forced against their will to attend Anglican services, a new generation had come to the fore, one which had only ever known the new ways, had been taught that the Church of Rome was a wicked heresy and that following its teachings was a sure way to hell. By Margaret's time, active Catholicism probably only existed in relatively few quarters.

Margaret Clitherow is now represented as a saintly figure (literally so, as she was canonised in 1970), but there are hints that Margaret's own views were seen as being towards the extreme end of the scale even among York Catholics. She could be outspoken and uncompromising, and may not have been overly popular within her own neighbourhood. Indeed, there are questions over how popular Margaret was even with her own husband.

Margaret Middleton married John Clitherow on 1 July 1571. She was probably just 14 or 15 (though one commentator says 18) at the time. We are told that she had light brown hair and a clear complexion, and Mush would refer to her 'sharp and ready wit'. She would grow into a very attractive woman, but biographer Margaret Monro suspected she had a quick temper and must have been 'about as self-willed and headstrong as a human being can be'.

Margaret's new husband was a widower, with two boys from his previous marriage. John was a leading citizen. A butcher by trade and a freeman of the city, he held at different times various civic posts, including churchwarden, Bridgemaster and, not long after the marriage, he (as Margaret's father had been) was made a chamberlain: a city official responsible for collecting and paying expenses. Morris tells us that the office of chamberlain 'entitles its bearer to the appellation of gentleman, and the title "Master" or "Mr"'. Thus, plain John Clitherow, butcher, became 'Mr Clitherow' and assumed the status of gentleman, something which then had a more specific meaning and carried far more weight than it does today.

The wedding ceremony was, naturally, an Anglican one, and took place at the same parish church of St Martin's where Margaret was probably baptized and in whose churchyard her father had been buried. Margaret moved into John's home in the city's famous Shambles.

It is not known quite when and why Margaret's spiritual life took such a divergent path from that of her family and her new husband. Even if she had Catholic leanings before John's proposal, it must be assumed that her actual conversion occurred after the marriage (unless she managed to hide her true religious sentiments from her husband-to-be), since it's surely unlikely that John would have knowingly married a Catholic. The story as it is usually told is that she was converted by Dorothy Vavasour, a leading figure in York's Catholic Underground movement.

Chapter 2

Mother of all the Good Wives in York

Dorothy Vavasour

Dorothy Vavasour and her husband, Thomas, were prominent among the Catholics of York in the second half of the sixteenth century. As with Margaret Clitherow, apart from the official records listing their fines for non-attendance at church and suchlike (and in Margaret's case, from John Mush), a good deal of what we know about them comes from a record left by a sometime fellow inmate in *Notes by a Prisoner in Ousebridge Kidcote*, which appears in Volume III of *The Troubles of Our Catholic Forefathers* by Father John Morris. This anonymous author was, in fact, William Hutton, a draper who lived in the same Christ's parish as Dorothy Vavasour and Margaret Clitherow. The fate of Hutton's wife, Mary, would become entwined with that of Dorothy Vavasour.

Hutton tells us that Thomas Vavasour, who had studied at Cambridge, was forced into exile because of his religious views during the reign of King Edward VI (1547–53). The best guess as to his birth date is 1536 or 1537, but this estimate must either be a little on the late side or he fled the country at the very end of Edward's reign, since even at the time of the king's death, he could have been only around 17. Thomas returned when the Catholic Mary came to the throne. He had spent his time abroad well, studying medicine in Venice. It has been said by some that this was merely a front for religious studies, but Thomas clearly took his medical training seriously and had qualified as a physician before returning to England.

During Elizabeth's reign, he was again put to flight, this time after the Northern Rebellion in 1569, so it's possible that Thomas was either directly involved in, or associated with, this uprising of Catholic nobles aiming to oust Elizabeth to make way for Mary, Queen of Scots. It was, however, an internal exile for him this time, since he is thought to have taken refuge at Spaldington in East Yorkshire, where his parents lived.[1]

Dorothy Vavasour may not have had her husband's medical training, but she did gain a reputation as an unofficial midwife to the young mothers of the city. Father Christopher Grene (quoted by Caraman in his *Henry Garnet*) describes her as 'the chief matron and mother of all the good wives in York'. Indeed, she it was who attended to Margaret Clitherow at the birth of (at least) her first two children. We don't know much about Dorothy's family, but there is a brief mention in Thomas's entry in the archives of the Royal College of Physicians to the effect that her maiden name was Kent and that she came from Hemlingford, Hampshire.

Thomas Vavasour came from noble stock: his father was a knight of the realm and his mother the daughter of a lord. His ancestors left their mark on the city when they helped to pay for the construction of York Cathedral.[2]

Other than Thomas's flight to the Continent, the Vavasours's troubles began in 1571, when they were listed as recusants and probably fined. ('Recusant' and its variations are words we will come across regularly in this story. A recusant was a Catholic who did not attend the Anglican church.) The following year, there was a complaint that the Jesuit priest Father Edmund Campion (who, as we shall see, would go on to tutor the Vaux children) was living with them.

The stakes were raised in 1574, devastatingly so for Dorothy, when their home was raided. At this time, they may still have been living in a house 'by the Common School House', on Ogleforth, halfway between York Minster and the city walls (Longley, *Trial of Margaret Clitherow*). Hutton, writing from his cell in the Ouse Bridge Kidcote, says this was not the first such occasion, but this one appears to have been unprecedented in its intensity and violence.

The story is that the Vavasours were informed against by a local schoolmaster. Thomas had been back in England for at least two years, but, aware that he was still of interest to the York authorities, had been living elsewhere in the county, slipping back only occasionally and

---
1. Hamilton, *Chronicle of the English Augustinian Canonesses*.
2. Hamilton, *Chronicle of the English Augustinian Canonesses*.

probably under cover of darkness. It may have been Dorothy who had emboldened her husband to make his regular returns home. Grene, quoted this time in Caraman's *The Other Face*, reports that Dorothy, 'knowing her husband's mind for faith and religion, and seeing him somewhat careful for her and his children ... did desire him to cast away all care and fear ... Herewith, he being marvellously encouraged, did take heart and comfort unto him and prepare himself, with God's grace, to suffer what persecution soever God should suffer to fall upon him.' And God would indeed suffer persecution to fall upon him.

Thomas, as the primary target, had time to hide himself before the raiders entered, but this left Dorothy and her children in the midst of a gang of armed men 'fearfully raging about every place of the house with naked swords and daggers, thrusting and porring [pushing or thrusting] in at every hole and crevice, breaking down walls, rending down cloths, pulling up boards from the floors, and making such spoil of their goods'.

This went on all day, and when Thomas's hiding place still wasn't found, the Lord Mayor of York set an armed guard to keep watch, thinking to starve him into submission. The doctor held out all that night and into the following day, but finally emerged voluntarily. Some accounts state it was to divert attention from a priest who was hiding with him, others that it was to avoid prolonging Dorothy's anxiety any further – which, if so, we know with the benefit of hindsight was a wise decision.

Thomas himself was initially put under arrest at the home of Matthew Hutton, the Dean of York (apparently no relation to William and Mary Hutton), where, for now at least, he was 'entertained very cordially'. Dorothy, unfortunately, didn't fare so well. The whole episode seems to have so severely traumatized her that she had some sort of nervous breakdown. Although Thomas was granted a compassionate interruption to his imprisonment so that he could return home and tend to his wife, the confinement resumed as soon as she recovered. He was next confined to the home of a local alderman for a few months, before finally being locked up in Hull Castle. Sadly for Thomas, 'finally' would prove to be a darkly appropriate term.

Despite the devastating effect the raid had on Dorothy, she not only recovered but stepped forward to single-handedly carry on the work of furthering the Catholic cause in York. The Vavasour house became 'a refuge for all afflicted Catholics', Grene reports, and Dorothy was probably one of the friends Margaret Clitherow would write to during her own imprisonment.

Priests were harboured there, but lay people also came to attend divine service and take the sacrament. As well as acting as midwife, Margaret facilitated the secret Catholic christening of newborns. Her house at this time has been described by biographer Mary Claridge as 'a Catholic maternity home'.

Dorothy's name (along with that of Margaret Clitherow) continued to appear in the recusancy lists. In 1577, the Archbishop of York and the Queen's commissioners undertook a survey of Catholics in the city, including their net worth. Dorothy was said to be 'worth nothing, but very wilful'.

In January of the following year, Hugh Graves, the new Lord Mayor of York, reminded the churchwardens of Vavasour's Christ's parish of the levy his predecessor had ordered upon their goods and those of other such parishioners, because they had 'wilfully absented themselves from their parish church'. There was to be no let-up:

'And also I ... command you, the churchwardens ... that you do levy of the goods of the said Thomas Vavasour, William Hutton ... and of all other persons within the said parish for every Sunday and other holiday that the wives of the said Thomas Vavasour, William Hutton ... shall from henceforth be absent from their said parish church, and will not come to the same ... and there remain orderly and soberly during the time of common prayer, preaching, or other service of God.'

As far as Thomas Vavasour was concerned, this was academic, since he was not destined to return home, but Dorothy continued to be a target.

In 1578, there was another surprise invasion of Dorothy's house. Since the last such occasion, the Vavasours had moved from the Ogleforth house to one that fronted onto King's Square, right in the heart of the city.[3] This intrusion was a rather more civilized affair than the traumatic

---

3. Longley, *The 'Trial' of Margaret Clitherow*.

1574 event, which had driven Dorothy temporarily out of her wits, and although several priests were caught on the premises, she herself merely had to endure an interrogation by the Archbishop of York. It is said that friends in high places helped to ensure that she did not join Thomas in prison. Nevertheless, the fines continued, and the climate in York by then meant that time was running out for Dorothy Vavasour.

She was supposed to 'behave quietly in matters of religion', which in a way she did – but the activities she 'quietly' continued to conduct led to what would prove to be the final raid on the Vavasour home, in 1581. It was a religious feast day, and the visit was no doubt deliberately timed to coincide with the presence of priests. A number of arrests were made, including not only Dorothy but her two daughters and her friends, Alice Oldcorne (said to be related to Father Edward Oldcorne, of whom we will hear more later) and Mary Hutton, wife of William, the writer of *Notes by a Prisoner*. The presiding priest was paraded through the streets to Ousebridge, wearing his vestments and with wax tapers carried ahead of him, to the jeers and mockery of the citizens.

The females were all condemned to the New Counter prison on Ouse Bridge, and it is often stated that Dorothy and the others remained there for seven years. However, Megan Hickerson, in her thesis *Female Recusancy in Elizabethan England*, has pointed out that the year after her arrest, Dorothy and her two friends were cited for staying away from church, and Alice Oldcorne again the year after – none of which could have happened had they still been incarcerated. It would appear, then, that they were released and then condemned to prison once again within a year or two.

All this time, Thomas Vavasour himself still languished in prison in Hull. Grene describes him as 'a man both grave, learned and godly', and tells us that he 'daily … passed his time in virtuous studies in contemplation and prayer, giving good counsel and ministering physic freely & cheerfully' to his fellow prisoners. But after Dorothy had served two or three years of her own sentence, she learned that her husband had fallen ill after being moved to Hull Castle and finding himself in an overcrowded, disease-ridden environment. When it became clear that his life was in danger, Dorothy applied for temporary leave to visit him, but this was callously denied. On 12 May 1585, after 'lying long with lingering pain',

Dr Thomas Vavasour died. He was roughly 50 years of age. 'Thus ended he his life in this noble cause, which he had nobly defended with a noble and valiant heart.' He was buried within the castle walls.

Back at the New Counter, where Dorothy could only grieve for her husband at a distance, there came a time when the authorities cooked up the malicious idea of displaying the heads of recently executed priests on stakes on a roof near to, and probably within view of, where Dorothy and her friends were imprisoned. However, these grotesque trophies hadn't been on display for long before some brave soul crept up in the dead of night and took them away (quite likely ensuring they subsequently received a proper Catholic burial). On the vague pretext that they were in some way linked with the operation, even though Dorothy and her fellow inmates couldn't possibly have been responsible, they were moved to a different location – a decision which ultimately proved fatal. (Some accounts say that newly elected, zealously anti-Catholic sheriffs were behind the move.)

Beheaded priests aside, conditions in the New Counter had been relatively tolerable. But now the Catholic prisoners found themselves in the 'low and filthy dungeon' of the Kidcote prison, also on the Ouse Bridge. Here, the dark, unsanitary and overcrowded conditions were similar to those which had ultimately killed Thomas Vavasour. They were at or below the level of the river, so dampness must have been endemic. Hutton says they slept on beds 'loathsome with filth', while Father John Morris (*The Troubles of Our Catholic Forefathers*) claims the women weren't even given any bedding. Predictably, illness soon spread among them, and even though they were transferred back to the New Counter – perhaps on account of their declining health – it was too late. Mary Hutton died on 25 October 1587, Dorothy Vavasour on the 26th and Alice Oldcorne on the 27th. If we assume that Dorothy was of a similar age to Thomas, she would also have been around 50 when she met her miserable end.

Dorothy, Mary and Alice were buried on Toft Green, a plot of land near Micklegate, a short distance from the south bank of the Ouse. 'Thus through hard usage and extreme dealing,' commented Hutton, 'these had their days shortened for professing the Catholic faith.' He calculated that in addition to the latest three of the thirty women sent to the Ouse Bridge prisons during the previous fourteen years, eleven others had died. An article in *Publications of The Catholic Truth Society* (Vol. 5, 1896) states that during the eleven years when Matthew Hutton served as Archbishop of York (1595–1605), forty out of the fifty-eight people imprisoned for refusing the Oath of Allegiance fell ill and perished in prison.

Chapter 3

Consider Well What You Do

The Trial of Margaret Clitherow

One wonders what Margaret made of the news of the first violent raid on the Vavasours' house and learned that one of the aldermen who had been involved was her step-father, Henry May, who had married Margaret's mother after her father's death. If Margaret was converted in 1574, the year Dorothy Vavasour was subjected to that traumatic event, she would have been one of the first in York to do so, since, according to Margaret Monro (*Blessed Margaret Clitherow*, 1647) this was the year the first priests slipped into York from the Continent.

From this point on, life began to take a different and dangerous course not only for Margaret, who had completely stopped attending services at the parish church, but also for her husband, John, who found himself in a particularly invidious position. Soon after Elizabeth I came to the throne, the Act of Uniformity of Common Prayer and Administration of the Sacrament was introduced to make attendance at church compulsory for all. Non-attendance was punishable by fine or imprisonment – and John Clitherow was one of the men responsible for administering the fines.

For a time, John paid the fines himself, but although he was comfortably off, the situation could not be allowed to continue and Margaret's eventual imprisonment was inevitable.

In November 1576, the Lord Mayor and aldermen of York met at the council chambers, situated beside the Ouse Bridge, to hear why Margaret and others like her had not been attending church. The explanations were almost all variations on the same theme and show the predicament people found themselves in thanks to the new laws. Lucy Plowman, wife of John Plowman, 'sayeth she cometh not to the church because she liketh not the priest nor the sacrament'; Gregory Wilson, felt-maker, 'sayeth he cometh not to the church because his conscience will not serve him so to do, for he will remain in the faith that he was baptised in'.[1]

Against their names was an assessment of their net worth and thus how much would be due in fines. This was not always a clear-cut matter: Elizabeth Portar, widow, 'sayeth she is a poor woman and of no substance, but we think her worth in clear goods is 40s'.

One of those listed, under Monkeward parish, was 'Dorothy Vavasour, wife of Thomas Vavasour, doctor of physic', who gave the same reason for non-attendance as Gregory Wilson (her conscience would not serve her to do so). A couple of entries later comes 'Margaret Clitherow, wife of John Clitherow, butcher', whose reason for failing to attend her local church 'we cannot learn, because she is now great with child and could not come before us'. However, the authorities did finally catch up with her, a marginal note against her name bringing her record up to date with '*in prisona*' (in prison).

Margaret had three children with John Clitherow, all of whom followed in their mother's Catholic footsteps and one of whom became a priest. It was probably her third child, William, who the above note refers to, and he may have been born in prison.

Margaret's first spell of imprisonment was in August 1577, the year after her appearance in the City Housebooks. She was committed to York Castle Prison. Dick Turpin would, years later, be its most famous inmate, while Daniel Defoe visited the place in the early 1720s and in his *A Tour Through The Whole Island Of Great Britain* declared it to be 'the most stately and complete of any in the Kingdom, if not Europe'. There are signs that by the time Margaret was incarcerated, husband John was beginning to feel the financial pinch from the repeated payment of recusancy fines, because he was imprisoned later the same month when he could no longer make a payment levied against Margaret. He only served three days, being released after committing to a £20 bond, but Margaret remained locked up for nine months upon John agreeing to pay two shillings each week to cover what was owed.

The money continued to flow out of the dwindling Clitherow coffers, and in April 1579 John was hit with a £40 fine on account of Margaret's

---

1. Morris, *Troubles of our Catholic Forefathers*, Vol. 3.

continued refusal to attend church. Needless to say, this was a huge amount, particularly bearing in mind that when their names had first appeared in the assessments only a few years previously, John's worth had been estimated at £6. Fortunately for him, the authorities – many of whom were probably acquaintances and possibly friends – took pity on him and reduced the amount to a more realistic forty shillings, on account of 'his poor estate'. It's apposite to mention here that when John Mush talks of how Margaret 'had spared no cost to maintain her religion' and had two hiding places or priest holes ('chambers') created – and how, when she was arrested, 'so much Church stuff had not been in a whole county as they found with her' – this must ultimately have all come out of John's pocket, in addition to the payment of fines.

Adherence to Catholicism and matters of conscience came at a price – obviously financial, but also no doubt emotional. We know that Margaret almost gloried in the sufferings she underwent for her faith, but nothing is recorded of how this all affected John, who had married a regular Protestant woman just a few years earlier, and who had a job and several children to care for during her periods of incarceration. John Mush reports that she asked for his guidance on the moral principle of harbouring priests (and the expenses thus incurred) behind her husband's back. It will come as little surprise that the priest told her that it was her duty to God, and so a higher priority than her duty to her husband.

How much did John Clitherow really know about what his wife was up to? His butcher's shop was both his and Margaret's place of work and their home, with the shop on the ground floor and the family areas at the rear and above. His civic duties must have sometimes taken him away, leaving Margaret to run the shop, and Monro surmises he would have been away for 'days at a time buying cattle for slaughter'. She also declares the Clitherow home to have been 'one of the chief Mass centres of York', with priests and lay people coming and going, children being taught in the basement, and having had a secret escape route to the next-door property created. John may have turned a blind eye to Margaret's activities, but he must surely have had at least some idea of the extent of them.

Margaret and other similar Catholic women 'organised their days round a demanding programme of private prayer'. She didn't get away from her husband's butcher's shop until 4.00 pm, 'but managed two hours of devotions and prayer every day as well as Mass and evensong' (Marie B. Rowlands, *Women in English Society*). As well as frequently taking in priests, we have already heard that Margaret set up in her basement or some lower-level room a school for the Catholic instruction of the children of neighbours, complete with its own resident teacher, a man called Stapleton. Naturally, when they were young, her own children were regular pupils.

Margaret found herself in prison twice more during the next few years, during which time she learned to read and write. This enabled her to study scripture, thanks to a recent translation of the Gospels which had been smuggled into the prison. She also used the time to help others, providing spiritual support as far as possible to those who were receptive, and somehow even helping out financially. Prison food then, and for centuries afterwards, tended to be not only of poor quality but sometimes barely enough quantity to survive on. Prisoners could supplement their diet if they could afford to, but for those who couldn't, the spectre of malnutrition and ill-health always hovered near, and Margaret did what she could to provide food and clothing where it was most needed.

The second incarceration was in October 1580, following which Margaret managed to avoid arrest for almost two years before being locked up again, in March 1583. This was to be her longest spell in prison, lasting about eighteen months. At around the same time, another priest who had acted as Margaret Clitherow's confessor was tried and sentenced to death, and she was one of the last people to have been blessed by him. She may well have watched him being dragged away, bound to a hurdle, for his hanging at the Knavesmire.

Claridge says that Catholic recusants were housed in one of two wings of a relatively modern building within the ancient castle grounds (the other wing being for general prisoners). The conditions do not appear to have been particularly severe or arduous by the standards of the day, and it seems that Margaret and her fellow recusant inmates, kept together as they were, lived as a Catholic community under the direction of a priest acting as a father superior.

Following her third release, in late 1584, Margaret dispatched her eldest son, Henry, to France so that he could receive a Catholic education, and he would eventually be ordained into the priesthood. This was done without the knowledge of husband John.

By now, Margaret's fervour for the Catholic faith was drawing so much attention to her that even Mush admits that 'her house became more notorious than the whole town besides', and it was an open secret that she was harbouring priests. It was a brazen flaunting of the law and the edicts of the local authorities, and was always going to end badly.

In March 1586, John Clitherow answered a summons to present himself to the authorities in York, which may have been a subterfuge intended either to protect him or to clear the way for what happened next – because while he was away from home, the sheriff and his men swept along the Shambles and swooped on the Clitherow home. Guy Fawkes biographer Nick Holland, quoting Peter Lake and Michael Questier in *The Trials of Margaret Clitherow*, says that it was Margaret's own father-in-law, Henry May, then York's Lord Mayor, who gave the order for this raid.

Margaret had suspected something was afoot as soon as John was summoned: 'They pick quarrels at me, and they will never cease until they have me again, but God's will be done.' John Mush was staying in her home at that time and it may have been because of her fears that he moved himself to the house next door, which no one seems to have thought to search before or after the events which were to follow. Stapleton the teacher, who, like Margaret, had served time in York Prison, had a lucky escape. He was in the middle of a lesson with Margaret's own children and others from the locality when 'a ruffian bearing a sword and buckler on his arm' burst in. Taking Stapleton to be a priest and thus a valuable prize, the man shut the door and went to get reinforcements. Thus warned, Stapleton slipped through the hidden passage between the Clitherow house and next door. When the sheriff's men returned and found him gone, the often melodramatic Mush declares that they took it as confirmation that he must have been a priest, 'raged like madmen' at his escape and began a search of the house.

Finding nothing incriminating, they targeted one particular boy, aged around 10–12, from among those rounded up. Stripping him naked, they threatened him with rods and soon intimidated him into talking. He quite understandably told them where the priest's secret chamber was located (the one in the Clitherow house, not in the adjacent property), and there they found all of the Catholic books and paraphernalia they needed to bring a charge against Margaret.

She and the other occupants were marched away. Maids and children were split up and sent to different prisons, while Margaret herself was taken directly to appear before the Council of the North. She, 'being merry and stout for the Catholic cause, thereby moved their fury vehemently against her, especially by her smiling cheerful countenance', Mush blusters. This may be his typical hyperbole, but if half of what he tells us about Margaret is true, it could well be an accurate representation of her demeanour (although, as we shall see, the York authorities were probably much more sympathetic towards her than he can bring himself to admit). Margaret almost seems to have desired to become a martyr. Was she so complacent, seemingly almost smug, because she had finally got her wish? At this time, she was in her early 30s, the mother of three children. Did this latter fact have no bearing on her thinking?

In the early evening, Margaret was sent off to York Castle Prison, where John was briefly allowed to meet her – though not in private. This must have been a trying time, but Margaret wasn't the first to be in such a situation and she would not be the last. Her husband could not have imagined it possible that this was the last time they would ever spend together.

Mush now sensibly went into hiding, and his report of what happened subsequently was gleaned by him from locals at a later date.

On Monday, 14 March 1586, Margaret was taken from the castle prison to the Guildhall, then called the Common Hall (a place where, in happier times, she had attended banquets with John), to appear at the assizes before two judges, Clench and Rhodes, and four members of the Council of the North. She was charged with harbouring priests, hearing Mass and various related offences. John Clench, the senior of the two judges, asked her: 'Margaret Clitherow, how say you? Are you guilty of this indictment, or no?'

'I know no offence whereof I should confess myself guilty.'

'Yes, you have harboured and maintained Jesuits and priests, enemies to Her Majesty.' It is worth noting that Catholic priests were always at pains to affirm their loyalty to queen and country, but it suited the authorities to tie that particular charge in with the religious ones, at least in part so that the gravest charge of all – treason – could be brought to bear.

Thus, it was that Margaret was able to honestly reply: 'I never knew nor have harboured any such persons, or maintained those which are not the Queen's friends. God defend I should.'

'How will you be tried?'

On the face of it, this question (in effect, 'How do you plead?') was a simple, routine part of the process, and might seem to be the least of her problems. It should – and could – have been a mere formality, yet history shows us that Margaret's very life hung upon her response.

The crucial factor at play here is that at this time, a prisoner was obliged to enter a plea of 'guilty' or 'not guilty' in order for a full trial to take place. Refusal to enter a plea was punishable by death.

'Having made no offence, I need no trial.'

The judge asked her again and again, but Margaret was resolute: 'I will be tried by none but by God and your own consciences.'

The horrific cruelty of her eventual punishment has given rise to the impression that the authorities in York were a heartless, bloodthirsty bunch, but (and contrary to his religiously influenced railings against them) Mush's own account of these proceedings shows that this was far from the case. In fact, many of those present could see with a growing sense of horror where this was leading and, clearly motivated by genuine human compassion, did everything in their power to persuade Margaret to enter a plea.

'Good woman, consider well what you do; if you refuse to be tried by the country [i.e., by a jury], you make yourself guilty and accessory to your own death, for we cannot try you but by order of law.' Clench, quite possibly exceeding his authority, even tried to reassure Margaret that she had little to fear from a trial: 'I think the country cannot find you guilty upon this slender evidence of a child.' But he added ominously that the court had no choice but to follow the law if she continued on her chosen path, 'which will condemn you to a sharp death for want of trial'. Whether intentional or not, whether he meant it or not, his reference to a 'sharp' death was to prove a grotesquely apposite pun.

But Margaret remained unmoved: 'God's will be done. I think I may suffer any death for this good cause.'

While there were attacks on Margaret for her beliefs from some of the assembled Council members, probably not locals, the judges themselves, and others present, were more interested in saving her skin, and continued to try to make her see what they saw as reason. She was granted the time to think on the gravity of her situation overnight, and brought before them again the next morning – but it was more of the same:

> 'Margaret Clitherow, how say you yet? Yesternight we passed you over without judgement, which we might have then pronounced against you if we would. We did it not, hoping you would be something more conformable, and put yourself to the country, for otherwise you must needs have the law.'

So again, it seems clear that the judges were driven by sympathy and charity, rather than religious intolerance and a determination to make Margaret renounce her faith. Clench once more reminded her of the weakness of the case to be brought against her, heavily based as it was on the statement of a frightened boy whom all present would have realized had been subjected to undue pressure. Margaret, even though agreeing with them regarding the weakness of the evidence against her, remained impassive. But why? Why not simply plead 'not guilty'?

It is claimed that one of her justifications was that by avoiding a trial, she would be protecting the souls of jury members who might find her guilty and pay the price in the hereafter. However, Mush also reports a conversation, which can only have been passed on to him by someone in prison with her at the time (probably Anne Tesh, who had been in Margaret's house and taken at the same time that she was), in which she said that going before a jury would have led to evidence being produced against her 'which none could give but only my children and servants', which would have been more grievous to her 'than a thousand deaths'.

On the face of it, this is an understandable explanation, but what would it have meant in practice? If Margaret had entered a plea, there would have been a full jury trial, during the course of which her children and servants may well have been called as witnesses, but that doesn't necessarily mean that they would have felt obliged to speak against her. She herself obfuscated when asked about the activities of priests in her home, and presumably they could have done the same thing. It's easy to say when one is not in Margaret's invidious position, but it might reasonably be said that in choosing a gruesome death rather than a trial with a good chance of acquittal, she was saving those close to her from the short-lived stress of that trial, but not necessarily anything worse than that. (Three years after these events, Anne Tesh was tried for harbouring priests and acquitted. On a later occasion, she was caught in a 'sting' operation attempting to convert someone to Catholicism and sentenced to be burned at the stake, but even that was commuted to life imprisonment.)

It has also been suggested that Margaret refused to enter a plea to avoid the exposure of the priests who had made use of her home, whose names might come out during the course of a trial. But again, she might simply have refused to name names – as she had done all along anyway. Even Mush understood that there was yet another layer to it, one alluded to earlier and which in a sense is more troubling to modern minds: *Margaret actually welcomed martyrdom, believing it to be a sure way to achieve heavenly salvation.*

Although scenarios similar to this one had been, and would continue to be, enacted in York, London and elsewhere during this turbulent period, there does seem to have been an extra dimension to this case which makes it unique, almost grotesquely so. It relates to Margaret's general demeanour and her apparent determination on self-destruction. Whereas we shall see in the lives of other people who will feature in this story – including the bravest and most determined Jesuit priests – who went out of their way to avoid capture and execution, on some level Margaret seems to have welcomed those things and perhaps even invited them. Consequently, it appears that, as her *Oxford Dictionary of National Biography* entry points out, despite the undoubted widespread sympathy for her, there was also a feeling that she might even be somewhat unhinged, suffering from a kind of religious mania. Her own stepfather described Margaret's choices at this time as being tantamount to committing suicide, which, as he would have known, was considered by Catholics to be a mortal sin. Even the Anglican Church denied suicides a Christian burial.

Be this as it may, Margaret's strength of mind in the face of enormous pressure and the dangling carrot of likely acquittal is admirable in a perverse sort of way. 'All the people about her condemned her of great obstinacy and folly,' says Mush, 'that she would not yield; and on every hand persuaded her to refer her trial to the country, which could not find her guilty.' But it had no effect.

The judge, his patience and options having run out, began to pronounce the only sentence legally available to him – but he was interrupted by a man among the assembled throng who rose to his feet and begged to be heard: 'My lord, take heed what you do. You sit here to do justice; this woman's case is touching life and death – you ought not, either by God's laws or man's, to judge her to die upon the slender witness of a boy!'

The speaker was neither friend, family nor even a member of the Catholic community. In fact, the interjection was from Giles Wiggington, a Puritan preacher. To his great credit, even this man, whose views were antithetical to Margaret's, could not bear to stand by and watch this chilling scene be played out to its inevitable and tragic conclusion.

Clench insisted that he had no choice in law but to pass sentence of death upon Margaret Clitherow.

'Who's [sic] law?' demanded Wiggington.

'By the Queen's law.'

'That may well be, but you cannot do it by God's law.'

Clench may well have privately sympathized with this view, but he was bound to proceed. Nevertheless, this new twist prompted him to yet again try to make Margaret reconsider: 'Good woman, I pray you put yourself to the country. There is no evidence but a boy against you, and whatsoever they do, yet we may show mercy afterward.'

Margaret maintained her uncompromising stance, whereupon Clench could delay the proceedings no longer:

> 'You must return from whence you came, and there, in the lowest part of the prison, be stripped naked, laid down, your back upon the ground, and as much weight laid upon you as you are able to bear, and so to continue three days without meat or drink, except a little barley bread and puddle water, and the third day to be pressed to death, your hands and feet tied to posts, and a sharp stone under your back.'

In fact, this wasn't quite how things played out, and a significant detail of what Clench actually said has been overlooked by most commentators.

It is usually assumed (perhaps because of the way things unfolded when the execution took place) that the intention was to lay the prisoner down and pile weight on until she was crushed. But Clench categorically states that she was to have as much weight placed on her as she was '*able to bear*' – not *more* weight than she was able to bear – and only after three days would the final, fatal weight be added.

Be that as it may, Margaret reacted to the pronouncement with typical sang-froid, 'without any fear or change of countenance', as Mush described it: 'If this judgement be according to your own conscience, I pray God send you better judgement before Him. I thank God heartily for this.'

This was a little unfair on Clench, and he was quick to defend himself: 'Nay, I do it according to law, and tell you this must be your judgement, unless you put yourself to be tried by the country. Consider of it – you have a husband and children to care for; cast yourself not away.'

'I would to God my husband and children might suffer with me for so good a cause,' she replied.

Mush reports that when some in York heard this, they interpreted it as meaning she wished a 'glorious' martyrdom upon not only herself but her family too; but she surely meant it in the sense that she had remained firm in her conviction, and hoped they would bear the suffering of their loss because of it.

The clearly troubled Clench, even after he had formally pronounced sentence, still gave Margaret another chance, perhaps hoping that the enormity of the torment he had described might have caused a last-minute weakening of her resolve: 'How say you, Margaret Clitherow? Are you content to put yourself to the trial of the country? Although we have given sentence against you according to the law, yet will we show mercy, if you will do anything yourself.'

Mush's purple prose has her 'lifting up her eyes towards heaven' in the manner of a religious icon, and replying with a cheerful countenance: 'God be thanked. All that He shall send me shall be welcome.'

Finally defeated, Clench ordered the sheriff to take Margaret away. Her arms were tied together and she was led from the hall under armed escort. When John heard of the outcome, 'he fared like a man out of his wits, and wept so vehemently that blood gushed out of his nose in great quantity, crying "Alas! Will they kill my wife? Let them take all I have and save her, for she is the best wife in all England, and the best Catholic also!"'

Even now, though, the attempts to make Margaret change her mind continued. A couple of days after the sentence was passed, she was visited by Sir Thomas Fairfax, vice-president of the Council of the North. We don't have an exact record of the exchange, but it is believed Margaret was told that if she would just attend the local church with him for one sermon, 'she should have a favour'. Predictably, this offer was politely but firmly refused. But there was a report of another matter being raised, a potentially dramatic development, yet which is rarely afforded the weight it deserves: Fairfax and others had heard a local rumour that Margaret might be pregnant.

Pregnancy would not in itself cause the death sentence to be annulled, but it would at least be grounds for a postponement until after the birth of the child. It hardly needs pointing out that if she were to be executed while knowingly pregnant, she would in effect be condemning her unborn child to die with her.

Margaret's reply, and the position she took in this matter is rather curious. Initially, she declared that she 'knew not certainly' whether she was pregnant, but 'thought *rather she was than otherwise*'. When they quite reasonably asked why she would not at least accept a temporary suspension of the sentence, she is reported as replying: 'I ask no favour in this matter. You may do your pleasure.' Unfortunately, this only adds fuel to the theory that Margaret Clitherow was determined to make herself a martyr, and that even to her, an intensely devout Catholic, an unborn child was not to be allowed to stand in the way of her destiny.

In the days that followed, family members also visited and tried to talk her round, and they, too, raised the issue of her possible pregnancy. They begged Clench not to allow the execution to go ahead now this new information had come to light. The judge, though, was now also under pressure from his own Council to not delay the execution, and was perhaps outnumbered in his sympathetic attitude towards Margaret. According to Mush (who manages to report Clench's magnanimous words throughout the whole business without giving the man one iota of credit for his consistently non-sectarian and humanitarian approach), Clench took the stance that, 'If she be with child, then I will not consent that she shall die', and ordered that 'four honest women' should examine her.

When the report came back that she was 'with child as far as they could perceive', Clench initially resisted strong calls from members of the Council to proceed. He would not have a pregnant woman executed, since, 'although she hath offended, yet hath not the infant in her womb. I will not for a thousand pounds, therefore, give my consent until she be further tried.'

Despite these bold words, Clench capitulated, under attack and perhaps suspecting he might anyway be outmanoeuvred by the Council. This humane and relatively powerful man (reputedly a favourite of Queen Elizabeth) sanctioned the execution.

Legally, Margaret should have been allowed a stay of at least twenty weeks until it became clear once and for all whether she was pregnant.[2] Ralph Hurlestone, one of the members of the Council of the North most vehemently and vociferously in favour of Margaret's early execution, wasn't even happy with that. He had worn Clench down, and as a compromise the judge put the execution on hold for a week – until Lady Day, 25 March – after which they must 'do as they think good'. In her biography of Margaret Clitherow, Mary Claridge understandably but perhaps harshly describes Clench as 'a kind man but not an heroic one'.

Mush tells us that when Margaret heard about the behind-the-scenes debates, she 'feared that she should escape death'. The never-ending procession of visitors hoping to help her do so continued. Anglican ministers and others came to debate with her both about the scriptural justification for what she was doing and the morality of her case if she did indeed prove to be pregnant. Giles Wiggington made an appearance, pleading with her, 'cast not yourself away', and, with sympathy, put forward a balanced and persuasive argument against her standpoint. (It's worth repeating here that it's highly likely that most if not all of these dignitaries and others at least knew of Margaret and John Clitherow, and in some cases were friends or acquaintances. One visitor, the Lord

---

2. Claridge, *Margaret Clitherow (1556?–1586)*.

Mayor, was her own stepfather.) Wiggington left saying, 'I am sorry that I cannot persuade you', but returned at a later date, like Fairfax begging her to just go through the motions of attending a single Anglican sermon, an act which would almost certainly save her life while not in any way undermining her own beliefs. Her response was that she would only do so if the sermon was preached by a Catholic priest, which they both knew was never going to happen. The persistent Wiggington came to make a third and final effort, and when it failed he sighed, 'I perceive you will cast yourself willingly away, without regard of husband or children', and left her for the last time.

There came a small glimpse into what lay behind Margaret's facade of cheerful imperturbability when the York sheriffs came to inform her that the execution had been set for just two days' time. She told a fellow inmate (probably Anne Tesh): '[N]ow I feel the frailty of mine own flesh, which trembleth at these [sic] news.' But she immediately began to pray, and her courage was soon restored.

There are two versions of Margaret Clitherow's final hours. As well as Mush, we have a briefer account by William Hutton, another Catholic recusant, in his *Notes by a Prisoner in Ousebridge Kidcote*. The two narratives agree in most respects, but differ on one or two points.

Since her appearance before Clench, Margaret had been eating sparingly of the food she was offered, which according to Mush consisted of water pottage, rye bread and small ale (whereas Hutton says they gave her only 'gruel porridge'). Whatever it was, after the sheriffs brought the terrible news, she stopped eating altogether.

On the eve of the execution, Margaret asked if one of her maids might be allowed to spend the night with her, 'not for any fear of death, for it is my comfort, but the flesh is frail'. This could not be granted, but Mrs Yoward, the gaoler's wife and the person to whom she had made this request, kindly stayed with her until midnight. When that time arrived, she watched as Margaret took off all her clothes and put on a plain white linen gown which she had been making over the course of the last few days in preparation for this moment. Margaret Monro, in *Blessed Margaret Clitherow*, must surely be correct when she surmises that Mrs Yoward was one of Mush's prime sources when he compiled his account. In this gown, Margaret knelt and prayed from midnight until 3.00 am. After spending a little time in front of the fire, she then went to bed until 6.00 am, but one wonders whether she managed to get any sleep.

Upon rising, Margaret removed her home-made habit and put on her ordinary clothes again, ready for when the sheriffs came to take her away. She asked Mrs Yoward if she would attend the execution, presumably for moral support, but the woman couldn't bring herself 'to see her die so cruel a death for all of York'. Yoward did, though, offer to shorten her suffering by engaging some of Margaret's friends to add heavy stones to those which would be piled upon her by the executioners, in much the same way that friends of people being hanged pulled on their legs. 'No, good Mrs Yoward, not so,' said Margaret. 'God defend that I should procure any to be guilty of my death and blood.' In the event, Margaret Clitherow's suffering was to be very much shorter than the three days of pain and misery described by Clench.

The sheriffs arrived two hours later and bound her hands with linen tape, which Margaret had also made herself. She walked barefoot, carrying her white gown over her arm, and as they emerged into the already crowded street and made their way to the designated spot, she tossed alms in the form of coins to the onlookers. In typical Mush fashion, he tells us that the spectators 'marvelled all to see her joyful countenance'.

She was taken to the tollbooth at one end of Ouse Bridge. It was a very short trip – just a few yards across the street from where she had spent her last night on Earth. Despite its name, by this time the tollbooth had been converted into a small prison or lock-up. (It was also known as the Ousebridge Kidcote, or the Kidcote Prison, 'kidcote' being a local term for a prison.) We know that the spot where the execution was to be carried out was open to the street, at least for this occasion; the final act of Margaret's life would be performed in front of as many witnesses as could crowd around the opening.

John Clitherow had been banished from York for a few days. It may have been an act of mercy to shield him from his wife's final agonies. It is not impossible that he felt the need to be near her and slipped back incognito on the day itself, but he was probably too well-known to have done so without being recognized. What we do know is that his and Margaret's own front door had been dismantled and taken to the tollbooth – Margaret's final indignation was that she was to be crushed to death beneath her own door.

The four sergeants designated to perform the task lost their nerve and paid a group of around eight local men and women, 'beggars' (and presumably Anglicans, as we shall soon see), to take their place. When Margaret was brought before them, they offered to kneel and pray with her. Perhaps she can be forgiven her response under the circumstances, but it was a rather cold and unmagnanimous one, and again perhaps an indicator of her character: 'I will not pray with you, and you shall not pray with me. Neither will I say Amen to your inferior prayers, nor shall you to mine.'

Margaret prayed out loud, ignoring a certain amount of heckling, which became particularly strident when she implored God to turn Queen Elizabeth towards the Catholic faith. When she had finished, Faucet, one of the sheriffs, ordered her to strip naked. It had been decreed that this was how she must die, and when Margaret asked to be allowed to wear the habit she had made especially for this moment, she was refused. Mush's rather contradictory-sounding story of this episode has caused some confusion about Margaret's state of undress at the time of her execution. He mentions that she was denied the habit, leading to a belief in some quarters that Margaret was totally naked when she was killed. However, he goes on to say that the women helping her undress 'put upon her the long habit of linen'. It seems that by this he means that rather than Margaret wearing it, the women laid it over body, though it only covered the lower half. Hutton states it much more plainly when he says that she wanted to wear the habit, but 'they would have her naked to the waist'.

Margaret laid herself down on the ground. As well as the garment covering her lower half of her body, a handkerchief was draped over her face. Then her own front door, the one she had passed through so many times in happier days, was placed over her body.

Margaret 'joined her hands towards her face', presumably in prayer, but once again she was ordered to desist. Using the cord she had made, her hands were tied to posts either side of her. As Mush pointed out, she now lay in a cross-shape.

The final, and in a sense cruellest, aspect of the execution now took place. Not content with crushing her to death, a fist-sized sharp stone (Hutton says it was 'made of purpose', so presumably an ordinary stone was fashioned to give it a flat base and an upward-facing sharp point) was placed under her back, level with her heart.

Now, with everything ready, the beggars loaded an enormous quantity of rocks on top of the door: 'five or six hundredweight' in Hutton's story, seven or eight 'at least' according to Mush (one hundredweight being 112lb, or 50kg). Margaret was a slightly built woman, and almost as soon as the first heavy stones were placed upon the door, driving her back into the sharp stone beneath her, she cried 'Jesu! Jesu! Jesu! Have mercy upon me!' These were to be her last words.

The punishment was not drawn out over the three days described by Clench. Indeed, it lasted no more than a merciful fifteen minutes. The enormous load splintered her ribs, some of the broken ends of bone piercing through her skin, and it's a reasonable assumption that on the inside they also penetrated her lungs, and perhaps her heart as well, which, combined with the heart-level sharp stone, would have caused catastrophic internal bleeding and explain the rapid loss of life. It was 25 March 1586 – Good Friday. In later centuries, Pope Paul VI would refer to her as the Pearl of York – the name Margaret being derived from the Ancient Greek for pearl.

*   *   *

Margaret's Clitherow's crushed, lifeless body was left in place from the time of the execution, 9 am, until 3.00 pm that afternoon. It would without doubt have then been buried in an unmarked grave, and according to the anonymous 'A Yorkshire Recusant's Relation' in *The Troubles of Our Catholic Forefathers*, Vol. 3, it was interred 'beside a dunghill in the town'. However, it was secretly exhumed six weeks later (and 'found without putrefaction') and spirited several days' ride away to where it lay for six more weeks before embalming materials could be acquired – all this time still miraculously without any decomposition taking place. It was then finally buried according to Catholic rites. Unfortunately, the secret of the location was so well kept that we have absolutely no clue as to the burial site, but one physical reminder of Margaret Clitherow may have been taken before her interment, and indeed may still be viewed today. A shrivelled and rather gruesome hand, said to be that of Margaret, is on display in an elaborate gold and glass container at the Bar Convent in York. According to Margaret Monro, who believed the hand to be a genuine Margaret Clitherow relic, it was donated to the convent by Father Mush himself. Also to be seen is a plaque that marks the spot on the Ouse Bridge where the execution took place.

After Margaret's death, John was allowed to take their children home. As we have heard, Henry, then aged 14, was already abroad, destined for the priesthood, and William was on his way to following the same path. Like his mother, William spent time in the prison at York Castle for his beliefs before being exiled to Rheims. Margaret's stepson, Thomas, wasn't so lucky. He too was educated abroad and returned to England, where he was also arrested and incarcerated in York Castle. He died during another spell of imprisonment, this time in Hull, in 1603.

Daughter Anne, who was about 12 when she was returned to her father after the death of her mother, perhaps found it hard to settle back into what was now a Protestant household, because about two years later she disappeared from the family home. John didn't hear of Anne for four years, then discovered that she was in prison in Lancaster. He used his influence with York's Lord Mayor to get him to write to Lancaster and beg for her return to York, where she would be 'conferred with by some learned and godly preachers'; if she still didn't see the error of her ways, she would be put before the courts there. Anne was duly obliged to return to her home city, but she was her mother's daughter and, predictably, the godly and learned men made no impression on her. She fled once more – this time to Louvain in Belgium, where she entered St Monica's convent.

John himself married for a third time. We don't know his latest wife's name, but according to Margaret Monro, this time it was a Protestant woman.

* * *

John Mush, a northerner himself, was a seminary priest who trained at the English college in Douai, Flanders, and in Rome, and probably arrived back in England to begin his mission three or four years before Margaret's execution. Claridge suggests that he had been a servant of Thomas and Dorothy Vavasour, through whose influence Margaret Clitherow converted to Catholicism. He and Father John Holtby were the leading figures of the priestly community in Northern England at this period.

Only a few months after Margaret's death, Mush himself was caught at a house in York. The householder, Richard Langley, was executed, but Mush, who seemed to lead a charmed life, somehow managed to escape from prison and remained at large, still very active writing and performing his priestly duties, for the rest of his life.

* * *

What can we make of Margaret Clitherow? Is it possible to see through John Mush's magniloquent hagiography? What is clear is that she was a divisive figure – not only among modern commentators but even during her lifetime, and within her own community.

Mush writes of her 'rare discretion in all her actions'. Brave and sincere though Margaret was, the 'discretion' label is debatable to say the least. It may or may not be that she endured a horrible death to avoid others having to suffer, but she also gloried in her martyrdom. We must be clear that Margaret Clitherow's execution was only indirectly one of religious persecution, and that matters would have unfolded in the same way if she had been arrested for stealing a loaf of bread. She was *not* put to death because of her Catholic faith, nor for her recusancy, for hearing Mass, nor for even sheltering priests, as is so often stated or implied, but solely because she refused to enter a plea. This made one liable to a death sentence, whatever the crime. The sentence of *peine forte et dure* (from the French for 'strong and hard punishment') and the method of pressing the convicted person to death, although rare, had been the prescribed penalty for around 200 years. For examples of true discretion, we must look to the Vaux sisters, whose own work in the Catholic Underground movement was getting underway at around this time.

There are signs that even among Catholics, Margaret seems to have been seen as a radical as regards her religious fervour, almost bent on drawing attention to herself, and perhaps even upon becoming a sacrificial lamb from a very early stage. Plenty of other Catholics worked quietly and effectively, unobtrusively, to keep the faith alive. From a modern secular perspective, the path Margaret (the probably pregnant Margaret) chose might almost be seen as a grotesque, and in a sense the ultimate, form of attention-seeking.

There is a story that John, having had a little too much to drink at a function in York, made disparaging remarks against Catholics which dismayed and angered his wife. He supposedly reassured her that his comments were of a general nature and not aimed at her personally, adding that 'she was a good wife in all but two things – her excessive fasting, and her refusal to go to church with him'. It is often said that new converts to a religion are much more zealous than those born into it, sometimes overly so. Even John's apology, with its reference to 'excessive' fasting, gives an indication of what we might today suspect to be a form of religious fanaticism.

Then again, it's unlikely, but not beyond the bounds of possibility, that John's outburst was staged. He was in a very difficult position. He had good standing in York, and it may be that he felt it politic to overtly distance himself from his wife's only-too-well publicized views. It would only be a short step from him seeming to be supportive of her to being seen as a Catholic sympathizer or even a secret Catholic himself. This in turn would risk not just losing his standing in the community, but could result in financial ruin.

* * *

Margaret Clitherow's York has changed a lot, but the Shambles where she lived has become a tourist attraction because it has changed relatively little, less than just about anywhere else in the city. Monro says that the Bishop of Middlesbrough, in whose diocese York is, bought 36 The Shambles after it had been 'satisfactorily identified' as Margaret Clitherow's house, and a shrine to her memory was established there. However, in later years it was realized that this identification was a mistake caused by the houses on the Shambles having been renumbered at some point. A house across the street, which has a priest hole next to the fireplace, is now believed to have been the Clitherow home.[3]

* * *

Not long after Margaret Clitherow's death, another northern woman, another Margaret, experienced similar horrors at the hands of the authorities, albeit in the capital rather than York.

---

3. https://www.insideyork.co.uk/what-to-see/shambles/margaretclitherowhouse.html.

Chapter 4

An Innocent Lamb

Margaret Ward

It's quite rare for us to be able to know so much about the life of an otherwise ordinary Elizabethan woman such as Margaret Clitherow. Unfortunately, Margaret Ward, who was put to death just a couple of years after Margaret Clitherow, did not have a John Mush or a William Hutton to fill in all the gaps.

All accounts of Margaret Ward's life tell us that she was born in Congleton, Cheshire, but none provide a source for this information. Bishop Challoner in *Memoirs of Missionary Priests* (1803) is possibly the earliest to mention it, and it is such a specific claim that it presumably has some reliable origin which has faded from view over time. A contributor to a local history magazine called *The Cheshire Sheaf* (Vol. 1, 1860) can be no more categoric than to inform readers that Margaret was 'said to be' of the Wards of Congleton, and surmises that she was the mother of John Ward of Capesthorne, 7 or 8 miles north of Congleton. He owned an estate in that place, thus indicating, if true, that Margaret was of a well-to-do family. She is sometimes referred to as 'Mrs Ward'. 'Mrs', as an abbreviation of 'mistress', could refer to social rank rather than marital status, but other accounts say that she had been married and widowed by the time of the events we are looking at.

Something took Margaret to London, where she is referred to in records as being 'in the service of a lady of distinction'. Being 'in the service of' does not mean she was a maid or servant, as the term later came to mean. Challoner tells us that she was from 'a gentleman's family' and elsewhere that she was a gentlewoman, which at that time indicated a person of rank. Margaret had her own servant, and her role in the lady's household was probably akin to that of a lady's companion. It's likely that the lady of distinction herself was from Cheshire, or had links with that county and spent time there, and took Margaret south with her. The lady whom Margaret served is usually named as 'Whithall' (amended to 'Whittle' in most modern accounts).

No one even knows whether Margaret Ward was a lifelong Catholic, whether she converted while still living in Cheshire or whether it was an encounter in London that led her to adopt the faith. We don't really get into the realms of solid facts until 1588 – the last year of her life.

She was probably in her 30s by then, another similarity with Margaret Clitherow, when she learned of the imprisonment of the Catholic priest Father Richard (or possibly William) Watson and began to visit him. Men like him were being locked up on a regular basis all over the country during this period, so the question arises as to why Margaret Ward took a special interest in this particular priest. Perhaps she read or heard about his arrest and her sympathies were somehow aroused, but a more likely explanation might be that she had received teachings from him, and that he had perhaps even been her confessor at some point before his capture. We might take the speculation a step further and wonder whether Mrs Whithall was one of those wealthy Catholic women who harboured priests in their large houses, he being a resident priest or at least a regular visitor. We will never know, but for whatever reason, Margaret Ward began making trips to the Bridewell Prison to spend time with Father Watson – and during the course of those visits, she began to hatch a bold and risky plan.

Father Watson was probably a similar age to Margaret. He was from County Durham, but like so many young men wishing to become priests he was obliged to go to the Continent to train. After being ordained in France, he slipped into England in 1586 ('in mariners apparell'), but lasted just a matter of months before being arrested. A major difference between Watson and Mush and most of the priests who will feature later in this story is that the former pair were not Jesuits, and in Watson's case it worked in his favour. The British Jesuits of this period are sometimes described as the Catholic 'guerrilla' wing or its special forces – certainly not in the sense of using violence (they were completely against the Gunpowder Plot, for example, despite highly effective government propaganda linking them with it), but because they were a small, elite, well-organized, theologically well-trained force, 'parachuted' in behind enemy lines to work undercover. And the government hated them.

One reason that Watson, as a non-Jesuit, was released and ordered into exile rather than being executed was that it suited the government, especially people like Walsingham, Queen Elizabeth's infamous spymaster (soon to be succeeded by his protégé, Robert Cecil), to show leniency towards, and curry the favour of, 'ordinary' Catholics as a way of weakening the power and influence of the Jesuits.

But there was a twist in the Watson story. For some reason, the authorities snatched him again before he could flee the country, and having originally been kept in the Marshalsea Prison he was now taken to the Bridewell, where he came to the attention of Richard Topcliffe, the feared priest-hunter whose delight in torturing his captives bordered on the psychopathic. Watson was later to write of his experiences in the Bridewell: 'All the plagues & torments of that place were inflicted upon me (whereof fewe I think were lefte oute, & some I dare say unknowen to her majesty or councell that ever I suffered, as whipping, grinding in the milne, withe the like).'[1]

Over the course of several prison visits, Margaret cultivated a friendship with the gaoler, which put him off his guard and allowed her to eventually smuggle a length of rope into Watson's cell.

The Bridewell Prison had been converted from a royal palace into a combined hospital and prison at roughly the time when Margaret was born. It backed onto the Thames at one end, running lengthways inland, with the River Fleet (which now flows beneath New Bridge Street) running alongside its eastern walls, and it was an enormous structure. The building took the form of a huge rectangle around 175 metres in length. It was built around a vast courtyard, which was divided in two by a central building running the full width of the yard. At one end of the rectangle, the accommodation was five storeys high, with more rooms in the attic, which had dormer windows. Accommodation in the other (southern) half was apparently more spacious, since it was around the same height but divided into only three storeys, again with attic rooms above. The prison section could accommodate some 200 people.

---

1. Law, *The Archpriest Controversy*.

So, with the Fleet on one side of the Bridewell and the Thames on another, Margaret's idea was to hire a boatman to be waiting at a certain hour on a specific day, at which time Watson would climb out of his window and lower himself down using the rope. The first attempt to put this plan into action failed when the boatman, well aware of the consequences should he be caught (as subsequent events would show), lost his nerve and failed to fulfil his side of the bargain.

Margaret then turned to Irishman John Roche. There is some confusion as to his background, with narratives referring to him as variously Margaret's servant, a priest or a boatman, and some playing it safe by simply calling him 'a young man'. (There are even doubts as to his real name – it may have been Neele.) His identity may be in doubt, but his courage isn't. He procured a boat and at the appointed time waited beneath the place where Watson was to make his escape.

When the time came, Watson emerged from his window. We don't know which floor of this tall building he was being held on, but he must have run out of rope and dropped the remaining distance to the ground, as he injured himself and possibly even suffered a broken leg. Roche agreed to swap clothes with Watson, and this may have led to his undoing. Watson successfully fled the area, but when the empty cell and dangling rope were discovered, regular visitor Margaret Ward was the obvious suspect. We don't know how soon after the escape the arrests took place, but Roche being found still wearing Watson's clothes is often cited as being the cause of his own capture. This would lead to the conclusion that the hue and cry went up very soon after Watson's escape. Roche and Margaret were tracked down and taken away, and, in Margaret's case at least, the torture began.

As well as being flogged, she was hung up by her wrists so that her feet barely touched the ground. As we shall see, this form of torture was said to have been devised by Topcliffe himself. It was an excruciatingly painful position to be in for any length of time, and one which could cause permanent injury. In Margaret's case it went on for hours, while she was interrogated about the destination of the man she had sprung from prison. Jesuit missionary Father Robert Southwell sent news to Rome that Margaret was 'crippled and half-paralysed', but bravely held out and gave nothing away.

She was tried at Tyburn, where she confessed to her role in springing Watson from the Bridewell, declaring that she had 'delivered an innocent lamb from the hands of those bloody wolves'. When it was suggested to her that she should ask for the queen's pardon, she replied that as far as she was concerned, she had done nothing that required pardoning, adding that 'the queen herself, if she had the bowels of a woman, would have done as much, if she had known the ill-treatment he underwent'.[2]

Even after this, Margaret Ward – like Margaret Clitherow – was thrown a lifeline, and it was one which Clitherow herself had been offered: she merely had to attend one Anglican service. But also, like Clitherow, she refused, telling the court that death was 'very welcome to her', and that she was 'willing to lay down not one life only, but many, if she had them, rather than betray her conscience, or act against her duty to God and his holy religion'.

So it was that on 30 August 1588, Ward, Roche and four other condemned Catholics were taken to Tyburn, singing the *Te Deum* as they went. They were hanged one at a time, each being blessed by one of their number – a Catholic priest called Father Leigh, who was the last to go to the noose.

* * *

Meanwhile, Watson rested at a secret location while he recovered from the injuries sustained in his drop from the rope which had saved him. His later life was one of flitting in and out of England, in and out of prison. He seems to have possessed good escapology skills, and for a time appeared to be living a blessed existence, until his luck finally ran out in 1603. Following the death of Queen Elizabeth, Watson was a leading figure in an ill-considered and ill-fated plot to kidnap the new monarch, James I, and force him to grant toleration to Catholics. There were a number of arrests and confessions, and the information extracted from these led the authorities to Watson. He was taken to Winchester, where he suffered a fate even worse than Margaret: that of being hanged, drawn and quartered.

---

2. Chalanor, *Memoirs of Missionary Priests*.

It's a common enough phrase for historical executions, but not everyone is fully aware of the full horror of the method. The idea was to hang someone for a time, but cut them down before they were dead, when the process of disembowelment (drawn) would commence. This done, the corpse was cut into four pieces (quartered), like a carcass in a butcher's shop. The key point is the length of time the hanging was allowed to go on for, which to a great extent was up to the individual executioner. If the victim was lucky, he or she would at least be unconscious from strangulation when they were cut down, or dead if one or more of the onlookers were allowed to pull on the condemned person's legs. But it will be seen later that there were instances when a particularly callous hangman might cut the rope only moments after the cart upon which the victim was standing was drawn away; the physical and psychological trauma in such cases is beyond imagination, as is the mentality of those who would wilfully instigate such torment.

* * *

Robert Southwell described Margaret Ward as 'this most shining martyr'. Like Clitherow, she was canonized by Pope Paul VI in 1970, and also like Margaret he gave her the epithet of 'pearl': she became the Pearl of Tyburn.

Chapter 5

Growing Greatly in Debt

The Vaux Family

The Vaux were a Catholic family with Northamptonshire roots going back to at least the fifteenth century. Nicholas, 1st Baron Vaux, had fought for Henry VII during the Wars of the Roses, and a young Henry VIII was a visitor to Harrowden Hall, the family's ancestral home just north of Wellingborough, 12 miles from Northampton. The machinations of that king were, of course, a major trigger for the train of events leading to the scenarios described in this book.

Nicholas's grandson, William, 3rd Baron Vaux, was born at Harrowden in 1535. His was a powerful and wealthy lineage, but that offered little protection in the face of its divergence from the state religion. William's adherence to the Catholic faith diminished his standing at court and led to a steady decline in the family's fortunes. William was just a child when churches around the country were forced to remove all traces of Romish frippery, and in the coming decades a new Anglican church service was imposed, with the sacking of recalcitrant priests and imposing of fines for non-attendance at church implemented with increasing vigour.

William Vaux married Elizabeth Beaumont, from another recusant family, and they had four children: Henry, Eleanor, Elizabeth and Anne. All would go on to play their parts in the English Catholic community, and two of them prominent roles in what would become the Underground movement.

It is likely that Anne's birth, in 1562, was a difficult one, because her mother died just a few weeks later. William Vaux then married another Catholic woman: Mary Tresham, aunt of future Gunpowder Plotter Francis. (The Vaux family's connections with the Treshams would play a significant part in the future course of events.) William and Mary would go on to have five children together.

* * *

Lord Vaux was a regular attendee at parliament during Queen Mary's Catholic reign, and when that queen's half-sister, Elizabeth, came to the throne, William was among those sent to join her retinue as she made her grand entrance into the capital. He did not, however, take his seat in Westminster for some years after her accession.

This may have been a pragmatic decision because of his Catholic inclination. Nevertheless, William was not a political animal, being more interested in the arts and hunting. He was not openly Catholic, but although he would have worshipped privately, it was all but impossible for a man in his position to keep his religious affiliations secret. In 1572, Elizabeth's spymaster, Walsingham, received a report about William's financial support for a priest who was 'favoured of a great number of papists',[1] and he was certainly on Walsingham's 'watch list' by this time, if not before. Not long prior to this, Lord Vaux took on a tutor for his son Henry.

Edmund Campion, a brilliant Oxford scholar, probably already had latent Catholic sympathies at the time of his being ordained in the Anglican Church in 1564. By the time he arrived at Harrowden, he was a confirmed (in the common sense of the word, if not the literal religious one) Catholic, and would soon need to flee the country. But in the short period before this, he not only taught the young Henry but became a family friend. Whether he taught the girls – Eleanor, Anne and Elizabeth – is a moot point. Some accounts say he did, but we know from surviving letters written by Anne that she was what might be described as semi-literate. (Although spelling back then was far more fluid than it is now, there was still something of a consensus over how quite a lot of words were spelt, whereas the adult Anne, intelligent and wise though she was, spelt in a largely child-like, phonetic way.)

---

1. Anstruther, *The Vaux of Harrowden*.

Campion's primary role was not to preach or provide religious instruction, but given Lord Vaux's own disposition and Campion's awakening, it would be surprising if the two men didn't at least discuss such matters. This makes it not unlikely that Vaux would have consented to, and perhaps encouraged, Campion to introduce his son to the finer points of the faith.

Anne Vaux would have been only about 5 or 6 at this time, but a few years later, nine years after the death of her own mother and with the children from Lord Vaux's new marriage beginning to populate the house, she and her three siblings were sent to live with their grandmother, Elizabeth Beaumont, at Grace Dieu Manor in Leicestershire. This is where Anne, Eleanor, Elizabeth and Henry would have continued their own education.

Around 1577, when she was about 17, Anne's elder sister, Eleanor, married into another staunchly Catholic family which had been playing a leading role in supporting priests and the cause in general. Her new husband was Edward Brooksby of Shoby in Leicestershire, a place just over 15 miles from where the Vaux offspring were then living. The Shoby house (like many others) had a private chapel and a priest in residence, but the family also owned a house in East Ham, where a printing press was set up at around the time when Eleanor and Edward married, and began churning out Catholic pamphlets and books.

The early 1580s were an eventful time for the Vaux family and Catholicism in England. In the summer of 1580, when Eleanor and Edward had been married for only a few years, two men arrived from the Continent, in disguise and travelling under false names, who were to play a role, albeit a brief one, in the lives of both sisters.

* * *

The port authorities at Dover had been tipped off that Gabriel Allen of the Douai seminary in Belgium would soon be trying to enter England, and on 25 June a man appearing to fit his description disembarked from a newly arrived ship. When he was intercepted, he told them his name was Edmunds and that he was a dealer in gems. Father Thomas Campbell, author of *The Jesuits 1534–1921*, describes the encounter with the port warden thus:

'You are Doctor Allen!'

'Indeed, I am not.'

'Well, you are a suspicious character at all events, and your case must be looked into.'

The suspect was taken away for questioning, and there is – at the risk of sounding cynical – a rather fanciful story recounting how he uttered a prayer begging to be allowed at least a little time to do God's work in England. Upon hearing this, a change came over his interrogator's stern countenance and he admitted to having made a mistake and released him without further ado. Whether it was God's work or the detainee's smooth talking, it is certain that the man was able to persuade the authorities that it was a case of mistaken identity, and he was sent on his way.

The port authorities had indeed been mistaken about the man's identity, but when they finally relented and released him, they had unwittingly let a bigger fish than Gabriel Allen slip through the net. The person they released was the recently ordained Jesuit Edmund Campion, formerly tutor to Anne and Eleanor's brother, Henry, and possibly the girls as well. He had intended to use the alias 'Mr Patrick', as he had in the past, but was talked out of it. It was a name probably inspired by St Patrick, and his friends feared that the name's Irish association would only increase his chances of coming under scrutiny.

Campion's companion was fellow Jesuit Robert Persons. They had arrived on the east coast clandestinely in the same boat, then made their separate ways to London. Persons's disguise was that of a soldier returning from foreign service. They had been sent to England on a mission to provide support for the Catholic network.

Others besides the Dover port officials were also on the lookout for a suspicious new arrival. Campion's heart must have missed a beat when he saw a man eyeing him up and down and then begin to approach – but when the stranger cordially greeted him as 'Mr Edmunds', he knew he was in safe hands.

Catholic helpers, one of whom was Lord Vaux's son, Henry, to whom he had once acted as tutor, had been waiting to whisk the two priests away to Edward and Eleanor and the safety of Shoby Priory. They did not, however, stay long. Fearing that their arrival had drawn too much attention to the Brooksby's home, they headed south for Hoxton, at the time a small village north of London, where the pair came into contact with Sir Thomas Tresham and William Catesby. Tresham, as we have seen, was Eleanor's uncle, and Catesby's son, Robert, would become another leading figure in the Gunpowder Plot.

Campion launched into his mission, travelling around Northamptonshire, Berkshire and Oxfordshire preaching and hearing confession. By December he had ventured north, and spent Christmas with the Pierrepont family at Thoresby in north Nottinghamshire, then venturing through Derbyshire, Yorkshire and Lancashire. Campion regularly changed his name and style of dress to avoid detection. The fact that he often found his appearance 'very ridiculous' was probably a small price to pay, since Campion soon became aware that Cecil and his spies knew he had entered the country, and in fact on more than one occasion read that he had been arrested. 'I cannot long escape the hands of the heretics; the enemies have so many eyes, so many tongues, so many scouts and crafts,' said Campion, as quoted by Godfrey Anstruther in *Vaux of Harrowden*. And he was right. The manhunts, the frequent arrests and the general atmosphere of paranoia affected his own morale and that of those around him. Campion continued: 'The house where I am is sad; no talk but of death, flight, prison ... nevertheless they proceed with courage.'

Things soon became very hot for both Campion and Persons, and their mission was to be short-lived. Just over a year after their arrival, Father Persons was worried that the south of England was now too dangerous a place to linger, and advised Campion to transfer his ministry to Norfolk. Heading north, Campion accepted an invitation to preach to the Catholic Yate family in Lyford (then in Berkshire but now within the boundary of Oxfordshire). The house, Lyford Grange, was a known Catholic centre, but, much against Person's better judgement, he gave Campion his consent, though urging him to stay for no more than one night.

He made his call and duly went on his way after his overnight stop, but was waylaid by a man bringing messages from a large group of Catholics who had arrived at Lyford too late to hear Campion preach, begging him to return. The priest's generous acceptance of this belated plea would lead to his downfall. Among Campion's audience on his return was a government spy, a man seeking to have a murder charge overlooked in return for snaring one of England's most wanted men. The spy alerted the local magistrate, who soon advanced on Lyford Grange with a posse. They were spotted as they approached the house, and Campion wanted to leave to avoid incriminating his hosts but was persuaded to hide in one of the Grange's priest holes.

The hiding place did protect him from the thorough search performed throughout the house, but when the pursuivants fell asleep after having been fed, the hostess sent to Campion to preach to her as she lay in bed, along with a few other guests. It was a rash and foolish idea, but once again, he felt obliged to fulfil his priestly duty. The whispered service passed without incident, but as the little congregation dispersed in the darkness, one of them tripped and fell, apparently causing others to stumble over him. The inevitable commotion alerted the slumbering pursuivants, and although they didn't catch anyone immediately, they now knew they were onto something and where to focus their search for a hiding place, which they did with renewed vigour. The searchers discovered and broke through a thin false wall, and Edmund Campion, along with several others, was finally in their grasp.

Campion was taken to the Tower of London, where he was sent to the 'Little Ease': more of a hole than a cell, admitting no natural light, its narrow confines making it impossible to stand upright or even lie down. (It is believed that thirty-odd years later, Guy Fawkes was placed there after his arrest). The priest was interrogated in the presence of the queen herself, and, as had happened back in his Oxford days, Campion made a favourable impression on her. She offered him his freedom, 'but under conditions which his conscience forbade him to accept', which presumably meant some kind of disavowal of his faith and possibly attendance at a Protestant service. Almost inevitably, Campion ended up on the rack, his captors demanding the names and opinions of those he had associated with.

This torture resulted in terrible injuries. According to Mendoza, the Spanish Ambassador, Campion was 'all dislocated and unable to move'. Worse still, if that were possible, there is a strong likelihood that racking failed to have the desired effect and he was subjected to 'pricking', a relatively innocuous-sounding practice, but which was actually quite horrific. It began with thin iron spikes being driven between the fingernails and the ultra-sensitive 'quick' underneath, and ended with the nails being torn out completely.

Campion was then sent for trial, where he was found guilty on trumped-up charges of treason (supposedly plotting to overthrow Elizabeth, the woman who had taken such a shine to him). At dawn on the rainy, bitingly cold morning of 1 December 1581, the priest was dragged to Tyburn on a hurdle. Two separate witnesses in a crowd said to have numbered in the thousands noted that he had no fingernails left when he went to his death, thus confirming Mendoza's claim.

Campion, then aged 41, was hanged, drawn and quartered, though it appears he was granted the mercy of being left to hang until he was dead before the butchery took place. That the horrendous pain under torture drove Campion to give up names is suggested by the number of those who had sheltered him being visited and questioned during the period between his torture and execution – these included Anne's father, Lord Vaux, Sir Thomas Tresham and William Catesby. This outcome may have simply been because the association between them all was known, but it's also possible that Campion was tricked into confirming the connection. It was not an uncommon ploy for interrogators to pretend to have already obtained the information from other sources, thus making it seem less imperative to the victim that he should endure further agonies to protect their identities.

Persons managed to avoid capture, but after the arrests of first Campion and then, shortly afterwards, Steven Brinkley, who had been operating the secret Catholic printing press, he realized that it would be impossible for him to continue operating in the current climate, and he was able to slip out of the country as surreptitiously as he had made his entrance.

Probably because of their status, Vaux and the others were initially placed under a form of house arrest in the homes of other members of the nobility in their locality, where there was to be preliminary questioning to see if their cases needed to be taken further. Vaux and Tresham were eventually taken to London, where they appeared before Lord Burghley and the Earls of Sussex and Leicester. Both refused to confirm or deny the story that 'Campion the Jesuit' had been at their houses, and were promptly committed to the Fleet Prison. They subsequently appeared before the Star Chamber, the judicial arm of the Queen's Council. Vaux put on a humble, almost obsequious performance, telling the assembled nobles that the man called Campion had been a teacher to his children but had not to his knowledge been at his house. Tresham also denied having hosted Campion. After some semantic exchanges about their refusal to swear this on oath (with Vaux protesting that a nobleman's word was as good as formally swearing), the pair were sentenced to be returned to the Fleet and issued with substantial fines: £1,000 for Vaux and 1,000 marks (around £666) for Tresham.

While Vaux was in prison, a further piece of misfortune befell him. A priest called Edward Osborn was arrested and committed to the Fleet Prison, where he was questioned about his contacts. Osborn had a chequered history, having achieved the almost unique distinction of being kicked out of both the English College in Rome and the order of the Franciscans. He came from Northamptonshire, the same part of the world as Vaux, and named the baron and his second wife, Mary Tresham, as being among those who had attended his Masses.

This led to Lord Vaux appearing before the notorious Richard Topcliffe. Among the many things written about him – none of them good – Anstruther describes him as an 'odious monster' who, regarding his cruelty, 'writers contemporary and modern, Catholic and Protestant, are in complete agreement'. Luckily, Vaux's rank afforded him a certain amount of protection, and he was meeting the fledgling torturer early in his career. When Vaux and the others were found guilty, the result was a relatively small additional fine. We shall be hearing much more of the exploits of Topcliffe.

It was also in 1581 that Lord Vaux's recusancy finally became 'official'. He had managed to keep his name out of the records of non-attenders at his local church until now, but he was finally cited in May, along with his servants, and came up with the creative response that since he owned and attended his own chapel, it was, in effect, his parish church. There doesn't appear to be a record of how this explanation went down with the authorities, but it's unlikely to have been a favourable one.

There was yet another significant event that year. With Eleanor's marriage just three years old, husband Edward fell ill and died. This would have been a crushing blow to any young, recently married person, but Eleanor was particularly badly hit and would never fully recover, as we shall hear.

She and Anne took up residence in the manor house at Ashby Magna, south Leicestershire, which she had inherited as her own upon Edward's death.

In 1582, Elizabeth Vaux, sister of Anne and Eleanor, was sent to Rouen, to join the Poor Clare community of nuns there, and three sons from Lord Vaux's second marriage – Edward, Ambrose and George – all made trips to France to receive Catholic tuition. We know this because these movements were noted by informants, and duly recorded in government papers. These visits were in contravention of the law, but with Lord Vaux still in prison anyway, the authorities chose to remain abreast of events for the time being without acting.

Lord Vaux was released in 1583, having spent just under two years in the Fleet, but he was not a completely free man. Rather like the modern Home Detention system, where prisoners may leave prison early and live under a type of curfew at a 'suitable address', Vaux was allowed to rent a house in Hackney, close enough to London to be kept tabs on. He was allowed to attend parliament, but otherwise he perhaps took the curfew side of things a little too literally, since he and members of his family who had joined him there were regularly fined for not attending church. There can be no doubt that they continued to observe Catholic worship and receive priests to provide instruction, take confession and conduct services, but the hunt for evidence of these activities among all known Catholic families was intensifying, with information pouring in from spies and even renegade priests. Vaux's friend Sir Thomas Tresham had his house in Hoxton raided, and much incriminating material was found.

Anne and Eleanor's father was beginning to feel the effects of the long spell of imprisonment and the relentless accumulation of financial penalties. In a letter to a friend, he admitted to 'growing greatly in debt', having been forced to 'sell divers lordships' (presumably meaning estates or manors).

At the end of 1584, two years after an increase in the fines for recusancy had come into effect, a bill was introduced which would make it an act of treason to be a priest ordained overseas since Elizabeth's accession. Vaux and Tresham, both still leading peers despite their trials and tribulations, took the risk of petitioning the queen herself about both this act and the general suffering of Catholics who had always been, and remained, loyal to the throne in all ways other than their faith. Their petition stated:

> 'If we shut our doors and deny our temporal relief to our Catholic pastors in respect of their function, then are we already judged most damnable traitors to Almighty God ... Behold, most gracious and liege Sovereign, into what straits we are plunged ... Suffer us not to be the only outcasts and refuse of the world ... Let it not be treason for the sick man in body (even to the last gasp) to seek ghostly council for the salvation of his soul of a Catholic priest.'[2]

The petitioners took the even bolder and rasher step (perhaps fearing that if their plea were sent through the normal channels it might not even reach the eyes of her Majesty) of concocting a plan to circumvent normal royal protocol and place their petition directly into Elizabeth's hands. Although understandable, it was not a wise move – as Richard Shelley, the man elected to deliver the document, found out when he intercepted the queen as she was taking the air in Greenwich. The outcome is neatly summarized in a single sentence added to a copy of Vaux and Tresham's document: 'The said Mr Shelley, for presuming to deliver it to her Majesty, not acquainting the right honourable of the Privy Council first withal ... [was] committed close prisoner to the Marshalsea where he died, which was the sum of the answer made to it.'

* * *

By 1585, the morass into which Lord Vaux had sunk came into sharper focus when a tax was levied specifically on recusants to help pay for the army. This, coming on top of the many forfeits already incurred, seems to have proved too much even for a leading man of state like the baron. He found himself in the embarrassing position of having to report that he was unable to meet the demand, and asked that some of the lands he owned be assessed for sale. There were further such humiliations, but in

---

2. *Ibid.*

matters of conscience Vaux remained unbending. At the end of 1585, he and Tresham were once again indicted for not going to church.

The following year, during which Margaret Clitherow met her awful end in York, what became known as The Babington Plot was exposed. This was an ill-conceived attempt to get rid of Elizabeth and replace her with her Catholic cousin, Mary, Queen of Scots, then in her eighteenth year as a prisoner in England. The conspiracy came to be named after Anthony Babington, who was not only one of its instigators but also engaged in 'secret' correspondence with Mary about it. But it was correspondence which Elizabeth's spymaster, Sir Francis Walsingham, knew all about thanks to his spies and code-breakers; indeed, he allowed it to continue in order to bring Mary down. When Walsingham finally chose to pounce, the news was a concern for Lord Vaux, because although he was not personally involved, he and son Henry were known associates of Anthony Babington. Fortunately, Walsingham chose not to investigate the link and the downfall of the plot did not add to Lord Vaux's many woes, though he almost certainly came under closer scrutiny from that point on.

At around this time, there was a development which would impinge directly on himself and his family as two more Jesuit priests surreptitiously entered England: Robert Southwell and Henry Garnet. Garnet, in particular, was destined to play a major part in the lives of Eleanor and Anne – especially the latter. In later years, to aid in their prime target's capture, the authorities issued a description:

> 'Henry Garnet, alias Walley, alias Darcy, alias Farmer, of a middling stature, full faced, fat of body, of complexion fair, his forehead high on each side, with a little thin hair coming down upon the middest of the fore part of this head; his hair and beard grisled. Of age between fifty and three score [he was actually probably not quite 50 by this time]. His beard on his cheeks close cut, and his chin very thin and somewhat short. His gait upright, and comely for a feeble man.'

Garnet was only in his early 30s when he arrived in 1586. When Weston himself was captured not long after their arrival, Garnet assumed the role of Jesuit Superior. At the time of the above notice he was still probably barely 50, and would show them just how 'feeble' he was.

From the beginning, the Jesuit Superior General in Rome, Claudio Acquaviva, well aware of the prevailing climate in England, issued the two young men with strict instructions aimed at keeping both them and the Catholics they associated with out of harm's way as far as possible under the circumstances. They were to confine themselves strictly to religious and pastoral duties, remaining aloof from politics and matters of state, and from criticism of the Queen or even allowing it from others in their presence. They might wear their soutane, or cassock, when it was safe to do so, but must not carry with them items for which ownership carried a death sentence, such as Agnus Deis (wax discs bearing impressions of a lamb and blessed by the Pope) and rosaries. (We know that rosaries etc. were found by pursuivants during raids, but presumably they were kept on the premises and not carried around by individual priests.)

For now, Garnet didn't spend long in London, where he had helped new arrivals such as Fathers Oldcorne and Gerard (covered in the next chapter) to settle in and set up an underground Catholic printing press. After visiting Hertfordshire, he travelled north to Eleanor's Leicestershire home. With Lord Vaux still confined to Hackney, it fell to his daughters to take the priest in. The widowed Eleanor Brooksby was now in her mid-20s, while Anne was about 22 and unmarried. Eleanor had two young children from her short-lived marriage, but when an aunt died not long after Eleanor's own husband, she had also adopted one of her relative's daughters.

Frances Burroughs was just 5 when this took place, but she would soon play her own part in the secret work being undertaken by the Vaux sisters. There is a description of how the adoption came to take place which was almost certainly supplied by Frances herself in later years. Eleanor was already godmother to one of her aunt's other children, and upon her death this was the child she had agreed to take in. But when Frances was brought to her, she seemed to see something in her that no one else did. Eleanor embraced the girl, and with tears in her eyes cried: 'I will have Frances! I will have Frances, for to this child God will give a blessing which none of the rest shall have.'

Anne and Eleanor were to regularly act as Garnet's hosts, and much more, during the course of the coming turbulent years.

* * *

Henry Garnet, as Jesuit Superior, had inherited a well-organized Catholic underground network from his predecessor, William Weston (who had the misfortune of being arrested just days after a meeting with Garnet by spies not seeking him but rather Anthony Babington). Philip Carman (*Henry Garnet 1555–1606 & the Gunpowder Plot*, p.36) states that every English county had bases where priests might be received, and estimates that there were about 300 such men active around the country. It was an amazing achievement in view of the equally well-established network of government spies and informants, but the life of a priest was still, as Weston himself discovered and as Garnet too would in time, a very precarious and often short-lived existence.

Ashby Magna became his first English base, but he was away from Anne and Eleanor a lot of the time as he travelled around the country overseeing the network, while at the same time trying to dodge the numerous raids on the homes suspected of harbouring priests. He stayed in London as little as possible, the capital being simply too hazardous for the time being. This was vividly illustrated when the authorities swooped on Lord Vaux's Hackney home, where Robert Southwell was then living. All of the priests secretly working in England used pseudonyms, and Father Thomas Campbell, in *The Jesuits 1534–1921* (Vol. 1), tells us that Southwell was going by the name of Cotton. The priest and poet had already given the slip to a man who had been tailing him, clearly hoping to be led to the house where his prey was staying. But shortly afterwards, the chief magistrate of London had learned of Southwell's location from the confession under interrogation of another priest; he and his men descended on the Vaux house, timing it with the intention of catching the family at Mass. The only thing that saved Southwell was the Vaux servant who answered the door, whose efforts to prevent the pursuivants from entering bought Southwell enough time to hide. Despite a violent and destructive search, they failed to locate him. Lord Vaux's eldest son, Henry, who was in the house at the time, was not so lucky. He had been studying for the priesthood, and while waiting to go abroad to ordain had been playing an active role in the clandestine lay Catholic movement. Once his identity was established, he was arrested and taken to the Marshalsea, a much less salubrious prison than the

Fleet, where his father had been held; the conditions there were to have a devastating effect on his health.

Lord Vaux and his wife were both present when the house was invaded. William bought Mary some time by interfering with the search until she could hide 'her little casket', which presumably held some relic or other religious items. It was she who sent a message to her husband's friend, Sir Thomas Tresham, and his lawyer asking what course of action she should take on behalf of her son. To Henry's credit, they advised that he should be allowed to speak for himself, since they were sure that his responses to the interrogators would be 'so wisely framed as he shall not need any other means of deliverance'.

At about the same time, perhaps acting on information from the same source, Ashby was also hit.

It was another early-morning raid. One of the two priests then present – probably Father Garnet – was taking Mass when all present heard a commotion below. Correctly guessing that priest-hunters had descended upon them, Anne, Eleanor and the adopted child Frances hurried downstairs to be met with the sight of armed men swarming through their home. We have no way of knowing whether Eleanor already had a naturally somewhat fragile temperament, but she never really recovered emotionally from the death of her young husband and was not up to confrontations with aggressive invaders. Normally it would be the doughty Anne who took the lead in such matters, even to the point of presenting herself as Eleanor – if not in name, then in her role as mistress of the house. But on this occasion, 11-year-old Frances, of whom it was later said 'her courage was such that she never seemed to be daunted or feared of anything',[3] surprised everyone by taking it upon herself to go head-to-head with the pursuivants.

'Put down your swords, or else my mother will die— she cannot endure to see a naked blade,' the girl cried.[4] The raiders are reported to have been suitably cowed by this surprise intervention. On the pretext of going off to get some reviving wine for her swooning adoptive mother, Frances secured Garnet's hiding place before returning with the drink.

---
3. *Ibid.*
4. Caraman, *Henry Garnet.*

When a further incursion took place later that year, it was Frances who came to the fore again, barring the searchers from going up the staircase. But these were of a different order to the previous band. Thinking to intimidate the young girl, a belligerent pursuivant held a knife to her breast, threatening to stab her if she didn't tell him where the priest was hiding. But he had met his match. 'If thou dost, it will be the hottest blood ever thou sheddest in thy life!' Frances retorted.

* * *

By May 1587 (three months after the execution of Mary, Queen of Scots), the health of Anne and Eleanor's imprisoned brother, Henry, had deteriorated. He is believed to have contracted tuberculosis, and was released from the Marshalsea and allowed to travel back to Ashby. It was intended as a temporary arrangement to allow him time to recover, but the illness was worse than anyone had realized and Henry died in November of that year. The large lump sum he left Anne would bolster her efforts to aid the Jesuit priesthood in the years to come.

And then came 1588: the year of the Spanish Armada.

The country was not taken by surprise, as reports of an increasing number of ships being assembled had reached England the previous year. An attack by Sir Francis Drake on vessels anchored at Cadiz helped to delay the Armada, but did not prevent it from going ahead at a later date.

Neither the Jesuits nor most other Catholics were inclined to support an invasion of their own country, and the queen and her ministers almost certainly knew this. Yet it did not prevent them from initiating a programme of interning the heads of recusant families. Lord Vaux was one of a number who were committed to the care of the Archbishop of Canterbury. He was not imprisoned, because he was classified as being one of those 'not so obstinate' Catholics. As we now know, the Armada was defeated and the immediate crisis soon passed, but there was a spate of Catholic executions afterwards, and the actions of the government had left people like Vaux and Tresham looking like latent traitors, skulking in the shadows while waiting for the right time to strike.

Chapter 6

Illustrious by Birth

Anne Vaux

On a rainy night in November 1588, three months after the execution of Margaret Ward at Tyburn, the dark outline of a ship, barely visible in the gloom, dropped anchor off the Norfolk coast. A boat was lowered and two men were rowed ashore. The boat returned to the waiting ship, which made all sail back to France.

The men who had been put ashore attempted to strike inland as far as they could before morning, but every path they took seemed to take them towards some form of habitation, setting off the barking of dogs. They decided to err on the side of caution and settled down to spend a cold, wet and uncomfortable night sheltering in some woods. Their ultimate destination was London, but when morning came they decided it would be safest to split up and make their own ways there. The two new arrivals were Fathers Edward Oldcorne and John Gerard. Oldcorne reached London first by some time, so the Jesuit Superior Henry Garnet, fearing that his companion had been captured, was very relieved to see Gerard when he finally turned up at his door.

* * *

Garnet liked to have two gatherings of the Jesuits under his authority each year, and, perhaps because of their growing numbers, he decided that a larger property than the Vaux sisters' current home in Ashby Magna was needed. He set about finding a suitable property, preferably in the same general area. This is how he, Anne and Eleanor came to make the move to Baddesley Clinton in Warwickshire, about 25 miles from Ashby as the crow flies. It was owned by a Catholic family and had its own ready-made concealed hiding place designed by the master priest-hole builder himself, Nicholas Owen. Owen was known to all and sundry as 'Little John' on account of his diminutive stature, and his mobility was hampered by a childhood injury to one of his legs, leaving him with a pronounced limp. He always accompanied Garnet except when sent away on a mission, and came to live at Baddesley with him. He was a skilled joiner and carpenter, and his reputation for designing priest holes whose ingenious locations and entrances defied discovery made him a man in great demand.

Unlike Great Harrowden Hall, where the sisters were born, Baddesley Clinton remains intact and can be visited today. Eight miles north-west of Warwick, it was and is relatively remote and hidden from view by trees. It takes the form of a hollow square (but for one open side) enclosing a courtyard, and is surrounded by a moat. It was easily big enough to host the twice-yearly Jesuit gatherings, and its warren of corridors, stairs, rooms and nooks and crannies had already defeated several determined searches by pursuivants in the past. It would need to do so again in the not too distant future.

The first raid on Baddesley Clinton about which we have any details took place in October 1591, when Father Garnet had gathered together all available priests to mark the Feast of St Luke. However, from what Anne Vaux was later to say, it seems clear that there had been previous such visitations. Writing about the event afterwards, Father Garnet said the meeting was held at the house of 'the widow and the virgin'. Garnet's reference to Anne as 'the virgin' conveyed more than merely her unmarried and chaste status. She was no mere shelterer of priests, but had by this time chosen to fully commit herself to the holy path, albeit as a householder. She had privately taken vows and was, Anstruther tells us, 'to all intents and purposes a nun. Her small property belonged to the community, and her life was directed by Father Garnet.' The Jesuit Superior himself described both sisters as being 'illustrious by birth, fidelity, and holiness and life, whom I sometimes in my thoughts liken to the two women who used to lodge Our Lord'.

Fortunately, the assembled priests received advance warning that a raid was imminent thanks to a drunken pursuivant – 'a filthy fellow who spent his days snoring in taverns', as Garnet's delicious put-down describes him – who took it upon himself to turn up alone one day before the meeting of the priests, demanding to be admitted. The servants, and possibly Anne, who tended to take the lead in these situations, engaged in their usual delaying tactics to allow all traces of Catholic paraphernalia to be hidden away. This, and the pursuivant's subsequent failure to find anything incriminating, caused him to be 'filled with sudden fury'. He told them that he had come as a friend, but after the way he had been treated he would be back in ten days with more men to 'break open the doors and shatter the very walls of the house'.

This put Garnet in an awkward position. He couldn't be sure whether the man really would go through with his threat once he had sobered up, but a number of priests were due to descend on the house from all parts of the country and it was too late to warn them off. The hope was that if the raid really did take place, it would be in ten days as threatened, since the visitors would then have come and gone before it took place.

The priests duly gathered and the feast of St Luke's Day was proceeding without incident, with the eleven visiting priests gathered at the table, when Garnet was suddenly struck by a premonition of imminent danger so clear and powerful that he advised those who could do so to leave Baddesley Clinton that very night. The Jesuits around Garnet had enough faith in their Superior to heed his advice. Four of them were in a position to get away that night, and the remainder prepared to leave first thing in the morning. Among those remaining with Garnet were Fathers Gerard, Oldcorne (who had lived with Anne and Eleanor for a while at the same time as Garnet but was now installed at nearby Hindlip Hall) and Southwell, the poet/priest with the distinctive auburn hair and boyish face who had arrived in England with Garnet.

They rose before dawn and settled down to breakfast at around 5.00 am while their horses were being readied. In the darkness outside, no one – not the servants airing the priests' cloaks and cleaning their leggings, nor even those saddling the horses in the courtyard – noticed a large group of men stealthily approach the house and then fan out to surround it.

The first hint that something was amiss came when a youth leaving the house spotted the shadowy figures flitting about in the distance, panicked and fled into the surrounding countryside. His precipitous flight alerted some stable hands, who grabbed pitchforks and shovels and challenged the trespassers before they could reach the main door of

Baddesley Clinton. The pursuivants' leader remained impassive (Garnet was magnanimous enough to later praise his calmness, reflecting that people like this were usually 'so brave if you show no fear, but so craven if you stand up to them'), assuring the defenders that he would 'deal gently' with the mistress of the house.

Meanwhile, news of the invasion had spread rapidly through Baddesley Clinton, galvanizing the inhabitants into action. Internal doors were locked, and rosaries and other Catholic paraphernalia were hastily secreted. An indication of how experienced the family and servants must have been in handling such situations is that even bed mattresses were turned over, in case any lingering warmth from the recent occupants should reveal the presence of guests. The priests themselves entered what looked like a well near the moat, but which had stone steps built into it leading to an underground passage, the only inconvenience being that they would be standing in a few inches of water. This was another Little John creation. Whether Little John accompanied them into his own priest hole isn't recorded, but it's possible that he stayed in the house and was passed off as a servant.

Eleanor, the elder sister and technically the mistress of the house, went into a different hiding place with her children. This was partly to protect them from being taken away, should it come to that, but there was another reason, and it was to do with Eleanor's still delicate mental state. As little Frances had already stated during a previous such occasion, she simply couldn't bring herself to confront the invaders. 'She is rather timid, and finds it difficult to cope with the threats and evil looks of the searchers,' Garnet would later say. Coming from one who was normally only ever full of praise and admiration for his two primary female supporters, this is quite a frank assessment – not that there is anything wrong with Eleanor's need to retreat from such events. In those situations, their very lives and the lives of those they loved were ultimately at stake, and few of us could know how well we might cope, regardless of how much we may imagine that we would remain as calm and defiant as had Frances. It also seems that stress and maybe chronic illness had aged Eleanor. Jessie Childs, in *God's Traitors*, refers to a reference in the local parish records to the death of the brother of 'old Mris Bruxby' (Mistress Brooksby). This was in 1587, when she was only around 27.

Be that as it may, Anne Vaux, herself now approaching 30 years of age and the younger of the sisters, put herself forward and assumed the identity of the widowed mother and mistress of the house. Once she was sure the decks had been cleared, Anne allowed the men at the door to enter – though initially just two of them. It must have taken some time to 'sanitize' Baddesley Clinton, because by this time the leader, who had initially been calm and respectful, yet probably well aware of the tactics being employed, was starting to show signs that his patience was being tested and complained about the length of time he had been kept waiting. Anne was not timid, but whereas Eleanor's problem was psychological, Anne's issue was physical. Like Margaret Line, she suffered from some sort of long-term ailment. Garnet writes of a 'chronic weakness' that she 'nearly always labours under'. He had noticed that she was sometimes so debilitated that it was an effort for her to even speak. Nevertheless, when the pursuivants arrived at her door, she always managed to find the energy and strength from somewhere. Garnet had known her to spend up to four hours holding her ground in stand-offs with such people.

She appeared to have decided that attack was the best form of defence on this occasion, peppering her uninvited guest with questions and accusations. Did he think it right and proper that he should be admitted to a widow's house before she or her servants or her children were out of bed? Where were his manners? Why come so early? Why did they keep making these hostile visits to her house? And so on. It worked, temporarily at least, putting the chief pursuivant on the back foot. (It has to be borne in mind that this man would have been socially inferior to Anne at a time when such things were of great moment. In any other social setting, he would have been expected to assume a deferential demeanour.)

'It's quite true,' the leader admitted to his colleague. 'I've always had courtesy from this lady.'

Garnet observed: 'The virgin always conducts these arguments with such skill and discretion that she entirely counteracts their persistence and their interminable chatter.'

But in spite of the apparent softening of his attitude, the leader wasn't to be deflected from his mission. He had seen an occupant of the house taking flight when his men arrived, which had convinced him that the youth must be a priest. He and his men would not be leaving until he was handed over, and if he wasn't, he told Anne Vaux that she would be the one taken away.

Now it was Anne's turn to be momentarily thrown. In the haste and confusion caused by the pursuivants' arrival, she had not been aware of anyone running away, so assumed he must be right about it having been one of the priests making his escape. (Ironically, the young fugitive was a layman, but did later become a priest.) Thinking quickly, Anne shrugged off the incident, explaining that they had merely frightened one of her relatives who had been due to travel with her that day. This was a particularly clever bit of impromptu invention, because it killed two birds with one stone – putting their minds at ease about the absconder, while also explaining away the extra horses being readied in the stables.

That particular situation had been diffused, but it didn't prevent the search from going ahead. In one sense, these raids were a kind of game. The pursuivants weren't striking randomly, groping in the dark. They knew who the Catholic families were, knew that priests traversed the country ministering to their flock, and knew that families like the Vaux harboured them in order to do so. The only thing they couldn't have known was the unusual extent to which Anne and Eleanor were involved, especially at this particular time. For their part, the Catholic families themselves knew that the pursuivants knew, and these sometimes polite games between the two sides were played out time and again.

On this occasion, 'Everything was turned upside down', Garnet reported. Rooms, cupboards, chests, even beds were examined. But whether skilfully so is open to question, since Anne later told Garnet that instead of conducting a careful and painstaking search, the pursuivants poked around displaying little thought or judgement, 'like a lot of boys playing Blind Man's Bluff'. Even on the few occasions when they came across incriminating items, they didn't realize what they were looking at. Anne must have looked on apprehensively when one found and picked up a silver pyx (a small lidded container in which consecrated bread was kept), examined it, then, presumably thinking it a decorative ornament, put it back where it came from 'as though it were the most ordinary thing in the world'. Another, sorting through a drawer of folded clothes, came across a dalmatic, a priest's outer garment, but paid it not the slightest attention.

After a time, Anne graciously treated the searchers to breakfast. During their conversations, the head of the pursuivants asked for the youth who had run away to be brought before them, reasoning that because of his holy vows, a priest could not deny that he *was* a priest. In fact, there was some debate about this very point within the Catholic Church, and Garnet himself believed that it was acceptable to answer the question in the negative – but in this case it was an academic point, since the young man had not been ordained. He was duly summoned, earnestly insisted that he was not a priest, and thus was released. Fortified by their meal, the pursuivants resumed the search. But with the second round proving no more fruitful, and with four hours having passed since their arrival, Anne was able to pay them off.

Garnet later said that he had so much faith in Anne, Eleanor and those around them that he had not been the slightest bit worried when he had hidden himself away. Now, emerging with the others, there was understandable relief and mutual congratulation. But though they had easily foiled the amateurish efforts of the local pursuivants, they would be confronted with far more determined, ruthless and professionally conducted searches in the future.

Chapter 7

To Die for Christ

Anne Line

In the spring of 1598, a large group of men headed by the Lieutenant of the Tower of London and the Knight Marshall (a senior royal official) descended on a large house in London. They spent two days searching the premises and grounds, but in the end slunk away defeated and empty-handed. There had, in fact, been a Catholic priest in the house, but so well hidden (very likely in a priest hole created by Nicholas Owen) that they didn't find him despite the lengthy search. Anyway, the priest then in residence wasn't their target. They were looking for two people, one of whom was Father John Gerard, one of the senior Jesuit priests in the country.

A later description of Gerard described him as being tall, upright and 'well set', with dark hair and complexion. He had a large face, 'his cheeks sticking out, and somewhat hollow underneath the cheeks; the hair of his head long, if it be not cut off; his beard cut close, saving little mustachioes, and a little tuft under his lower lip'.

The other was the woman who had been in charge of running the house and tending to the numerous priests who had been coming and going for quite some time. Her name was Anne Line, and although she avoided capture this time, she was already living on borrowed time.

* * *

Anne Line's heritage has caused genealogists a bit of a headache over the years, but the consensus of opinion is that she was born Alice Higham or Heigham, changing her Christian name to Anne when she converted to Catholicism and her surname when she married Roger Line in 1583. If, as seems probable, Alice Higham and Anne Line are one and the same, she was the daughter of William Higham. Until recently, Dunmow in Essex has been considered to be the place of her birth, but recent Anne Line biographer Martin Dodwell (*Anne Line: Shakespeare's Tragic Muse*) has suggested Hazeleigh, a parish 20 miles south-east of Maldon in Essex, as being the correct place. The family owned the manor house of Jenkyn Maldon — Dunmow being a later address. Anne is strongly associated with an elegant Grade I Listed Elizabethan building in Dunmow known as the Clock House (presumably on account of the clock tower on its roof), but originally called Goston Lodge. It's the kind of place an Elizabethan gentleman like her father might have owned, but the author of *Francis Clark: a Man of his Time*[1] says that she was merely a housekeeper there (and that she is said to still haunt the place!).

Anne's father, William, was a member of the landed gentry and a devout Protestant; so devout that when Anne not only turned away from the faith of her birth and her family but also married a Catholic man, he withdrew her dowry and ensured that she would not inherit any of the estates he owned. Anne left Dunmow to work for the family of a nobleman who was a courtier to Elizabeth I, and it was almost certainly her new-found faith that led to her leaving that position.

The union of Anne and Roger was ill-starred in ways other than the financial losses inflicted on them because of their Catholicism.

They married young. Anne is often categorically stated to have been 19, but this must be regarded as an unreliable figure, since while the year of her marriage is known, her birth year definitely isn't. The idea may have arisen because Roger himself, according to Anne's *Oxford Dictionary of National Biography* entry, was 'a recusant gentleman under the age of nineteen' when he married Anne, so Anne's age may have been extrapolated from this.

Be that as it may, these undoubtedly young and committed people were destined to spend less than two years together. Roger, like Anne, had been disinherited by his family because of his conversion and missed out on the inheritances that would have been due to him when both his father and uncle died. One day in December 1586, Roger Line attended Mass

---

1. https://fitzroyhistorysociety.org.au/wp-content/uploads/2022/03/francis-clark-amhart-2015-2022-1.pdf.

with Anne's brother, William, and both were caught, arrested and sent into exile. Anne would never see her husband again. Biographer Martin Dodwell believes that before the couple's enforced separation, Anne gave birth to a son, John, and that the child was taken from her, willingly or otherwise, and brought up by Roger's family.

Roger went to Belgium, and for some reason was awarded a pension by the King of Spain, out of which he was able to send Anne a small amount of money. But with Anne's own family disowning her financially and otherwise, it was probably not enough. When Roger died in 1594, she was, as Father Gerard says in his autobiography, 'without a friend in this world and was entirely dependent on God's providence'. Although Anne is said to have worked for Father Garnet, it was now that Gerard took Anne under his wing. He had been staying with Sir William Wiseman and his wife, Jane, probably in a house called Braddocks, near Thaxted (about 7 miles north of her old home in Dunmow, a place also still standing), and he arranged for her to live with them for a while.

This would seem to have been a somewhat risky move, since Braddocks had been raided by pursuivants about three years previously while Gerard was in residence – but then again, there were few large houses of known Catholics that hadn't been targeted at some point or other. Unbeknown to Gerard and the family, however, soon after his arrival one of their servants had betrayed them to the authorities, and the priest was in the act of preparing for an early-morning Mass on Easter Monday, 1 April 1594, when they heard the thunder of horses' hooves outside and discovered that the house was surrounded by troops, with local justices of the peace at their head. While the staff barred the doors for as long as they could, Gerard frantically gathered everything from the altar, along with incriminating books and papers, and hid them in a priest hole. There was another hiding place accessed from the dining room which he wanted to take refuge in himself, but Jane Wiseman persuaded him to go into another which was upstairs, near the family chapel. The priest hole there was one of Little John's finest creations, the entrance being ingeniously concealed beneath the grate of the fireplace. A small supply of food was always stashed in it in case of emergencies such as this.

Gerard had not been shut up inside the hiding place for long when he heard the front door being smashed open and the heavy reverberation of many boots on the wooden floorboards as the invaders poured in and spread out through the building. Jane Wiseman and her daughters (husband William doesn't seem to have been at home) were locked in Jane's bedroom while the men got to work. They were clearly experienced in such matters because they knew to tap the walls and floors, listening for tell-tale hollow sounds, and they measured walls externally and internally – a shorter internal than external measurement might indicate a false internal wall.

The house was virtually pulled to pieces on the inside, the searchers not hesitating to smash walls and floorboards whenever they thought they might have found a cavity. They ripped plaster from walls, and, Gerard later recorded,

> 'set a man to work near the ceiling, close to the place where I was ... So they stripped off the plaster all round, till they came again to the very place where I lay, and there they lost heart and gave up the search. My hiding-place was in a thick wall of the chimney, behind a finely inlaid and carved mantelpiece. They could not well take the carving down without risk of breaking it. Broken however it would have been, and that into a thousand pieces, had they any conception that I could be concealed behind it.'

At one point they had explored the fireplace which provided the entrance to the priest hole, even to the extent of putting a ladder inside and tapping with hammers. Gerard heard one of them muse, 'Might there not be a place here for a person to get down into the wall of the chimney below, by lifting up this hearth?' His colleague didn't think so, but speculated that there could be an entrance behind the chimney they were currently exploring. He kicked the brickwork, causing Gerard to fear they would detect the hollow response, but 'God who set bounds to the sea, said also to their dogged obstinacy, "Thus far shalt thou go and no further"'.

When two days of this intense searching revealed nothing, it was decided that Gerard must have left before their arrival. The magistrates decided to stand the search down, but left a few men to guard the house and took Jane Wiseman, her daughters and some servants, away with them to be questioned. By now, Jane was beginning to worry that

Gerard's meagre rations would soon run out. In the frantic rush to conceal incriminating evidence, food for the priest hole had been a low priority; all Gerard had was a couple of biscuits and some quince jelly. Before being shut in, he had told Jane that he would starve to death rather than emerge and be caught – not for his own sake, but because of what would happen to her family if he was found on the premises. With this in mind, before being taken away she took aside one of the servants who was to be left behind and told him to sneak into a certain room, quietly call out Father Gerard's name and help to get him away from the house when he emerged. What she didn't know was that the servant was the traitor who had betrayed them.

The man rushed off to tell the magistrates, and the search was quickly resumed, with, of course, special attention given to the room Jane Wiseman had told the servant to go to. But such was Little John's skill in building and concealing the entrances to his hiding places that even then, after a further two days' exploration, they failed to find it.

It seemed that Gerard had escaped their clutches again, until a couple of men who had been set to guard the room overnight began to feel the cold, and decided to light a fire. Little John had created a false bottom to the fireplace, but it was made of wooden boards; even though they were painted and covered with bricks to make it all look like a conventional hearth, and firewood had been laid on top to make it seem ready for use, it was obviously never intended to be lit. Gerard's heart sank when the chilly guards took advantage of the conveniently prepared fireplace.

As the men sat idly chatting and warming their hands against the flames, the wooden boards under the bricks began to warp and shrink from the heat. This caused the bricks to start shifting until they were on the verge of crashing down into the priest hole. Finally, the guards noticed that something was amiss in the fire and began to poke at it to see what lay beneath.

Gerard listened as the pair discussed their discovery, but was relieved to hear them reach the conclusion that it was too dark now to investigate properly, agreeing to put off further exploration until the morning. By now, the wooden cover to the priest hole was close to burning through completely, forcing Gerard to press himself to the side of the narrow space so that the falling hot embers didn't land on his head or clothes.

Miraculously (no doubt Gerard would have believed literally so!), it didn't completely collapse, but in broad daylight the entrance to the priest hole would be glaringly obvious.

But they never came back. The general search resumed the following day, and although Gerard never found out why, his room, the very one identified by the traitor and now featuring a suspicious fireplace, was left alone. It can only be assumed that, having undertaken a night shift, the two men who had come so close to finding Gerard were not among those called back for duty the next day. In fact, those who did recommence the search eventually discovered the very priest hole in which Gerard had originally wanted to hide, but they left without locating their prime target and Jane Wiseman was finally allowed to return to her battered home. As soon as she arrived, she barred the doors and helped Gerard out of his hiding place. The priest was sore, aching and cramped from his time in the confined space, as well as wasted and weak with hunger. He then discovered that his hostess had herself refused to eat during the entire four days to give her some idea of Gerard's condition and judge whether he could still be alive.

This crisis over, the Wisemans provided Anne Line with free board and lodging, while Gerard supported her in all other respects. Anne repaid the family by acting as teacher to their children. In a short and troubled life, she had at least landed on her feet for the time being.

As an interesting aside, Sir William Wiseman's own mother, an elderly widow also called Jane, had been sentenced to the same *peine forte et dure* crushing death as Margaret Clitherow, but when news of it reached the ears of Queen Elizabeth, she was appalled and made it clear that the sentence was not to be carried out.

* * *

After Anne had been living with the Wisemans for a time, Gerard felt he needed a house better suited to serve as a hub for visiting priests. He found one in London which he felt matched his purposes, took out a tenancy and furnished it, and decided that Anne Line would be the ideal person to run it for him. He gave her the pseudonym of 'Mrs Martha', and she was put in charge of the general housekeeping, including the finances and dealing with visitors – of whom there would be many, since this would be a staging post for priests newly arrived in England or returning to commence their missions after training, as well as those travelling around England who happened to be in the vicinity.

It must have been a constant physical struggle for Anne, because her health was never good, to say the least. In a letter to his superiors in Rome, Father Gerard wrote: 'More than once I myself have seen her completely exhausted and apparently dead; in fact her infirmities reduced her almost to the extreme stages of physical weakness.' He was never specific about the problem or problems ('She was always suffering from one ailment or another') but Richard Challoner, in *Memoirs of Missionary Priests*, provides a little more detail. She was said to be 'troubled with almost continued head-aches, and, withal, dropsy'. This latter condition is now called oedema, or water retention. It is usually a sign of a problem with organs such as the heart or kidneys, but it can also be caused by malnutrition.[2] It's highly likely that (like other devout Catholic women) Anne Line fasted regularly, perhaps at times overdoing it, which may have contributed to her health problems, although that's not to say there wasn't some other underlying disease. It is interesting to note, however, that one of the most obvious signs of dropsy was swelling of tissues, especially in the arms and legs. Yet when Anne died and her clothing was removed, her limbs were observed to be 'as thin as the rope that hanged her'. She was apparently prone to falling ill every spring and autumn, to the extent that her friends often feared she would not survive. Anne herself told Father Gerard:

> 'I naturally want more than anything to die for Christ, but it is too much to expect that it will be by the executioner's hand. Possibly Our Lord will let me be taken one day with a priest and be put in some cold and filthy dungeon where I won't be able to live very long in this wretched life.'

To one of her confessors, she once revealed a vision in which she had seen 'of our Lord, in the blessed sacrament, bearing his cross, and inviting her

---

2. *Cambridge World History of Human Disease* (2008).

to follow him; which seemed to promise her this martyrdom to which she aspired, and which she at last obtained'.

* * *

Despite avoiding capture at Braddocks, the pursuivants did eventually catch up with Gerard, but they weren't able to hold him for long. That story is told elsewhere, but by the time he regained his freedom, Gerard decided it was time for Anne Line to move on again. In explaining why, the priest was frank to the point of implying criticism of his faithful helper:

> 'During my imprisonment people had come there in far greater numbers than I would have tolerated myself if I had been free. Too many people, in fact, knew about it … So the house which was meant for myself and my close friends became a place of call for many people, some of whom were no friends of mine at all and might even have been traitors … It was this that forced me to make other arrangements. As it seemed advisable to scotch the idea that Mistress Line kept an open house for anybody and everybody, she took a lodging by herself in a rented room in a private house.'

For the most part, Gerard extolled the abilities and virtue of Anne Line, yet here it sounds as if he is accusing her of laxity or carelessness in a situation where lives depended on extreme discretion. Tellingly, the very scenario the priest highlights as the reason for closing the house she had been running is the same one which would later lead to her arrest.

Gerard, even more highly sensitive to matters of safety and secrecy than usual after his narrow escape from certain execution, had one particular reason to be worried.

After escaping captivity, he was pestered by a priest called William Atkinson (who was later to renounce the Catholic faith), whom Gerard had assisted in the past but who, for reasons Gerard wasn't aware of, turned against him and had even somehow managed to engineer his transfer from the Clink Prison in Southwark to the feared Tower of London. Atkinson had wanted explanations on various matters, which Gerard doesn't describe in detail, but were presumably theological in nature. Gerard initially tried to help, but Atkinson was never satisfied and continued to badger Gerard. The priest reached the point where he felt he had no more to say, and decided the best way of discouraging the constant demand for answers was to stop replying altogether. But Atkinson failed to take the hint and persisted, and when he sent a messenger to Gerard requesting a meeting, the latter relented and agreed.

The understandably wary Gerard insisted on meeting outdoors, at night and away from his current address. But while waiting for Atkinson to arrive on the appointed evening, pacing the field where the rendezvous was to take place, it suddenly struck Gerard that he had wandered close to the home of the Archpriest, the head of the Catholic priesthood in England. He feared that if Atkinson – whom Gerard didn't fully trust – saw him in that vicinity, any problems arising out of the meeting might also rebound on the Archpriest if Atkinson thought he had been visiting him. Gerard's apprehension came too late. Atkinson arrived as Gerard was walking away from the vicinity of the Archpriest's house, which only served to give Atkinson the impression that he had just left the premises, thus bringing it under suspicion.

The meeting with Atkinson was no more productive than the correspondence had been, but shortly afterwards, there were two raids: one on the house which Atkinson already knew Anne Line had been running, and the other on the unfortunate Archpriest's residence. Luckily, neither raid resulted in an arrest. Anne Line had already moved out, and the Archpriest managed to secrete himself in yet another cleverly built priest hole, which defied the efforts of the pursuivants even after two days of determined searching. It's often stated that the pursuivants descended on Anne's address just a couple of days after she had moved out, but this is a mis-reading of Gerard's own account. The raids did happen shortly ('three or four days') after Gerard's nocturnal meeting, but he clearly states that 'this [the back and forth between himself and Atkinson after his escape] went on for six months' before that – whereas Anne Line had left his house soon after his escape from the Tower.

* * *

Anne Line had established herself in the new house, taking in priests again as before, but also as before she let her enthusiasm for her faith take precedence over the need for caution and secrecy. On 2 February, Catholics celebrate Candlemas Day, or what was then known as The Purification of Our Blessed Lady (or The Blessed Virgin Mary). It was an important date in the calendar, and on this day in 1599 Anne entertained 'an unusually large number of Catholics', enough to attract the attention of neighbours, who alerted local constables.

The officers of the law acted quickly. A swoop was made and the house secured before anyone could flee or even clear away the incriminating altar which had been set up for the Mass. However, the priest, Father Page, had a lucky escape. He was standing near the door, and when one of the pursuivants opened it he took his chance and darted out and up the stairs to where he knew there was a priest hole. The hiding place did its job and Page was never found. There could be no better testament to the work of Little John that once again the searchers knew a person they were after was somewhere in a house, yet were defeated by his ingenuity. Anne Line wasn't so lucky.

Gerard and Jesuit lay brother John Lilly were present in an upstairs room. When a constable tried to open the door, they held tightly onto the latch, which convinced him that it must be locked.

'Perhaps the manservant who sleeps in that room may have taken away the key. I will go and look for him,' Anne Line, who had accompanied the constables, helpfully suggested.

'Oh no you don't,' the constable replied. 'You don't go anywhere without us, or you will be hiding something away.' They went off in search of the key, allowing Gerard to scuttle out and take refuge in a priest hole in the roof space. Lilly bravely stayed behind to take the blame for Catholic items in the room; he even allowed them to believe that he was a priest himself in order to further divert attention away from Gerard. His reward was a trip to the Tower and torture by Topcliffe. Even then, Lilly managed to be useful. At some stage during his imprisonment, he was told by William Waad (sometimes spelt 'Wade' in modern accounts), Lieutenant Governor of the Tower and a man with a reputation almost as black as that of Topcliffe, that they knew of the Jesuit house in Spitalfields, and Lilly somehow managed to get a warning out.

Anne and the rest of the attendees of the Mass were taken away and imprisoned, although some were subsequently released on bail. Anne Line was arrested and tried as 'Martha Anne'. It seems that the authorities never did realize they were trying her under a pseudonym, and when Father Garnet, her first spiritual mentor, wrote to her in prison, he addressed his letters to 'Mrs Martha'.

She was kept in prison for several months before being tried at the Old Bailey, by which time her physical condition, always fragile and no doubt now exacerbated by prolonged confinement and poor prison food, meant that she was bedbound. Anne had to be carried into court in a chair, there to face the accusation of harbouring priests. Although she declined to give a clear answer to the charge, as was usual in such cases, what she said next was tantamount to both a confession and signing her own death warrant: 'My Lords, nothing grieves me more but I could not receive a thousand more.' She was found guilty and sent to Newgate Prison to await execution by hanging.

Gerard says she 'received the sentence of death with manifest joy and thankfulness'. Anne was subjected to the same pressure as Margaret Clitherow to renounce her faith as she was led to her execution on 27 February 1601, but she gave them short shrift: 'Away! I have nothing in common with you.'

The location was Tyburn, then a junction of two country roads on the outskirts of London, but now the vicinity of a busy junction and the site of Marble Arch. To the assembled crowd, echoing what she had said at her trial she exclaimed: 'I am sentenced to die for harbouring a catholic priest, and so far I am from repenting for having so done, that I wish, with all my soul, that where I have entertained one, I could have entertained a thousand.'

She kissed the gallows, then mounted the cart and the noose was placed around her neck. Upon a given signal, the cart lurched away. Anne crossed herself as she fell, and it is said that she continued praying to her dying breath – which, because of her frailty, was a mercifully short time in coming. A Benedictine monk called Mark Barkworth who was to be hanged, drawn and quartered after Anne's hanging wasn't so lucky. As we have heard, in theory the butchering took place before the victim was quite dead from hanging, though they were at least usually semi-conscious if not unconscious or dead from sympathetic souls pulling down on their legs. But the rope around Barkworth's neck was cut almost as soon as the cart was pulled from under him; he fell to the ground barely injured and jumped to his feet, screaming 'Oh Lord! Oh Lord! Oh God!' as the disembowelment commenced.

Garnet had sent someone to try to get a relic from the body of the woman who would become Saint Anne Line. His agent managed to cut a piece of the sleeve of the gown she was wearing, and he dipped this in the blood of Barkworth and another priest who had been executed at the same event. As was usual, Anne's body was dumped in an unmarked grave by the roadside, in her case with a few executed common criminals. A group of Catholics surreptitiously retrieved it and reburied it in a secret location, possibly with a priest present to perform the necessary Catholic rites. Anne Line's biographer, Martin Dodwell, says this was done at the behest of the Countess of Arundel, who will later play her part in this story, and it's tempting to wonder whether Anne's final resting place was somewhere in the grounds of Arundel House, or even the more extensive grounds of Arundel Castle.

Anne Line was included in the list of forty martyrs (which included several other people involved in this story) canonized by Pope Paul VI in 1970. There is a Catholic church dedicated to Anne in her birthplace of Great Dunmow, and a school named after her in Basildon.

* * *

As for Father John Gerard, he now needed yet another new location which would serve as a refuge and headquarters. He didn't want to impose upon the Wisemans again, even though they were keen to take him in, because 'It seemed that I would always be causing those good and dear friends of mine some sort of trouble.' At around this time, while he was on his travels around the country he happened to visit a home in Northamptonshire which he had been to several times before. The owner of the house had died, and he discovered his widow 'completely over-wrought' by her husband's death, unable to even set foot in the part of the house where he had died. Other members of her family confided in Gerard that if he was to make his new home there, it would allow the widow to 'put aside her long mourning'. There was already a priest in residence (who happened to be Guy Fawkes's cousin, though that name probably wouldn't have meant anything to Gerard at the time) and he had his doubts about the arrangement, but was ultimately persuaded to stay.

The widow, 'a devout and pious soul', was Eliza Vaux, the sister-in-law of Anne Vaux.

Chapter 8

Graceful Comeliness

Anne Dacres (Lady Arundel)

Robert Southwell, one of the priests who had been hiding with Garnet, may have escaped the attentions of the pursuivants at Baddesley Clinton, but his freedom was short-lived.

For a few brief years, yet another pious Catholic woman would provide this young Jesuit priest with the same refuge and support that the Vaux sisters had to Father Garnet and others. Formally, she is generally referred to as Lady Arundel, but she was born Anne Dacres in Carlisle in March 1557, and her father was Thomas, Lord Dacres. (The family name is often spelt 'Dacre'.)

After the death of Thomas's wife, Anne's Catholic grandmother, Lady Mounteagle, took the responsibility for her upbringing. It was a rather strict environment, with Lady Mounteagle 'not permitting such liberties as many do to the ruin of their children', according to her descendant and anonymous biographer (*The lives of Philip Howard, Earl of Arundel, and of Anne Dacres, his Wife*, p.169). 'She reprehended them sharply for their faults, and chaff'd with her own hands, by which means they came not only to know what was evil, but also to have a fear and horror to do it.' However, Lady Mounteagle also instructed Anne in spiritual matters and instilled a sense of virtue and humility, lessons which informed her attitude and behaviour towards others, especially those less well off than her, for the rest of her life.

Anne's stepfather, Thomas Howard, 4th Duke of Norfolk, keen to make a good match for her, betrothed her to Philip, the eldest son of the Earl of Surrey, when they were both only 12. There was a contract and ceremony of sorts, but the ceremony had to be performed again a couple of years later when the children were both legally of age. This 'second marriage', though now perfectly legal, was carried out in great secrecy, the reason being that the duke was in deep trouble with the queen and feared royal intervention should Elizabeth become aware of the match. In what would be one of numerous contretemps between the monarch and the family, Howard had not unreasonably incurred Elizabeth's wrath for his part in the Ridolfi Plot, whose aim, like the earlier Babington Plot, was to oust her and put Mary, Queen of Scots on the throne. Ultimately, the duke was executed as a result of this, soon after the union of Anne and Philip.

Their marriage got off to a rocky and inauspicious start. Once he was old enough, Philip went off to study at Cambridge, after which he became part of Elizabeth's court, living in London and doing his best to ingratiate himself with the queen (who was his second cousin, once removed). Like many young men with ambition, he was trying to get himself accepted into the inner circle of her favourites. It was widely recognized at court that the young bloods who surrounded Elizabeth were unlikely to make much progress if they 'shew'd any love for their wives'. But it seems that Philip's distancing himself from Father Southwell's future patron went beyond a mere selfish and overly ambitious desire to advance himself, and took the form of a calculated and callous rejection of his wife. A distraught and lonely Anne eventually went to live with Philip's sympathetic grandfather, the Earl of Arundel. When he died, Anne, already the Countess of Surrey through her marriage, also became Countess of Arundel.

This did nothing to heal the rift with Philip, which must have seemed permanent to Anne, leaving her with nothing but a bleak and isolated life ahead of her – which makes it all the more surprising that eventually Philip not only rejoined her, but that a genuine affection soon blossomed between the couple. It's true that Philip only returned to the marital home because his attempts to curry favour with Elizabeth had failed miserably, but he was easily wealthy enough and owned property enough to continue to have maintained a separate lifestyle. With growing maturity – probably realizing that he had been behaving like an idiot, and also no doubt discovering that although the marriage had been a politically arranged one, he really did like Anne – Philip was humble enough to ask for forgiveness. She welcomed this change of attitude, and the relationship was blessed with a new beginning. The couple had two children, and even their religious outlooks came to converge.

Philip was raised a Protestant, and in spite of the Catholic education she had received from her grandmother, Anne was ostensibly one too – not unusual among those of the nobility wishing to keep on the right side of Elizabeth. Anne first began to think seriously about Catholicism after hearing stories about the two Jesuit pioneers in England, Edmund Campion and Robert Persons. She then met Father Gaspar Heywood, said to have been the first Jesuit to actually set foot in England. This, though, proved to be a false start, since Anne allowed herself to be influenced by 'some who buzz'd many things against them' (i.e., the Jesuits). A meeting with Father William Weston helped to bring her round again and she ultimately allied herself with Robert Southwell, who, like Henry Garnet to Anne Vaux, thereafter became not just her chaplain but her 'constant friend'.

When Lady Arundel's confidence and strength in her faith led her to become openly Catholic, she feared Philip's reaction, not realizing that he himself had already converted after meeting Weston. Philip arranged for Father Southwell to take up residence at their home in Arundel Castle, but Elizabeth hadn't finished with the couple yet.

When the queen, now aware of their conversion, heard that Anne was pregnant, she ordered her to be placed under house arrest with Sir Thomas Shirley until after the baby was born. The child, a daughter, was then forcibly baptized in the Anglican Church.

In the meantime, Philip, aware that he was being linked to yet another conspiracy to rid the country of Elizabeth and put Mary on the throne (the Throckmorton Plot), decided to flee to save his skin and boarded a boat on the Sussex coast. As his vessel sailed into open waters bound for France, Philip must have let out a sigh of relief, believing himself safe. Nevertheless, in another example of how far the tentacles of the state spread, details of the mission had reached the authorities and the boat was intercepted. Anne's husband was tried on a variety of charges, ultimately leading to that of high treason. The sentence for such a crime was, of course, death. However, during the time that Philip was kept in the Tower he was unaware that Elizabeth had not signed the warrant for his execution. Perhaps the time he spent fawning over her at court had made some impression after all.

He was not allowed visitors – especially not Anne – but learned that Robert Southwell was being held nearby. The two were kept apart, but Catholic prisoners were nothing if not inventive. Philip had been allowed the company of Anne's dog, which rather bizarrely was allowed to roam freely, and the two men came up with a way of using it to pass messages between themselves (presumably hidden beneath its collar).

Anne, alone once more, was being cruelly fed stories that her husband was leading a debauched life in the Tower, straying from his faith and even being allowed, and enjoying, the freedom to fraternize with women. To what extent she believed these improbable stories is hard to say, but they must, as they were designed to do, have added to the stress and despondency she felt at her indefinite separation from Philip.

Although Elizabeth never did enforce the sentence of death, if she had done so it might have been a blessing, because Philip lingered in isolation in the Tower for ten long years until finally falling ill and dying in mysterious circumstances. Some accounts ascribe his death to dysentery, but there was also a rumour that he was poisoned.

It's clear that despite her leniency towards Philip, Queen Elizabeth harboured a personal animosity towards Anne. Other imprisoned noblemen were allowed visits from their wives, but Anne's appeals to do so were always rejected. When Philip died, Anne should legally have inherited his lands and estates, but Elizabeth would not countenance it. She saw to it that the Crown took possession of Arundel House (not to be confused with Arundel Castle, it was a house just off the Strand in London, a grand place and the former London residence of the Bishops of Bath and Wells). This left Anne having to rent a house in Romford with 'nothing but the Beds on which herself and a few servants were to take their rest, and those only lent her for a time'. She experienced the humiliation, for one of her station, of having to sell her jewellery in order to feed and pay the few staff she was able to keep on. After much imploring, the queen grudgingly allowed Anne a pension of £8 a week, 'and that many times so ill pay'd that she was often compell'd to borrow and make hard shifts to procure necessary provisions', her biography reports. Eventually, after a protracted and expensive legal battle, Elizabeth was obliged to restore Philip's land and properties to his widow.

This must have come as a great relief, but the death of her husband, coming as it did after years of separation and ordeals and battles with the monarch, made Anne ill. We might today call it depression or perhaps post-traumatic stress disorder, but to her biographer it was a 'rising of vapor, and other infirmities following' which kept her bed-bound, for a time even unable to sit up, let alone stand.

But one quality these women shared was resiliency. Anne not only regathered her strength, but was able in some degree to reinvent herself. Rather than remarry, she decided that from now on she would commit herself to the Catholic cause. As Anne Vaux had done, she took a vow of chastity and devoted herself to living the life of a lay sister. As well as attending Mass twice a day and evensong, she spent much time in her chapel in prayer and meditation. She became a committed provider of alms to the poor and sick, supported Catholic schools and colleges at home and overseas, and, of course, supported priests – and not just Jesuits, but secular priests. On one occasion, she even saved the skin of the Archpriest George Blackwell (a man of whom Garnet had a rather low opinion).

Blackwell was chaplain to one Mrs Meany, who lived in Westminster, and when pursuivants swooped on her house he was obliged to take refuge in her priest hole. The initial search failed to find any trace of the priest, so, knowing that he must either be fed or brought out at some point, a watch was posted in the house. Mrs Meany may well have been a friend of Anne's, or at least part of the same Catholic network, since word came through her about Blackwell's plight. There were fears that even if not captured and executed, the Archpriest might well choose to starve rather than get Mrs Meany into trouble, so Anne took it upon herself to intervene.

Either in person or through messages, she dangled a big enough purse before the leader of the raid to secure Blackwell's escape. A secret deal was struck that during a 'changing of the guard', when one set of watchers was relieved and another brought in, two of Anne's servants would spirit the Archpriest out of the house. Blackwell was whisked away to Anne's London residence, where she looked after him while he was rested and refreshed after his ordeal, then arranged for him to be taken to a new location. Anne was so pleased with the cooperation of the chief pursuivant that she continued to send him venison pasty every Christmas.

But it was the Jesuits to whom Anne owed her strongest allegiance. Her biographer refers to the 'very large almes' she gave to the Society, telling us she had one or more priests in her house for over forty years. Anne also bought a place in Ghent, Belgium, to house Jesuit scholars serving their probationary period. Most of all, she is associated with Robert Southwell, who as we have seen became friend and confessor to both herself and husband Philip. Anne took Southwell under her wing in around 1588. He probably spent time as her chaplain in Arundel, but was also given the use of Arundel House in London. It was likely here that Southwell started an underground printing press and published many of his works. One of these was *A Shorte Rule of Good Life*, which Anne came to adopt as her spiritual manual. However, Southwell's time as Anne's mentor was not destined to last long.

In the summer of 1592, only three or four years after Anne had taken him into her home, Garnet sent word for Southwell to join him again in Warwickshire. Unfortunately, an act of spiritual charity on his journey north was to cost him his life. He received an invitation from Anne Bellamy to perform Mass at her parents' home in Uxendon Hall, near Harrow, a place he had visited in the past. What he didn't know was that she, a Catholic, had lured him into a trap, although the circumstances behind the betrayal are shrouded in mystery. It is often stated that Anne Bellamy was arrested for recusancy and ended up in the hands of Richard Topcliffe, who raped her, leaving her pregnant. He cynically used this development to trap Southwell, promising to marry her and look after her family if she made sure that the priest was at her home on a certain date.

This story neatly fits both the overall picture of Catholic persecution at the time and Topcliffe's malignant and Machiavellian character. However, there is also a troubling suggestion that Anne Bellamy was not violated but seduced, and willingly gave up Southwell. She married not Topcliffe but one Nicholas Jones, a keeper of the same Gatehouse Prison that Southwell was committed to. When Southwell was indeed captured, Anne Bellamy became, in effect, his assistant gaoler.[3]

---

[3] Morris, *Troubles of our Catholic Forefathers*, Vol. II.

Before being locked up in the Gatehouse, Southwell was taken to Topcliffe's own house with its torture chamber, where he was brutally treated even by the standards of the day. He was finally held in solitary confinement in the Tower, which he endured for more than two years in stinking and filthy conditions, becoming bedraggled and lice-ridden. His father even wrote to Queen Elizabeth, saying that if Southwell was guilty of anything he would rather be quickly executed than linger in such a state. To her credit, the queen did intervene: an order was issued that Southwell should be moved to better quarters, and his father was allowed to take him clean clothes, as well as a copy of the Bible and the works of St Bernard.

In February 1595, after three years of imprisonment, he was put on trial for treason. Southwell was physically and mentally frail, and begged forgiveness for memory lapses resulting from the ten sessions of torture he had endured. All of his responses to questions were scorned by Topcliffe, who bore such enmity towards the prisoner that he had to be restrained from attacking him on several occasions. Predictably, Southwell was found guilty. He was returned to Newgate and the next day, without any advance warning or time to prepare himself, he was taken to Tyburn to face the horror of being partially hanged and mutilated while still alive. Mercifully, he was dead before the butchery began; even so, it was not a quick death. He had time to make the sign of the cross several times after the cart was pulled from beneath him, leaving him swinging by the neck. When the executioner made to cut the rope with Southwell still clearly alive, the crowd's vociferous disapproval stayed him. Finally, onlookers rushed forwards and pulled on Southwell's legs to put him out of his misery. He was 34 years old.

* * *

Anne, Countess of Arundel, may well have been acquainted with Anne Vaux, since the latter consoled the countess after the death of her infant daughter when the two met, either by chance or design, in London.

Her unnamed biographer describes Lady Arundel as being known for her beauty, with a good complexion and taller than average. In her later years, she was said to look younger than her age, and despite becoming 'something corpulent', it was 'without deformity, it rather adding a kind of graceful comeliness'. She eschewed make-up and jewellery, and dressed well but modestly.

Towards the end of her life, Anne moved to the manor house in Shifnal, Shropshire, probably to be cared for by her son, Thomas, and his wife. The house had been in the hands of the earls of Shrewsbury and came to Thomas when he married Alathea, daughter of the 7th Earl of Shrewsbury. Here, Anne's health gradually declined, and she died on 16 April 1630, aged 73. Her body was transported to Arundel, where she was laid to rest beside her husband in a vault she herself had had made.

The author of her biography reveals that he was a Jesuit and with her at the end, which indicates that the writer may have been a priest. However, although Anne may have dictated the story of her life to him as she lay for those two years at Shifnal, the wealth of detail in the account – relating to both Anne and her husband, Philip – raises the possibility that the author was son Thomas, his wife, Alathea, or one of their children. The latter two were already men of substance by then and probably no longer at Shifnal, however, making them less likely candidates.

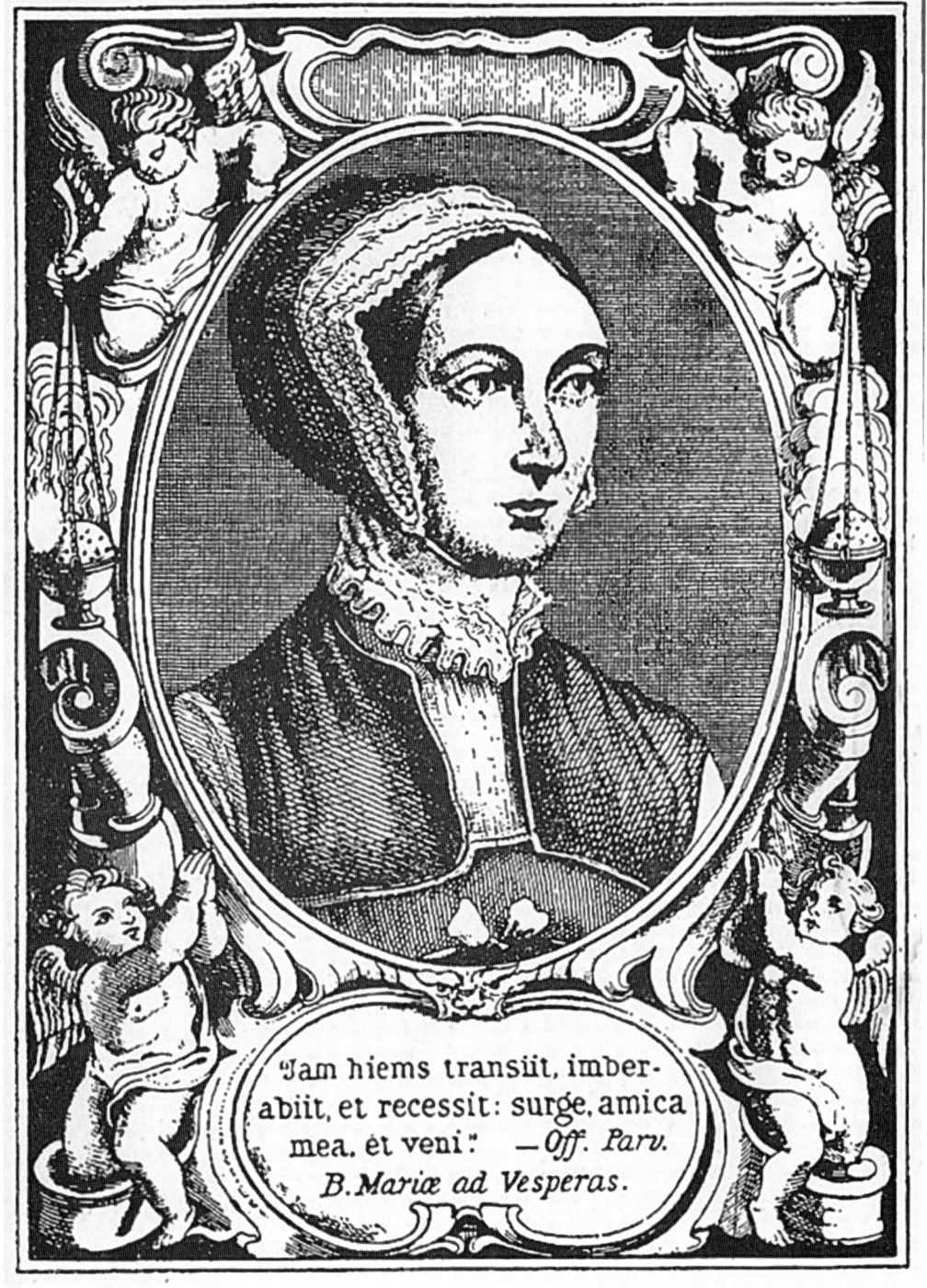

Margaret Clitherow. (*Unknown engraver, c.1750, based on an older illustration; Wikimedia Commons*)

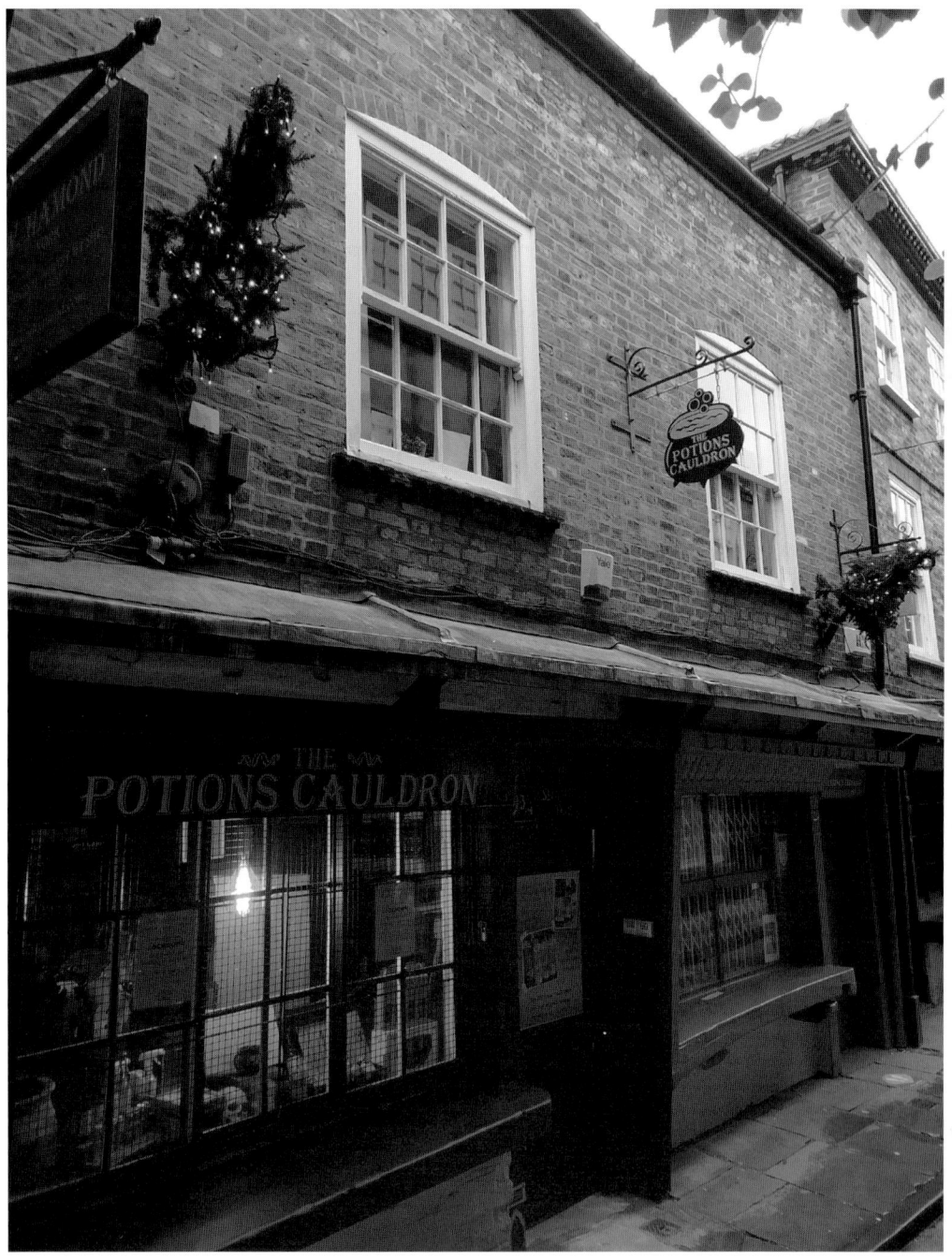

10–11 Shambles, York, where John and Margaret Clitherow had their shop and home. (*Warofdreams, Wikimedia Commons*)

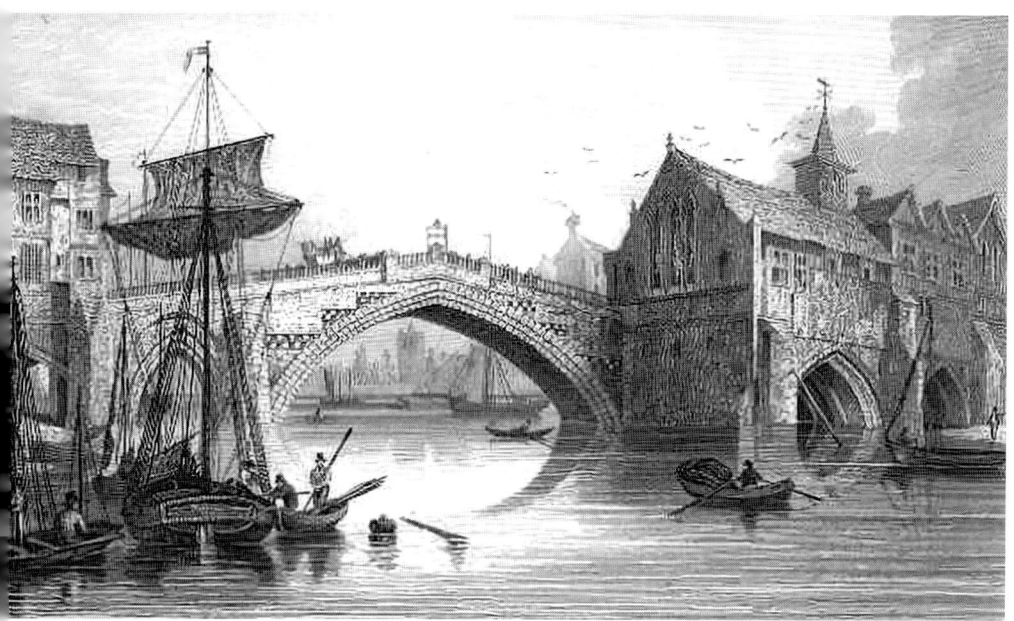

The old Ouse Bridge, York, where Margaret Clitherow was executed. (*Anonymous, Wikimedia Commons*)

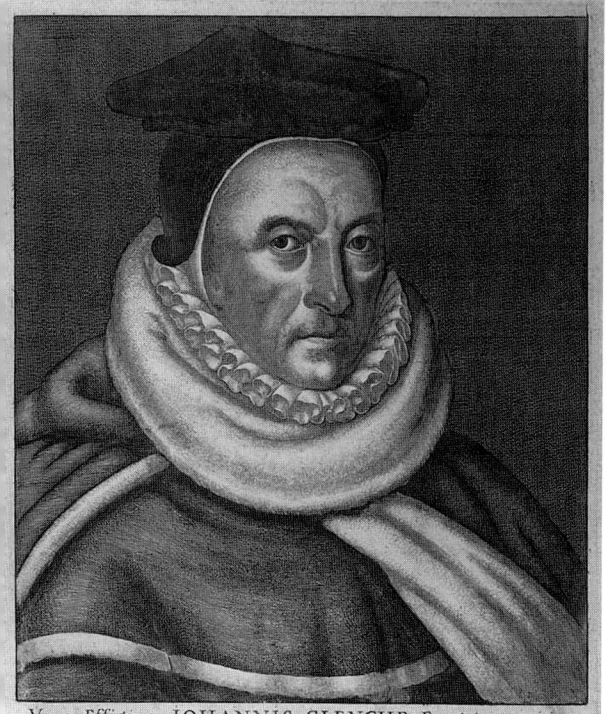

Judge John Clench, who pleaded with Margaret Clitherow to avoid execution by entering a plea. (*Wenceslaus Hollar, Harvard University Library; Wikimedia Commons*)

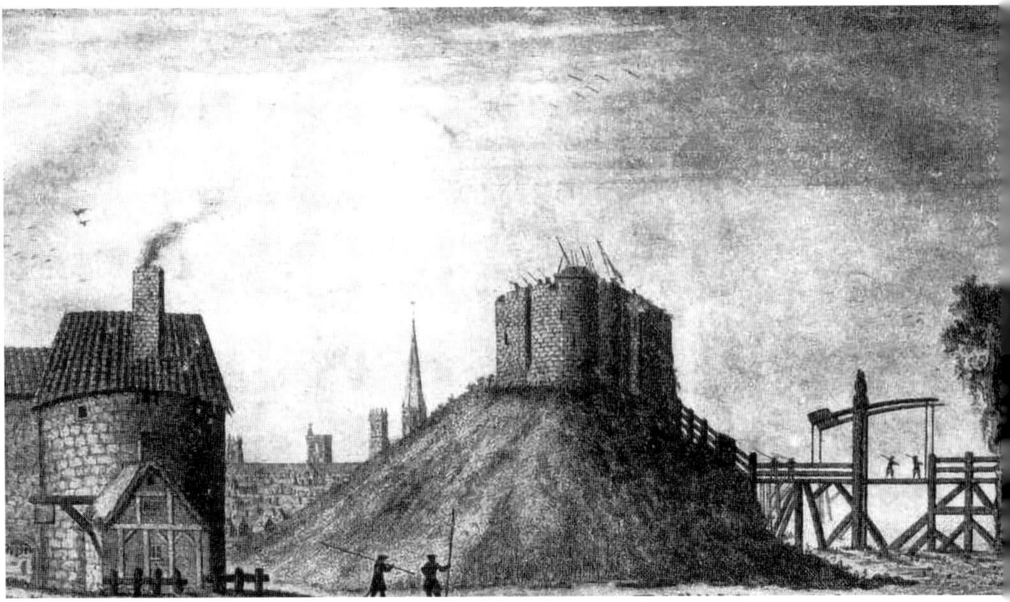

York Castle. The building on the left is where Margaret Clitherow was imprisoned. (*W.H. Toms after Francis Place, Wikimedia Commons*)

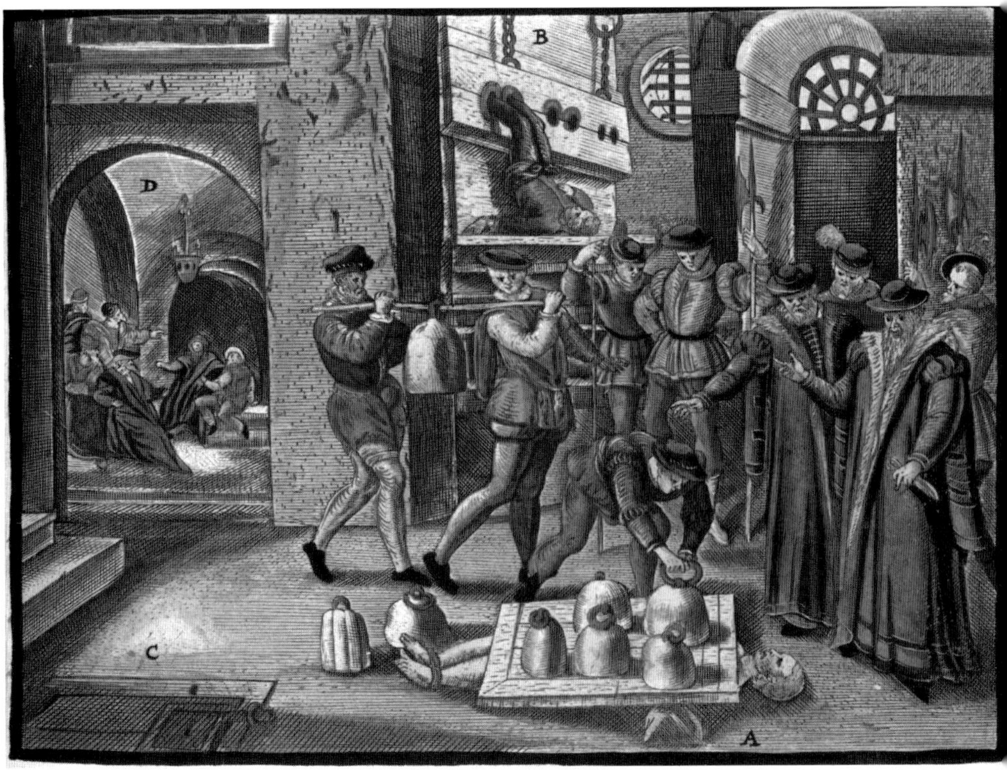

An image said to depict the pressing to death of Margaret Clitherow. (*Richard Verstegan/Richard Rowlands, Wikimedia Commons*)

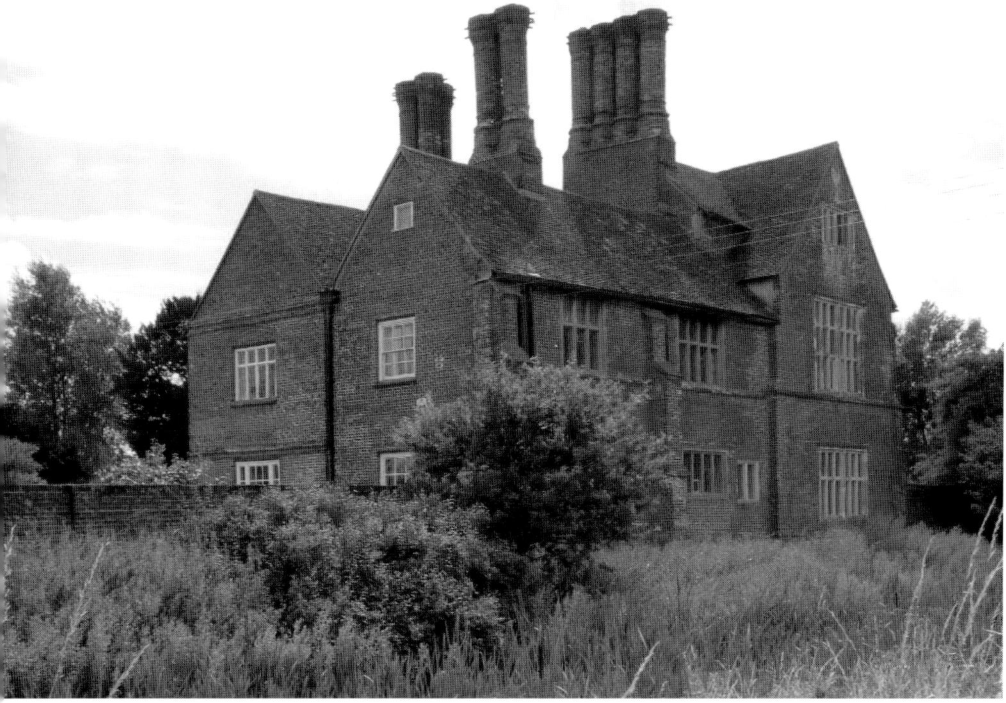

Baddesley Clinton. (DeFacto, Wikimedia Commons)

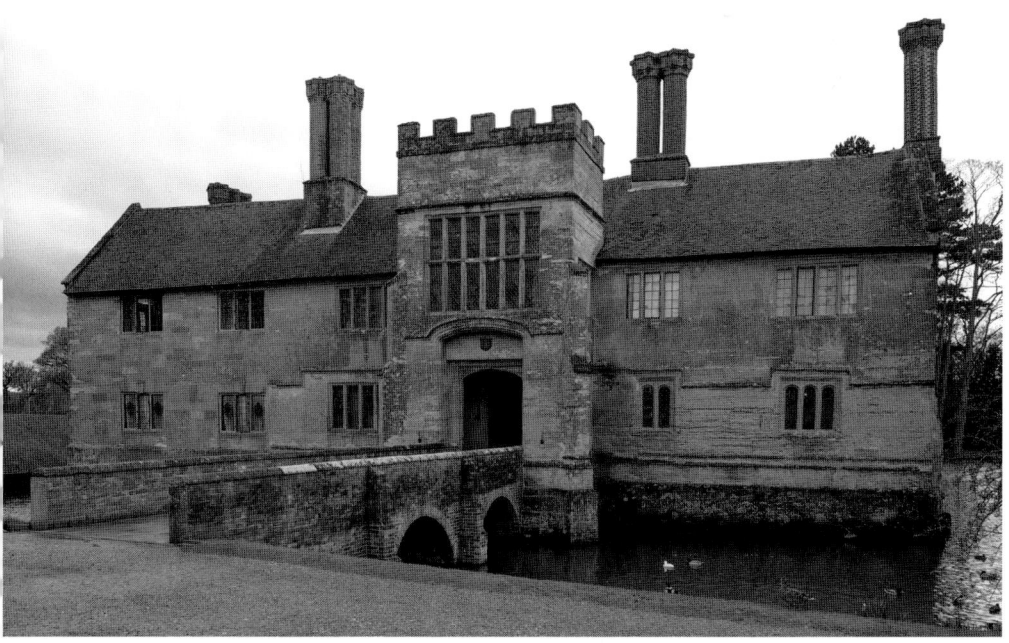

Harrowden Hall. (*The Vaux of Harrowden*, Godfrey Anstruther)

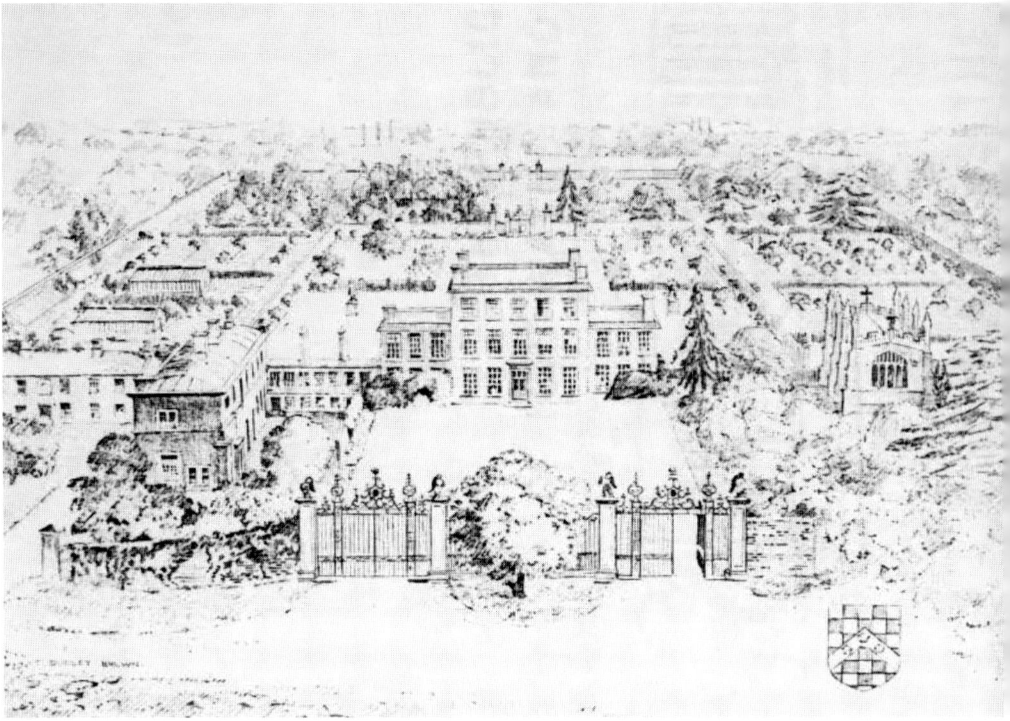

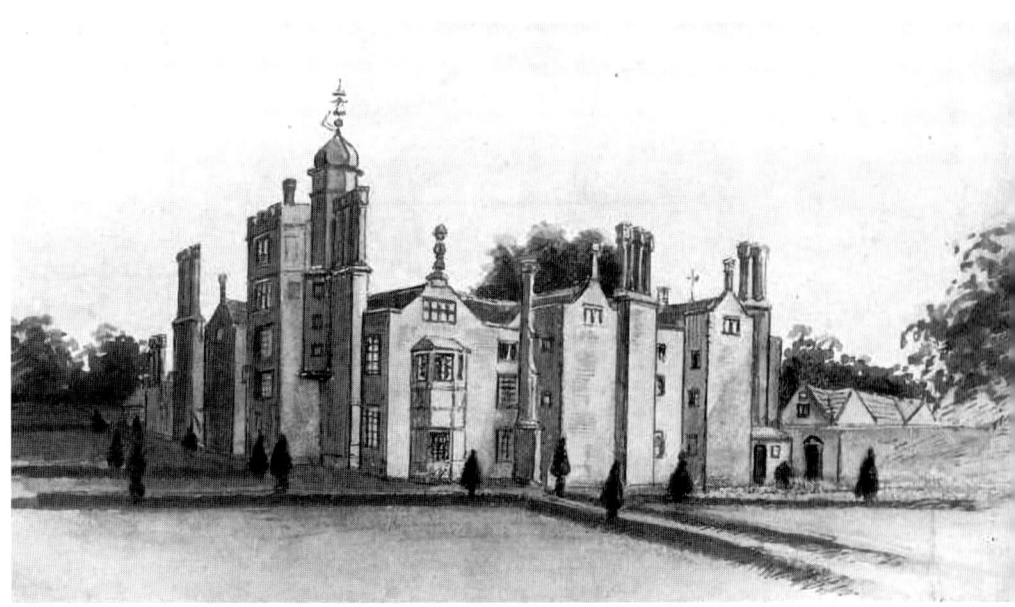

Hindlip Hall. (*Secret Chambers & Hiding-Places*, Allan Fea)

Braddocks, home of the Wisemans. (*Courtesy of Martin Dodwell*)

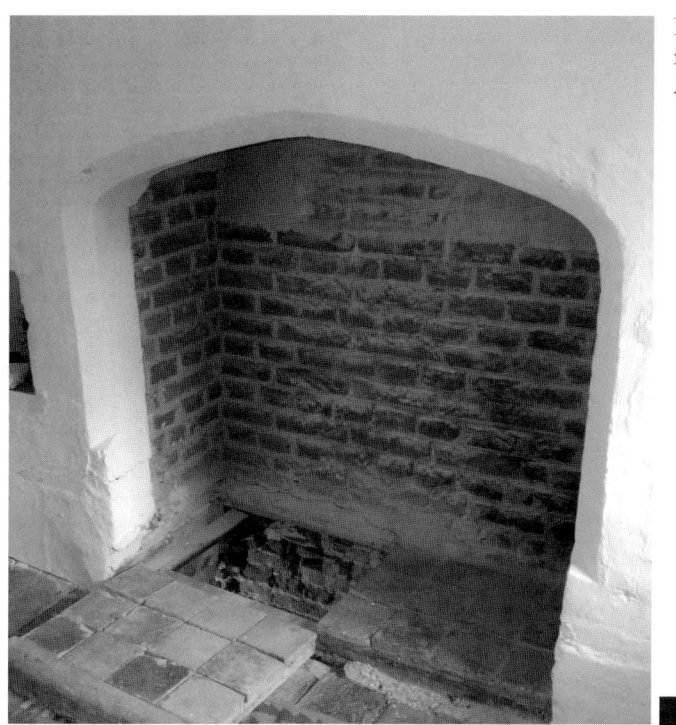

Braddocks, secret entrance to fireplace priest hole. (*Courtesy of Martin Dodwell*)

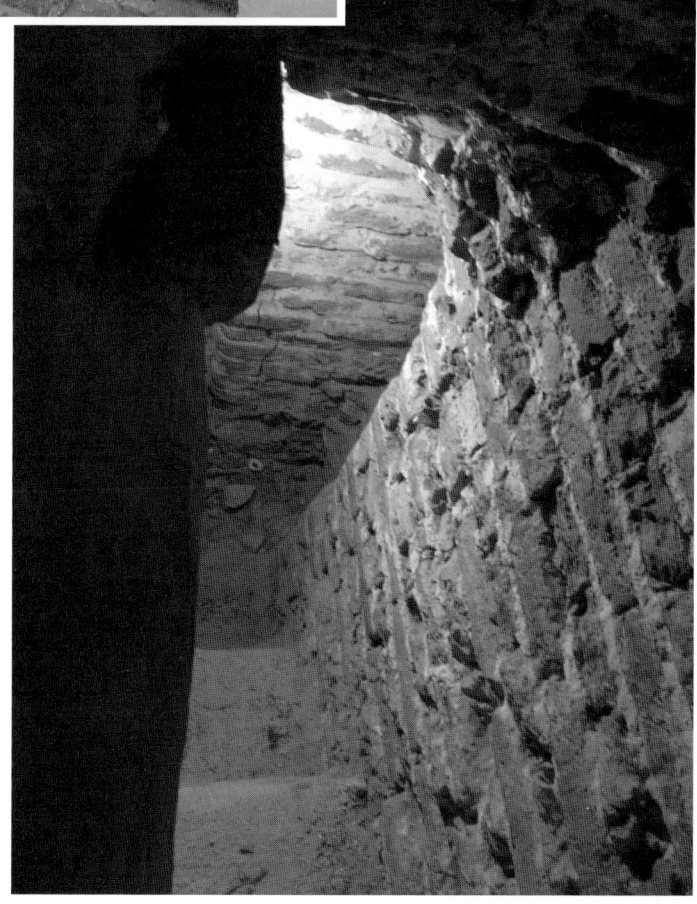

Braddocks, steps down to priest hole. (*Courtesy Martin Dodwell*)

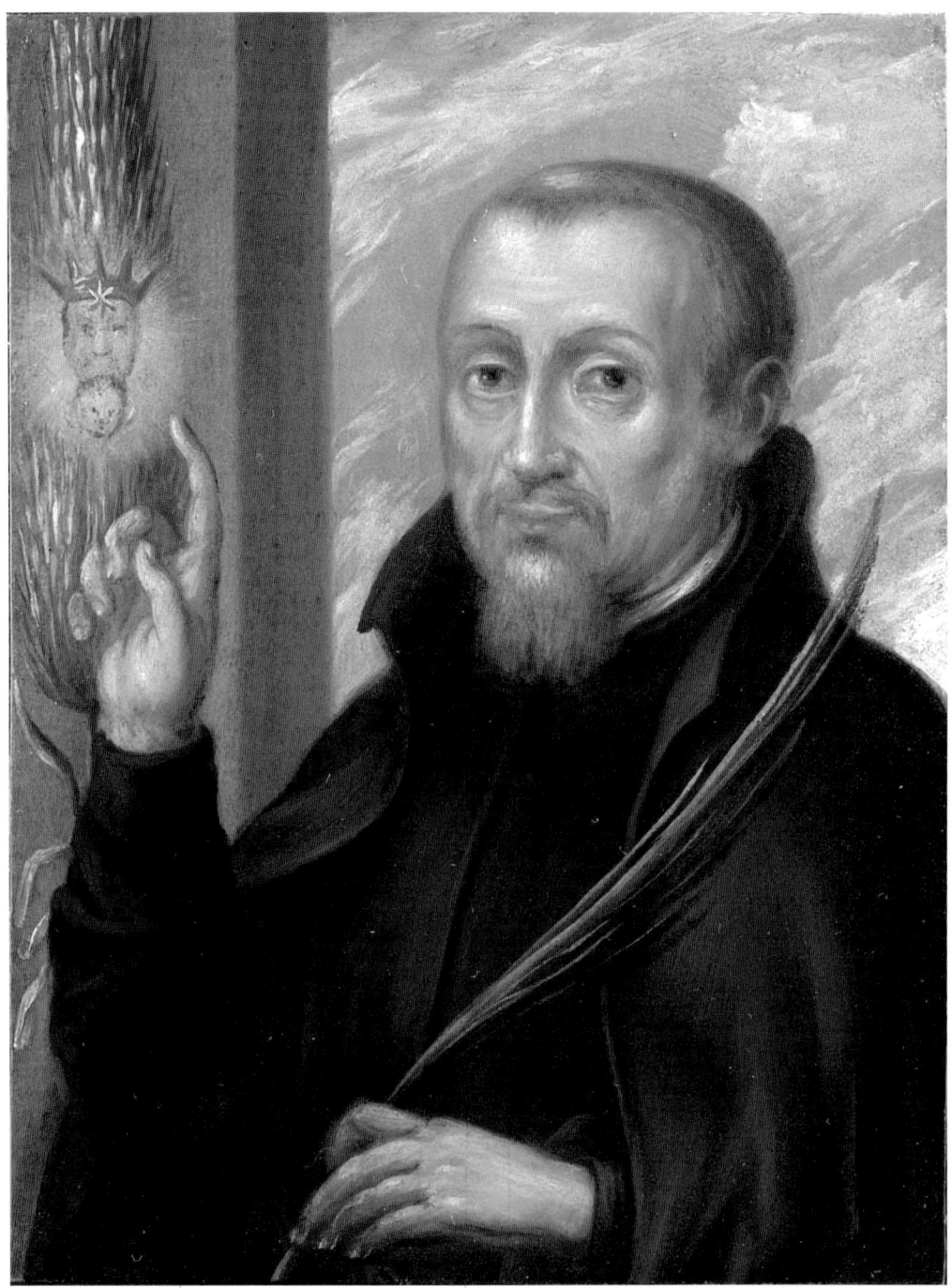
Father Henry Garnet. (*Unknown, Wikimedia Commons*)

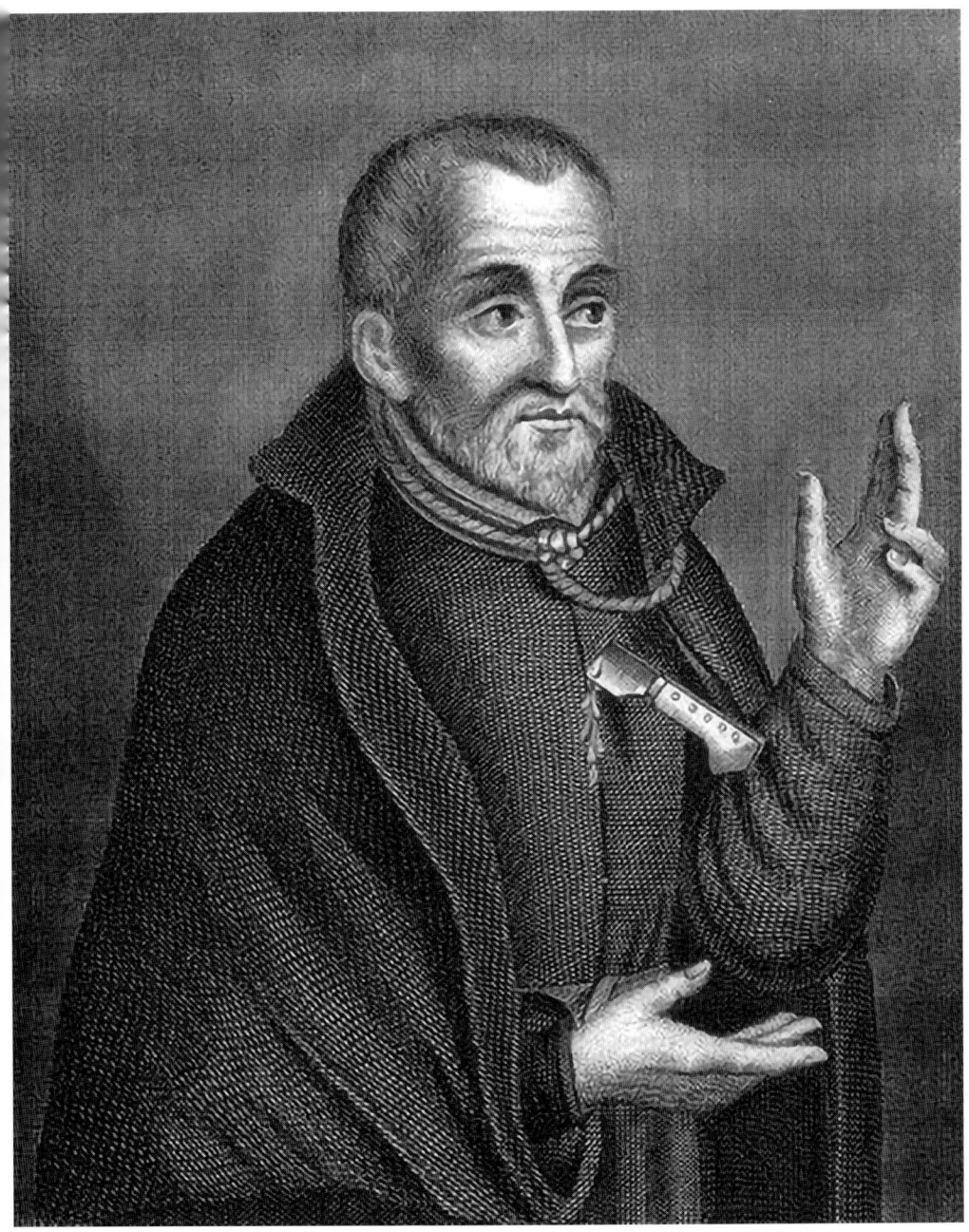

Father Edmund Campion. (*Unknown, Wikimedia Commons*)

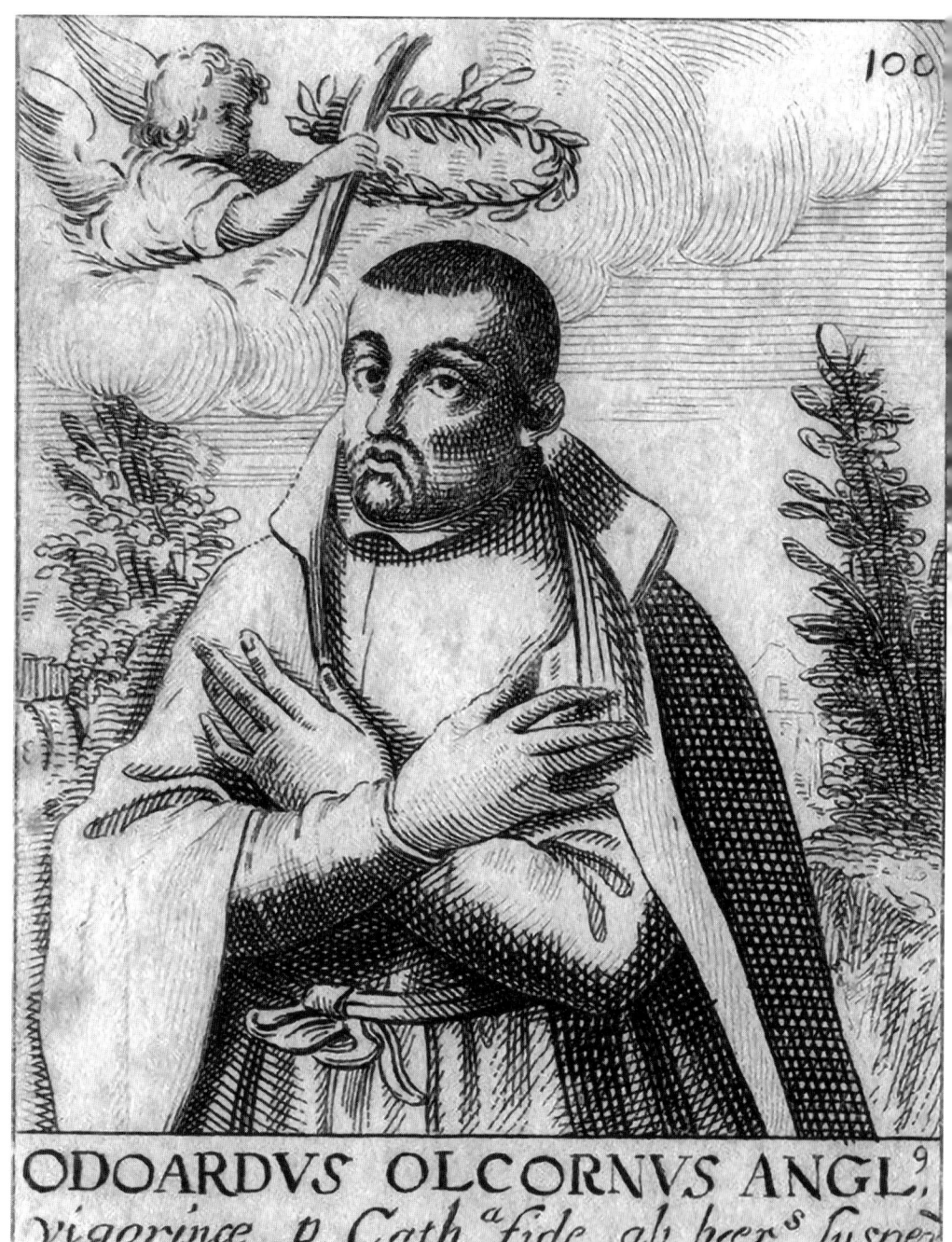

Father Edward Oldcorme. (*Unknown, Wikimedia Commons*)

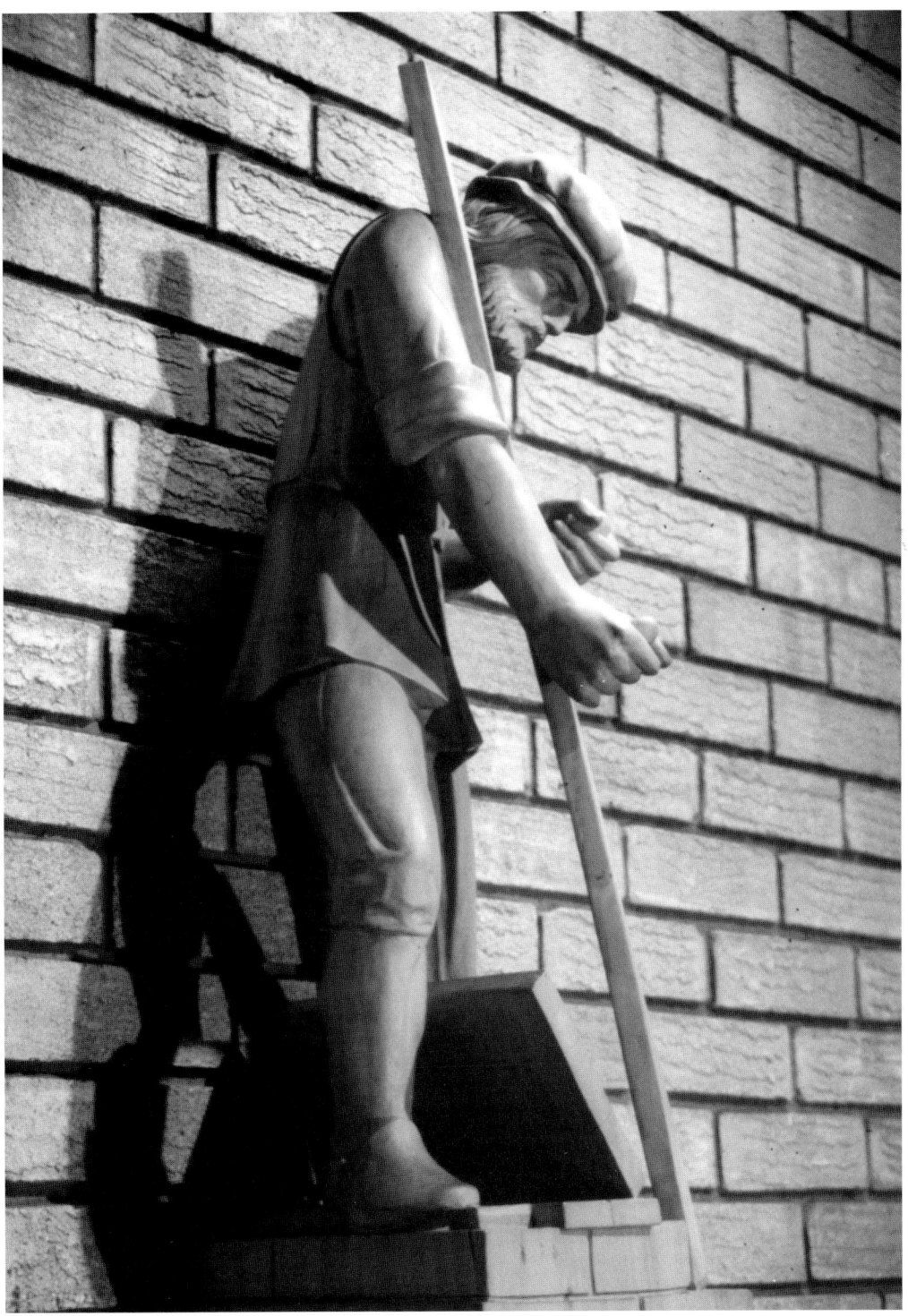

Nicholas Owen. Carved by Dennis Mitchell, St Joseph's Roman Catholic Church, Wednesbury, West Midlands. (*Sjukmidlands, Wikimedia Commons*)

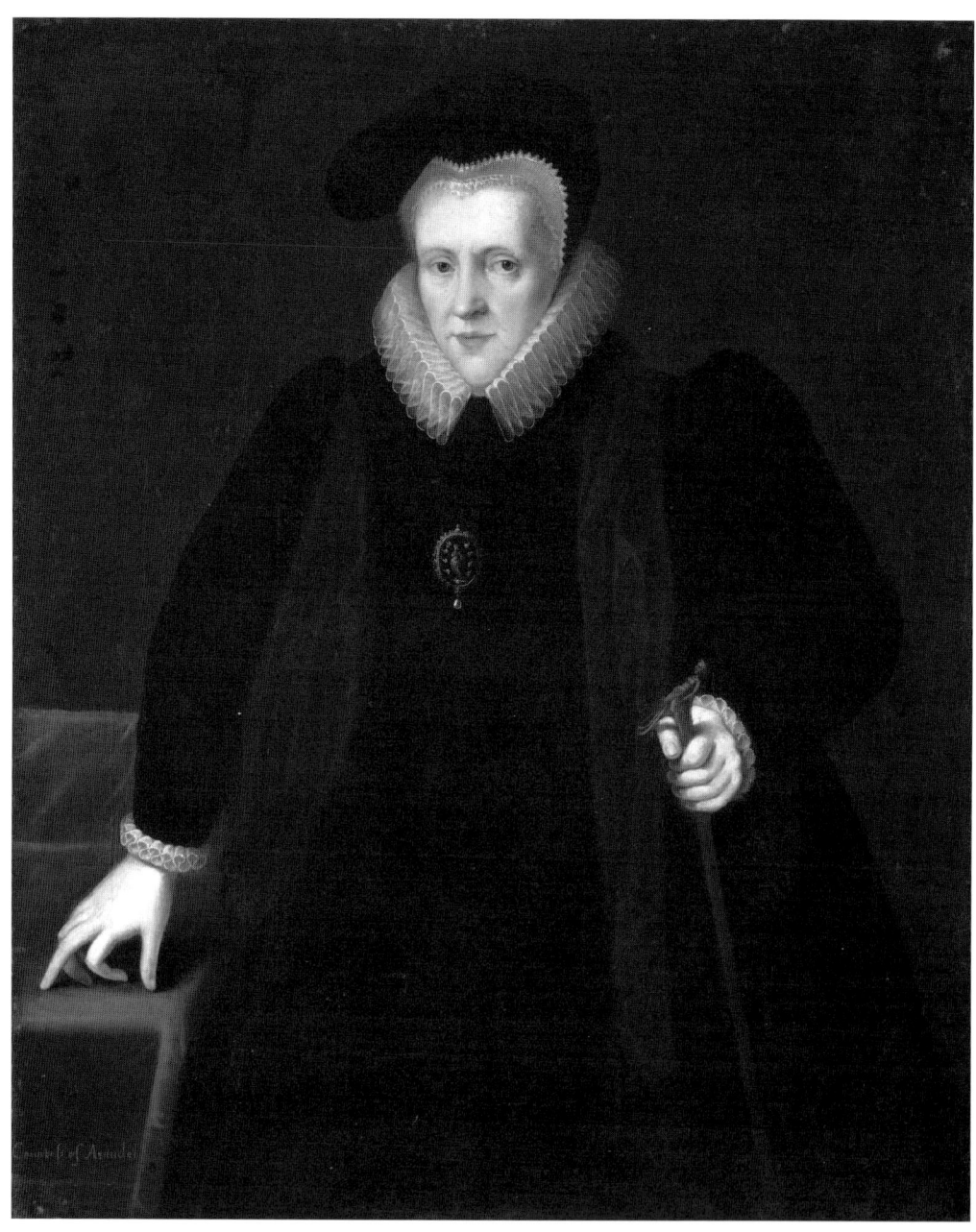

Anne Dacres, Lady Arundel. (*Anonymous, Wikimedia Commons*)

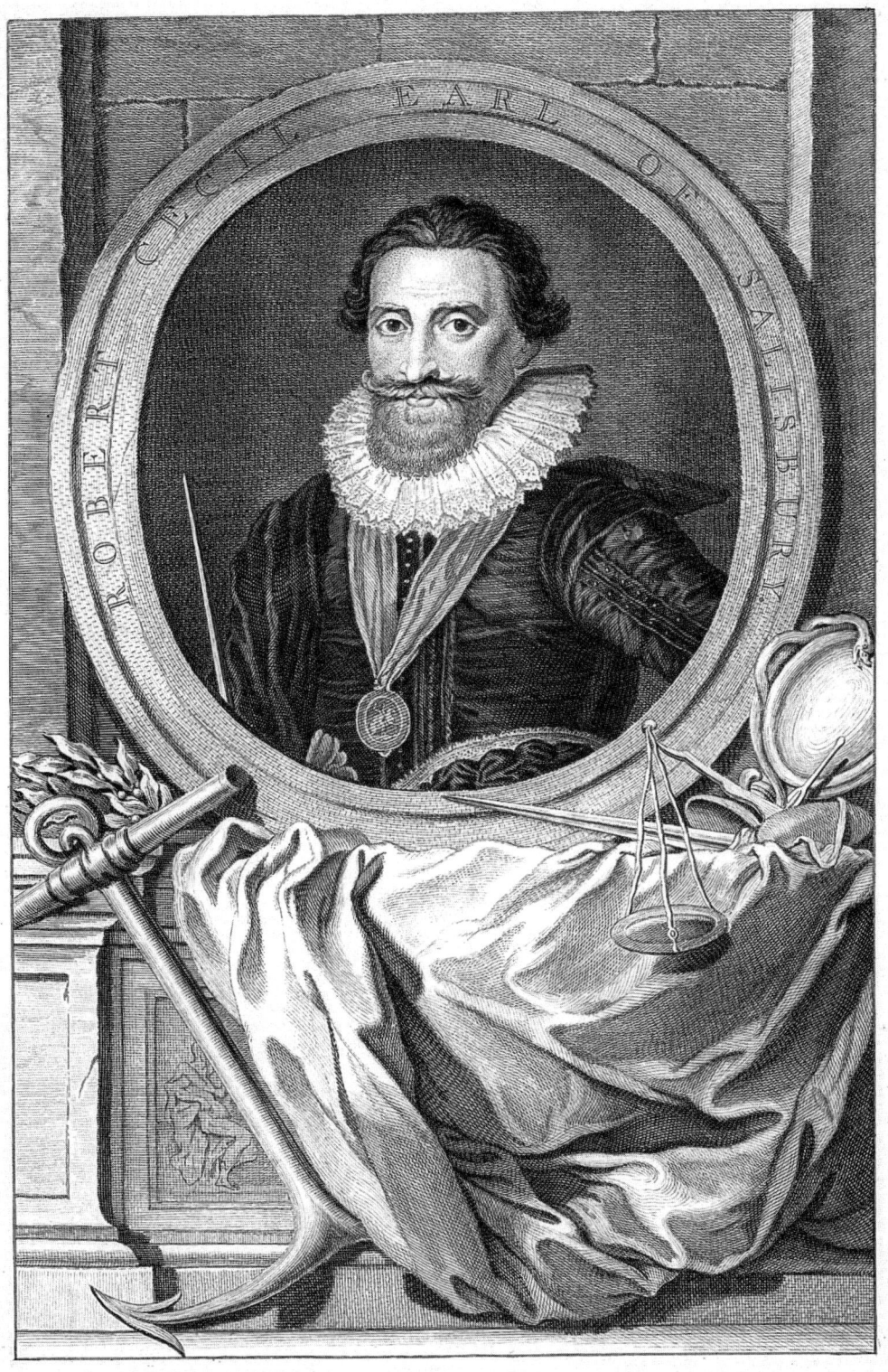
Robert Cecil. (*Jacobus Houbraken after John de Critz, Wellcome Collection*)

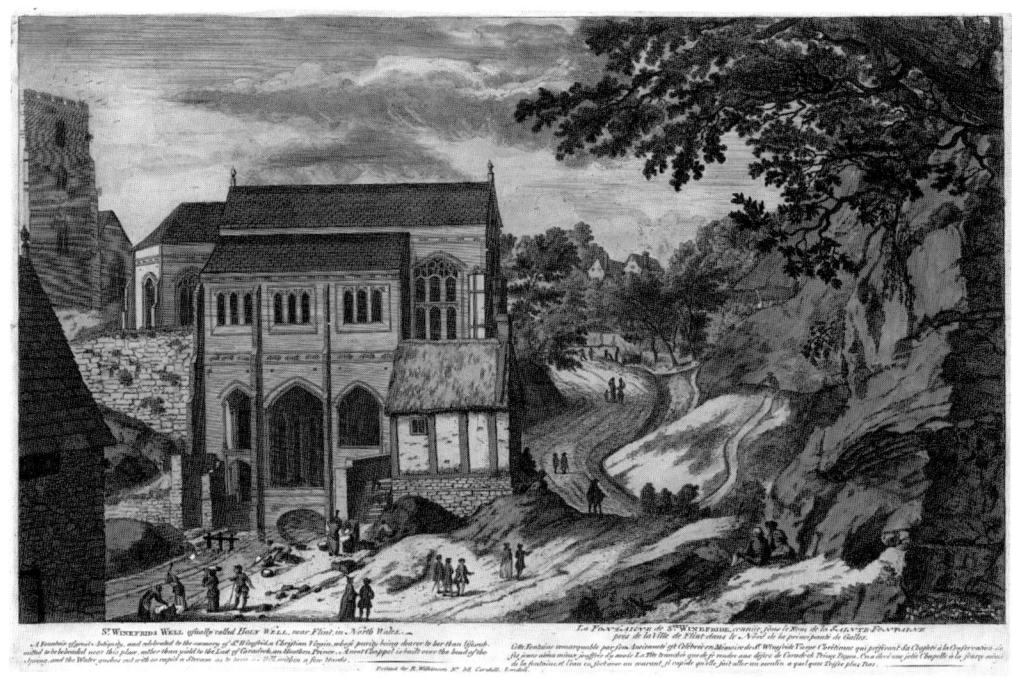

St Winefride's Well. (*Robert Wilson, Welsh Landscape Collection; Wikimedia Commons*)

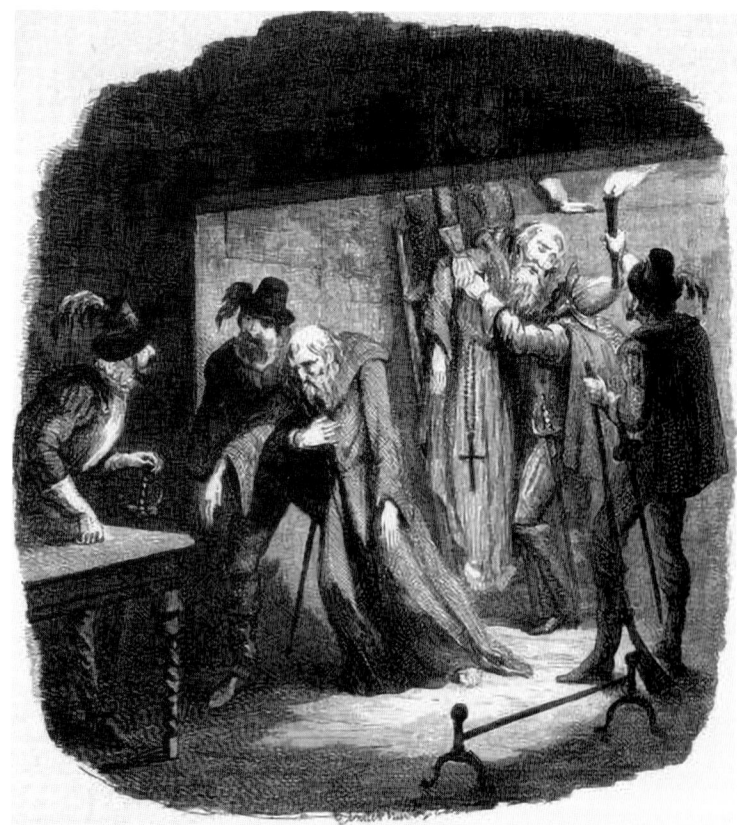

The Discovery of Garnet and Oldcorne. (*George Cruikshank, Wikimedia Commons*)

Part of letter from Anne Vaux to Father Garnet in prison. (The Vaux of Harrowden, *Godfrey Anstruther*)

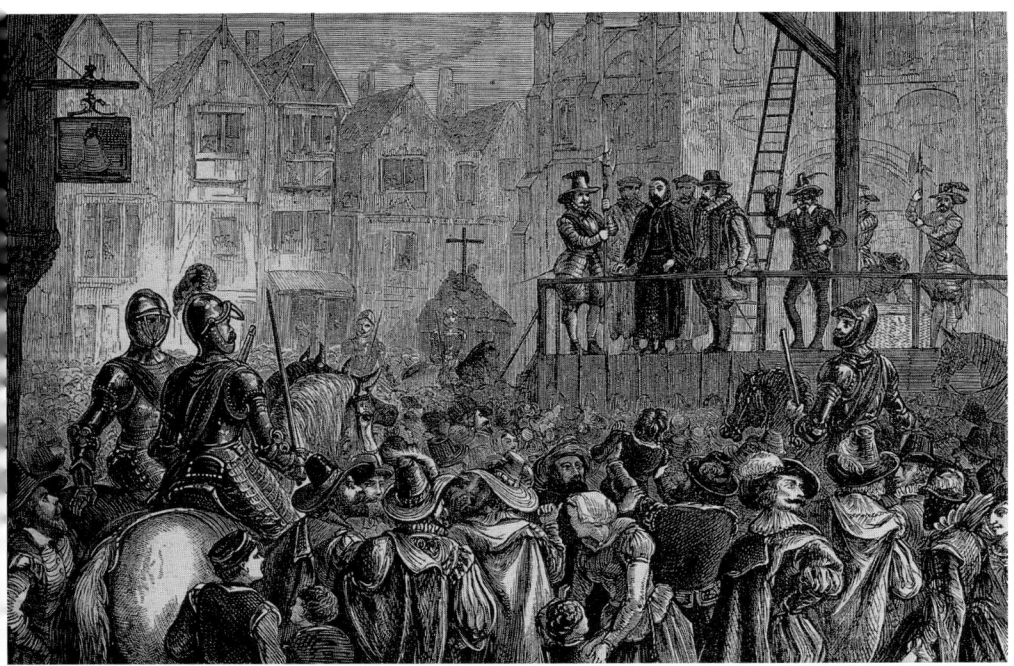

Execution of Father Garnet. (*Wood engraving, unknown artist; Wellcome Collection*)

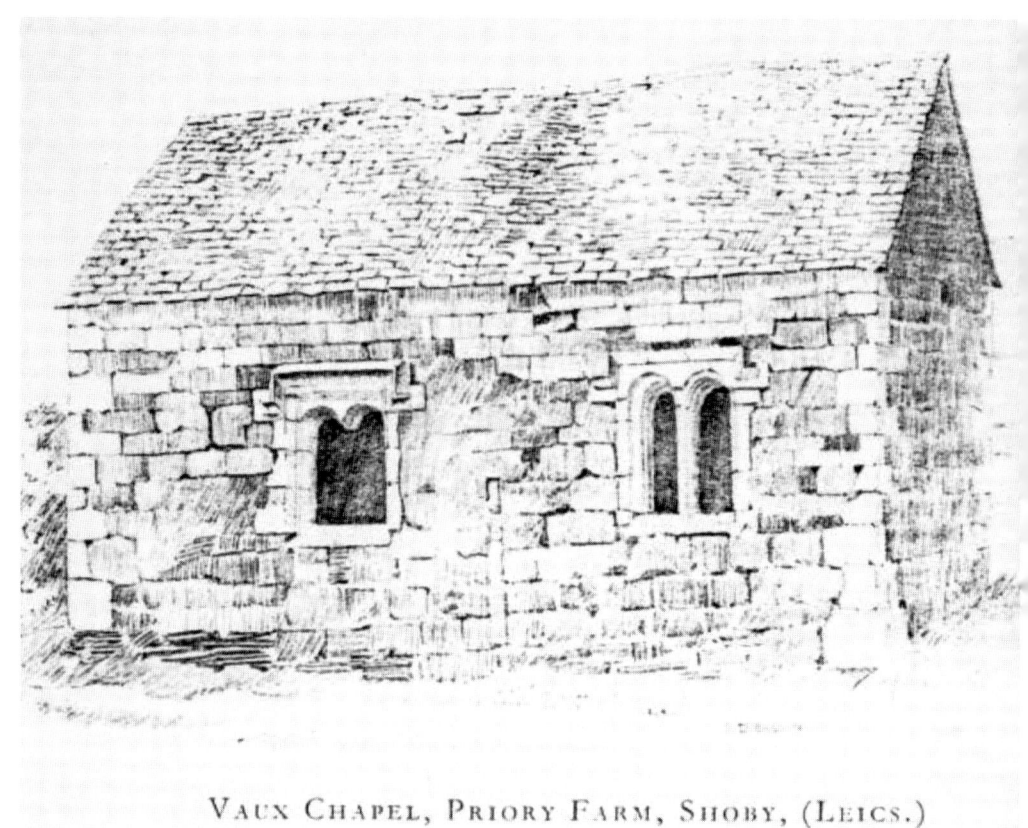

VAUX CHAPEL, PRIORY FARM, SHOBY, (LEICS.)

Chapel at Shoby, in the grounds of one of Anne Vaux's last known homes. (The Vaux of Harrowden, *Godfrey Anstruther*)

Chapter 9

A Man of Cruelty

Richard Topcliffe and Father Gerard

Returning to Anne Vaux, whether it was related to Southwell's arrest or perhaps a feeling that Baddesley Clinton was now considered to have been compromised, she, Eleanor, Garnet and the little community around them moved on. They often had to do so, but it is surprising that their next destination was London. Presumably there was some pressing reason for it, since the capital was a much more dangerous place for such a group than rural Warwickshire. The heat was increased in 1593 when the anti-Catholic laws were ramped up once more in the form of the Act for Restraining Popish Recusants. As if to balance things out a little, there was also an act against Puritans; some Quakers, for example, also did not attend their local parish church. Catholics could now be imprisoned rather than fined as previously, not just for attending Mass, but merely for not attending their Protestant church. Furthermore, they would remain incarcerated until they agreed to obey the law relating to such matters. If they continued to refuse to 'conform', they would be forced to 'abjure the realm' (i.e. go into exile). If they didn't, or if they left the country and returned, they faced the death penalty. Additionally – and this may well have been aimed directly at people like the Vaux family and Garnet – recusants had to register their address with the local authorities and weren't allowed to travel more than 5 miles from it; if they did, they would forfeit their lands and goods.

When this Act was passed, Lord Vaux was still alive, and his financial situation had certainly not improved. In this year, he was summoned to attend parliament and he told Lord Burghley in a letter that he couldn't even afford to dress as befitted a member of the House of Lords: 'My debts and miseries beyond measure multiplied, I am come up raggedly suited and clothed ... Yea I protest to you that I am moneyless and creditless.' Even his parliamentary robes were in pawn, and he couldn't afford to get them back.

Fortunately for Anne and Eleanor, along with their other sister, Elizabeth, William Vaux, perhaps aware of the declivitous path his financial situation was taking, had shrewdly taken steps to safeguard a large sum for them. He had set up an agreement whereby Sir Francis Tresham, his friend and brother-in-law (and friend of Garnet), would receive £1,500 (paid in annual instalments); acting as trustee, Tresham would pay the sisters £500 either upon getting married or in the event of William's death.

Lord Vaux and Tresham may have been on good terms, but it seems that Anne and her sisters never warmed to him. Eleanor received a payment from Tresham after marrying Edward Brooksby, but only 'above eight score pounds' (i.e., £160), which was less than a third of the promised amount. Elizabeth never married, but was given £300 after becoming a nun – oddly, almost double that given to Eleanor. Anne had received nothing.

Even though she had not and would not marry, Anne, who had chosen a path of chastity very similar to that of Elizabeth, felt that she too should have received her share by now. And she did mean her full share of the money her father had intended her to have, rather than the unsatisfactory amounts awarded to her sisters. By 1594, with Tresham's disbursement still not forthcoming, Anne instigated legal action against him.

Her problem was that the document drawn up by Lord Vaux all those years ago was found to have been poorly and ambiguously worded, leading to a dispute over its validity. Furthermore, Tresham claimed not to have received from William most of the £1,500 intended to be apportioned between his daughters. Nevertheless, Anne must have made a convincing case because the Court of Chancery found in her favour. However, there was a proviso. The court required Anne to 'acknowledge her obligations to Tresham, beg a continuance of his good opinion towards her, and pray his furtherance in helping her to the £500' (Anstruther, p.222). Anne, as the daughter of a baron at a time when social status was everything, felt that she should not be forced to go cap in hand to a knight in order to obtain what was rightly hers. But the court remained steadfast on this point.

According to Tresham, whose account of what followed is the prime source of information on it, Anne fulfilled her obligation, but with bad grace. He invited her to meet him at his daughter's home, but she ignored this and arrived unheralded at his house in Hoxton, catching him alone (apart from a couple of servants) so that, according to him, 'her submission might be swallowed up in secret'. Anne, he complained, had on her side 'old Broksbie and a pettifogging formal solicitor'. It's possible that 'old Broksbie' was Eleanor, but it's more likely to have been a relative of her late husband. Tresham went so far as to accuse Anne of timing her arrival for when he was about to have dinner, and says that over the course of four hours, while his stomach rumbled she managed to pull off the almost mutually exclusive feats of fulfilling the requirements of the court that she should 'beg a continuance of his good opinion towards her' while at the same time haranguing him as if he were a recalcitrant servant. One of her gripes appears to have been that Tresham pressured her sister, Elizabeth, into joining a convent.

An interesting aside that came out of this affair was Tresham's report that Anne supposedly told him that she had remained single because of poverty, and 'she hath not her marriage money in her own custody'. If she really did tell him this as a way of justifying why she wanted the money, it was disingenuous to say the least. Tresham, like many others in the Catholic community, knew full well that she had remained unmarried because she had committed herself to a holy life by choice. Tresham also knew that Anne received a regular allowance from Lord Vaux, was often helped out by her eldest brother and had received £500 and an annuity upon the recent death of her grandmother. To be fair, Anne did spend an awful lot of what money she had on the Catholic Underground: renting and maintaining houses, helping impoverished priests, bribing gaolers and the like. This wasn't quite the end of the matter of Tresham's role as trustee of monies intended for the Vaux sisters.

* * *

Meanwhile, in the same year of 1594, after two years of Anne, Eleanor and Garnet managing to remain under the radar in the capital, a priest was arrested in York and brought south for interrogation. He revealed under torture that Father John Gerard was living in London in a house owned or rented by 'Mrs Vaux'. He did not reveal the whereabouts of the house, and indeed probably did not know. Having got all they could from the priest, he was returned to York and executed.

Gerard was not in fact with Eliza Vaux at this time, but the authorities were closing in on him; the danger for him and those around him came from an enemy within.

'There was another … who brought great trouble upon us,' Gerard reports ominously. John Frank was a Protestant but a servant to Thomas Wiseman, William's brother, and known to and trusted by the Wiseman extended family. Gerard and members of the Wiseman family regularly used to stay at his house in Goldings Lane, Lincoln's Inn Fields, London. Despite Frank's impressive credentials, and Gerard having no specific reason to suspect him, the ever-cautious Jesuit still made sure never to 'let him see me acting as a priest, or dressed in such a way as to give him grounds to say that I was one'. Frank was, nevertheless, shrewd enough to discern the truth for himself, in particular noting Thomas Wiseman's deferential demeanour towards Gerard. In search of a generous reward, the man reported his suspicions to the authorities, who sent him to snoop on the family and note in particular the comings and goings of anyone associated with them whom he believed to be priests.

Once Frank had provided them with sufficient intelligence, the home of Jane Wiseman, Sir William's widowed mother, was the first to be targeted. This was on Boxing Day 1593, when, fortunately for her, the priest she had been sheltering managed to hide in 'a privy place in a chimney' and avoid capture, but Jane was nevertheless taken away to London to be examined. At her trial, she, like Margaret Clitherow, refused to enter a plea – Gerard says she was sure the jury would have to find her guilty and did not wish them to have her death on their consciences – and she was duly sentenced to be pressed to death. However, 'on account of her rank and the good name which she had, the Queen's councillors would not let such barbarity be practised in London'. She thus avoided the death sentence, but did spend several years in prison, where 'she pined in a narrow and filthy cell'. Her release came about when she was one of those who received the traditional pardon upon the coming to the throne of a new monarch, in this case James I.

In the meantime, John Frank was still secretly keeping the magistrates informed of Gerard's movements. In March 1594, he told them that the priest was soon to arrive at the Golding Lane house in Lincoln's Inn Fields. Gerard was, in fact, spending some time with Father Garnet; he had informed the household of when to expect him back, and Frank came to know about it. As luck – or God – would have it, Garnet persuaded Gerard to stay another night. The raiders found only Gerard's servant and a few others.

Gerard now needed to find alternative accommodation, and Garnet dispatched Little John, the man who had built the ingenious hiding place that had once saved him, to help Gerard find a suitable new house. During this period, they stayed at a house called Middleton's, the home of a Catholic supporter in Holborn, yet again unaware that there had been a betrayal.

At midnight on St George's Day, Gerard and Little John had retired to bed (they were in the same bed, it being very common in those days for men to share beds when travelling away from home) when they heard noises below, then footsteps coming up the stairs. Gerard guessed what was happening, but there was no other exit and Little John had no choice but to open the door to them. 'The room was at once full of men armed with swords and staves,' Gerard reported; so many, in fact, that a number still on the landing outside were unable to fit in.

The pair were separated, with Little John being taken to prison while Gerard spent a couple of nights in the home of one of the pursuivants. He was tempted to escape by making a rope from the bedclothes and climbing out of the window, but feared being spotted by a man in the next-door room assigned to guard him. He did plan to attempt it on the second night, but fate intervened when his arms were manacled together.

Gerard was taken before the authorities and questioned. He initially gave a false name (possibly 'Brooke', a name he was known to have used), but when it was put to him that one of his captors knew he was Gerard he dropped the pretence, admitting both to his name and to the fact that he was a Jesuit priest. He told them he would answer their questions honestly in matters relating to him, but would not say anything that might jeopardize the safety of anyone else. Therein lay the dilemma, because it was Gerard's knowledge of other priests and those helping them that his interrogators were most interested in.

There was a lot of predictable back and forth about religious matters and the loyalty or otherwise of Gerard and other Catholics to the queen, before he was finally formally charged and taken to the Counter Prison. There were two 'Counter' (or 'Compter') prisons in Elizabethan London, and it is not clear to which one Gerard was sent, but he did leave a description of his cell. It was a tiny garret room, whose sloping roof meant that it was impossible to stand up straight anywhere but beside the bed, the sole item of furniture. Gerard, then about 33, was a tall man, which obviously didn't help matters. He did have a window, but he reports that it was always kept open, admitting 'foul air' when it was dry and water when it rained. One thing responsible for the foul air was the privy next door, used by numerous other prisoners. Even the hardy Gerard was kept awake at nights by the stench.

After three or four days, he was taken for questioning by a magistrate who, ominously, had Richard Topcliffe sitting beside him. Even the magistrate seems to have been cowed into near-silence by the presence of Topcliffe. He was wearing a sword, indicating his status as a Queen's Messenger, and it was he who did most of the talking. Gerard joins the list of those who had nothing good to say about Topcliffe: 'He was a man of cruelty, athirst [sic] for the blood of Catholics ... an old man, grown grey in wickedness'.

The magistrate opened the proceedings, but when it came time for Topcliffe to talk, he first made a show of removing his sword and placing it on the table in front of Gerard. The priest knew the gesture was intended to unnerve him, but he was not so easily intimidated; indeed, the display only served to make Gerard abandon his usual polite demeanour and adopt a testier, more combative manner, scornfully batting away all of Topcliffe's claims and accusations. The arch-torturer changed tack. He scribbled out a document accusing Gerard of, among many other falsehoods, being on a political mission to turn people into traitors of their country, and said he was going to present it to the Privy Council. When Gerard asked for a pen and paper to formulate his own reply, Topcliffe's tone suddenly changed, softening, and he called Gerard a 'reasonable man'. The priest easily saw through this act, however, knowing that what had really cheered Topcliffe up was the prospect of getting a sample of Gerard's handwriting to compare against documents found in various pursuivant raids. The priest was one step ahead of him, writing his riposte in a 'feigned hand'.

Topcliffe literally shook with fury when he saw he had been outwitted. Initially, he disingenuously offered to copy it out, but Gerard knew his man and wasn't going to allow his only chance to put his case before the Privy Council be twisted by additions and inventions. Furthermore, he signed his name close beneath the last line of his memorandum, leaving no space for anything to be inserted once the document was out of his sight. This was more than Topcliffe could stand.

'I'll get you put into my power and hang you in the air and show you no mercy,' he growled, 'and then I shall see what god shall rescue you out of my hands.' These would be chilling words coming from anyone, but doubly so when uttered by Richard Topcliffe – and the outcome of the scenario he suggested would become manifest in due course.

Gerard was taken back to his cell, and on Topcliffe's orders his legs were shackled. He was kept like that for three months, a period which, when he wasn't being questioned (though not yet tortured), he devoted to prayer and contemplation. During that time, Gerard's servant and Little John were both tortured in the manner the priest knew awaited him – having their hands manacled above their heads supporting the whole weight of their bodies, their feet being some way off the ground. Such a position, especially when inflicted for hours on end, as it was here, was not only excruciatingly painful but hampered breathing, restricted circulation to the hands and damaged ligaments. Little John probably suffered more than most, since he is known to have had a hernia. The purpose of the torture was to extract names, but both men managed to hold out and Little John, his captors being focused on priests and unaware of what an important player they held, gained his freedom. His reputation as the master priest-hole builder of the age may have yet been unknown to the authorities, but his skills were highly valued within the Catholic community and a wealthy noble made his gaoler a financial offer he couldn't refuse.

Thanks to the intervention of friends and another generous bribe to a gaoler, Gerard was moved to the Clink in Southwark, where he was among other Catholics. It was a place he considered to be 'paradise' when compared to the Counter, especially when his leg irons were removed.

More clandestine payments meant that the priest was soon allowed a great deal of freedom and was even able to receive and visit other prisoners, take confession and set up a little chapel. It couldn't last, of course.

When the man in overall charge of his detention died, responsibility for Gerard was transferred to William Waad, who immediately set about removing Gerard's freedoms and reprimanding his lax gaoler. A little later, Gerard was moved once more, this time to the Tower. He had been there just three days when his new gaoler arrived, saying that the Attorney General and the Queen's Commissioners had arrived and wanted to see him. Gerard knew what this meant, and even the gaoler seemed troubled. It was time for the torture to commence.

He was taken to the apartment of the Lieutenant of the Tower, Sir Richard Barkley, which was within the confines of the Tower complex of buildings, and after some preliminary questioning which led nowhere, Gerard was shown the warrant authorizing his torture. He was then taken 'in a sort of solemn procession', candlelit because of the gloom, to an archetypal underground chamber, an extensive room where there were 'diverse sorts of racks and other instruments of torture'. In a scene reminiscent of a Bond film, he was first treated to a short tour of these fiendish devices and told he would 'have to taste them, every one' unless he gave them the information they demanded – the main piece of intelligence they wanted being the whereabouts of Father Garnet, the leader of the Jesuits in England. 'It is out of my power to satisfy you,' Gerard told them. He then sank to his knees and began to pray.

And so it was that John Gerard was led to one of the wooden pillars that extended from the earthen floor to the ceiling and formed part of the internal structure of the building. Manacles were attached to Gerard's wrists, a set of steps were placed at the foot of the beam and he was told to mount them. Iron staples protruded from the beam well above his head, and he had to raise his arms while a bar was threaded through staples and manacles. The steps were removed, and maybe for a moment Gerard thought his luck was in; being much taller than average, he could still make contact with the floor with his toes. But as soon as his captors saw this, any hopes of a relatively easy ride were dashed when they simply dug away the earth beneath his feet.

The pain, mostly in his arms and hands, but also chest and abdomen, was such that when he tried to pray aloud he could barely stammer the words out. At first, unsurprisingly, he didn't think he would be able to bear it for much longer. He left a graphic description of the sensations:

'It seemed to me that all the blood in my body rushed up to my arms and hands, and I was under the impression ... that the blood had burst forth from my hands. This, however, was a mistake; the sensation was caused by the swelling of the flesh over the iron that bound it.'

It was in this state that his interrogators left him and retired to Barkley's residence, every so often sending someone to see if there had been any developments. Remaining with him were 'three or four strong men, to superintend my torture'. His erstwhile gaoler also stayed. It didn't seem to Gerard that he had to do so, and when the man used his own handkerchief to dab away the torture-induced sweat trickling down Gerard's face, he suspected that the official was a compassionate man who sympathized with his prisoner's plight.

Gerard hung like this for a whole harrowing morning until finally reaching the limits of physical endurance and passing out. The steps were placed beneath his feet, but this was just a temporary respite; as soon as he started mumbling a prayer, they were removed again. This process was repeated several times, until at about 5.00 pm Waad reappeared to find out whether his prisoner's resistance had been broken. When Gerard made it plain that it hadn't, Waad stormed off, snarling: 'Then hang there till you rot.'

This proved to be an empty threat, however, because the bar holding his shackles in place was soon removed and he was lowered to the ground. Gerard found that even his free-hanging legs and feet had been affected by the ordeal, and he could barely support his own weight. But this was far from the end of the nightmare.

The friendly gaoler supported Gerard as he staggered back to his cell, then made a fire and brought him some food. The following morning, the priest was summoned by Waad. Attempting to dress, he discovered that his hands were too swollen to pass through the sleeves of his shirt, and all he could do was wrap a cloak around his shoulders.

The devious Waad told him that he was commanded by the queen herself and Cecil, her chief minister, to tell Gerard that, on the queen's honour, they knew for certain that Garnet *did* interfere in political matters and *was* an enemy of state – thereby presenting Gerard with the option of doubting the word of her Majesty or continuing to stick to his story. This was a crude piece of psychological chicanery, and Gerard would almost certainly have been aware that it was merely a variation on a commonly used ploy: 'We already know the truth – all you have to do is confirm it and the torture will be over.' Moreover, he had spent enough time in Garnet's company to be sure that he was being told lies about his superior, and he calmly told Waad so.

In another clumsy theatrical ruse, Waad sent next door for 'The Superintendent of Torture', who just happened to be a big, powerful, menacing-looking man. It was patently another move designed to intimidate Gerard, but unfortunately for Waad his prisoner happened to know that the newcomer was not the chief torturer but a master of artillery in the Tower, who had clearly been dragged along because of his size and physical presence. It was another failure on Waad's part.

Nevertheless, while it might not have been his day job, the artillery man was assigned to supervise the next round of torture: from now on, Gerard was to be racked twice daily until he told them what they wanted to know.

Technically speaking, Gerard was not 'racked' in the usual sense of the word, which we associate with a wooden bed with cogs and ropes at both ends used to stretch arms and legs simultaneously. The term, which Gerard himself used, seems to have been employed loosely back then, and the post with the iron staples to which he was returned was known as 'Topcliffe's Rack'. It is said to have been a form of torture invented by him and which he boasted was even more painful than the conventional rack. This time around, Gerard's hands and wrists were so swollen that the manacles weren't big enough to pass over them. Fortunately for the torturers, the flesh marking where they had been fastened the previous day remained crushed, and they were able to open up the manacles and refasten them there.

Gerard's body was still incredibly sore, and being suspended from the manacles this time was like having salt poured into an open wound. Gerard lost consciousness, but unlike the previous day he couldn't be revived and his attendants thought he was dead.

The next thing Gerard knew, he was sitting on a bench with someone trying to force warm water down his throat. Barkley, the Lieutenant of the Tower, was one of a large group standing around him. He once again attempted to persuade Gerard to talk, and once again the priest refused, stating: 'I have but one life, and if I had more I would offer them all for this cause.' So it was back to the torture chamber, although Gerard was too weak to walk and had to be half-dragged, half-carried. By this stage, he knew only too well what agonies he was about to go through – and would apparently continue to go through – and he displayed an almost unimaginable strength of mind and spirit.

But now came a surprising – almost astonishing – turn of events. Gerard was hung up again, but after little more than an hour he was let down. He kept expecting this to be just a blip, a temporary change of routine, but it gradually sank in that the torture was over.

Initially, Gerard speculated that Barkley, who had seemed to Gerard somewhat 'sorrowful' when condemning him to a further round of torture, had given up in frustration, but much later he would be told a very different story. Soon after these events, Sir Richard Barkley resigned his post (replaced as Lieutenant of the Tower by Waad), and there was an unsubstantiated rumour that even he was so disgusted by what he was expected to do that his conscience would no longer allow it. If true, a certain sneaking admiration for Gerard's fortitude and strength of faith might have had something to do with this, but perhaps also the enormity of what he was doing to a man whom he knew to be breaking the law in a religious sense, but whom he also surely knew deep down was *not* part of some anti-government, anti-Elizabeth plot, which was the main charge against people like him and Garnet.

The compassionate gaoler was in tears when Gerard was brought back to his cell. He cut up his prisoner's food and fed it to him like a baby, since Gerard had lost the use of his hands and fingers. Three weeks would pass before he could even begin to handle a knife to cut up his food, but the overall effects would last much longer.

Gerard was fed quite well now, and the gaoler was able to get certain specific food items for him. Among them were oranges. It was partly a reward for his helper, since he knew the man liked oranges. Gerard was probably sincere in this, but he also had an ulterior motive: 'I meditated making another use of them in time.'

He fashioned crosses from the orange peel, and the gaoler took them to various Catholic prisoners, but that wasn't the only plan Gerard had for the fruit, and was secretly squeezing the juice into a jug. Might he be allowed a quill, he wondered, just to make a toothpick out of it, and some paper in which to wrap the rosaries and crosses that he was handing out? Oh, and might he be allowed to write a line or two on the wrapping paper, asking the recipients to pray for him?

What he was actually doing was establishing lines of secret communication by using the orange juice as invisible ink. It was a tactic well known in the Catholic Underground movement, so the recipients knew to hold the paper against their fire to reveal secret messages. Some of the messages were to fellow prisoners, but a few were smuggled out to his supporters. Gerard hadn't survived so long without being a cautious and astute man, and he didn't push his luck too far in case the subterfuge was discovered (which it eventually was). He never used real names, and only fairly routine messages were exchanged for some months – although if Gerard had known that the gaoler, who made a show of carefully scrutinizing all the visible messages, was actually illiterate (as Gerard eventually discovered), he might have advanced his plans more quickly.

One significant secret note asked a supporter to buy his friend John Lilly out of prison. At the time, it was merely a good deed, but having Lilly on the outside would prove useful in other ways in time to come.

In spite of the humanity shown by the gaoler and the generally relaxed regime he was now enjoying, Gerard was under no illusions; he fully expected to be tried and executed before long.

One of the Catholic prisoners Gerard came to know was a man called Arden, who was being kept in the nearby Cradle Tower. He had been sentenced to death, but the authorities had somehow never got round to doing the deed and he had now been languishing in the Tower for ten years. Eventually, he had been allowed to go out onto the leads, a flat roof area next to his cell, to exercise. Gerard was in the Salt Tower, which had a direct line of sight with the Cradle Tower. There was a garden between them, but the distance was less than 50 metres. Gerard could see the man from his window and they were close enough to be able to exchange signals. Arden took to kneeling so that the priest could provide him with a sort of remote blessing.

After a great deal of persuasion (and the changing hands of a little money), Gerard was allowed to cross the garden area between the two towers (the Privy Garden) and visit Arden in his own cell, and even stay the night there. Initially, his only intention, apart from the company (Gerard was not allowed visitors from outside), had been to minister to the lonely Arden. But when he gazed out of the window of this room and took in the lie of the land, an audacious idea came to him: one not dissimilar to that employed by Margaret Ward in trying to free Father Watson. But would it end in the same disastrous fashion?

The Cradle Tower was and is at the Thames end of the complex, close to its south-east corner and built into the outer perimeter wall. The moat lay beneath it, followed by another wall. Beyond that was a strip of land (The Wharfe), and then the Thames. Might not someone with a decent length of rope, Gerard asked his new companion, be able to clear moat and wall and reach the outside? Arden was sure it could be done, 'if a man had some true friends to help him'.

'There is no want of such friends,' Gerard assured him. Two such were the now-free John Lilly, through whom Gerard got a secret letter to Father Garnet, seeking approval for his scheme. The Jesuit Superior was all in favour, just as long as Gerard felt sure he could accomplish it safely.

Gerard enlisted Lilly, as well as Garnet's servant Richard Fullwood. The plan was for them to row a boat to the bank of the Thames nearest the Cradle Tower at midnight on an appointed date.

When the day came, Gerard again persuaded his ever-helpful gaoler to allow him to visit Arden and spend the night in his room. The first problem arose when the gaoler, before leaving them together, locked not only the door to the room, but also the one which led out onto the roof. Gerard and his companion got their knives and worked away at the stone into which was fixed the metal loop into which the bolt was inserted, until it became loose enough to pull out.

The two men knew someone was always on guard at night in the garden below, so they crept as quietly as they could across the roof until they reached the edge nearest the Thames. At close to midnight, they saw the ghostly outline of a boat approaching. As it came closer, peering through the darkness, Gerard saw that in it were John Lilly, Richard Fulwood and the boat's owner, whom Gerard recognized as having been his gaoler at a previous prison. Then disaster struck. Just as the boat approached the riverbank ready to moor, a man happened to emerge from a nearby cottage. He caught sight of the suspicious craft and called out to them. Their response seemed to satisfy him and he went back indoors, but the encounter had spooked the men in the boat. They waited for signs that the man had gone to bed, but it took so long that Gerard's would-be rescuers lost their nerve and the operation had to be aborted. To make matters worse, the three men in the boat almost drowned trying to get away.

They had to pass under the arches of London Bridge, but by now the tidal flow had increased. The old bridge at that time was notorious for how the water was forced between the piers at the base of the narrow arches, increasing the flow and causing turbulence. There were numerous deaths through drowning because of this, and when Lilly, Fulwood and the boatman entered the maelstrom, they were soon in danger of adding to the tally. With the boat being tossed about and ready to capsize, the three had to abandon all pretence at stealth and yell desperately for help. Gerard and Arden could only stand on the roof, looking in the general direction of the scene, since the boat had passed out of sight. But they did hear the commotion, and Gerard could make out Fulwood's voice. Help arrived, and although the boat finally did turn over with one man left on board, he was also dragged to safety.

The next day – 4 October 1597, his 32nd birthday — Gerard got a letter from Lilly saying they would try again that night. He was once more able to talk the gaoler into letting him stay with Arden, and this time he wrote three letters, to be left behind in his cell, including one exonerating the gaoler.

The boat arrived again at the appointed hour, and this time there was no one around to disturb them. According to the prearranged plan, Gerard threw down a lead ball with a length of string attached. The boatmen grabbed it and tied one end of their own stouter rope to the ball and string, allowing Gerard and Arden to haul it up, where they attached it to a cannon on the roof. They wound it around securely enough, but didn't tie a knot because they planned to shake it free and retrieve it when the mission was accomplished, leaving the authorities with less chance to work out how the escape had been accomplished. The boat party secured the other end to a stake in the riverbank.

They now had a zip wire-type arrangement in place, but because of the distance between the Tower and the riverbank, the rope was at a shallower angle than Gerard had bargained for. It soon became clear to the two men that rather than letting gravity do the work and sliding down freely, they would need to haul themselves along the thick and heavy rope.

Arden went first. Young and strong, he managed it without too much trouble. But his weight had slackened the rope, making things even harder for Gerard. He straddled the rope face-down, grasping it in his hands and wrapping his legs around it, and set off. He hadn't gone far before he lost his balance and overturned, finding himself hanging upside down. This was almost certainly the better position for such a task. His arms and hands were far from being recovered from the manacles, which is probably why he had tried to pull himself along on his belly first. He struggled through the pain to keep a grip, but soon felt himself losing his grip. Pausing to compose himself, Gerard started to shuffle along, hand-over-hand, but it wasn't just the weakness in his hands that made the task difficult and dangerous. Even discounting the torture he had been subjected to, Gerard had by now been cooped up in various prisons for several years, and it had told on his fitness and stamina. His progress was painfully (literally, in his case) slow; he struggled and gasped to around the halfway point, then had to rest and regain his breath. With the saints working for him, as he saw it, and the rescuers below praying for him, Gerard pressed on and cleared the inner wall, only to come to a stop once more when his strength and burning lungs failed him.

He was over the moat now. A fall would have been noisy, but not necessarily the end of the escape attempt. Gerard, determined to complete his labours, struggled on. By the time he reached the outer wall, the last barrier to freedom, the rope had become so slack that it was almost horizontal. He was dangling beneath the top of the wall and had reached the limits of endurance, no longer having the strength to pull himself up and over.

Luckily, the men waiting on the other side realized what had happened. John Lilly managed to scramble up the wall (he later told Gerard he had no idea how he managed it) and manhandled Gerard to the other side, where he was lowered to the ground so exhausted that he couldn't stand unaided. They shook and pulled on the rope with all their might to bring it in, but even though it hadn't been knotted, the two men's efforts had somehow tightened or snagged it around the cannon, and it wouldn't come free.

This was a small price to pay. Against all the odds, Gerard and Arden had achieved what very few ever had and escaped from the Tower. They were free men.

* * *

The two escapees now split up. Lilly took Arden to the house being run by Anne Line, while Gerard rendezvoused with Little John. Before his removal to the Tower, Gerard had been visited in the Clink by Little John, who is widely thought to have been one of the planners of the escape stunt. Although no one involved stated as much categorically, it certainly bears the hallmarks of his resourceful mind. Whatever thee truth, he and Gerard made their way to Uxbridge, where Henry Garnet was currently staying. But Gerard's mind was still on his escape from the Tower, and in particular into what kind of jeopardy he might have put his gaoler. He dashed off and dispatched a secret letter to the man, explaining what he had done and why, and arranged to have someone waiting with a horse at an appointed spot to take him to a safe house. Moreover, Gerard guaranteed that he would provide him with more than enough money to compensate him – 200 florins a year – for his help and kindness, and to help him out of the difficult position in which he would undoubtedly soon find himself.

When Gerard's messenger intercepted the gaoler on his way to the Tower the morning after the escape, he was not yet even aware that two of his prisoners had fled. He was approached by a man bearing a letter, who told him in hushed tones: 'This is for you, and not for anyone else.'

When the puzzled gaoler asked who had sent it, the messenger simply replied: 'A friend of yours.' Only now did it emerge that the gaoler was illiterate, and had to sheepishly ask the messenger to read the contents to him. The poor man, as might be expected, was both shocked and scared, and had no hesitation in accepting Gerard's generous offer. It was just as well, because before he could even quickly visit the Tower to summon his wife to join him, one of his colleagues came up to him, saying: 'Be off with you as quick as you can, for your prisoners have escaped and the Master Lieutenant is looking for you everywhere. Woe to you if he finds you!'

The gaoler was therefore whisked 'all in a tremble' to a waiting horse, and thence embarked on a 100-mile ride to yet another safe house assigned to him by Gerard. It seems his wife later joined him, and that the gaoler himself converted to Catholicism and was never caught.

Chapter 10

A Wise Woman

Eliza Roper

In 1595, before Gerard's escape, Anne and Eleanor's father, by now financially ruined as well as mentally and physically broken, had died in Irthlingborough, aged 61. In the words of Godfrey Anstruther, he had left his children 'an impoverished estate and a vast ocean of debts'. Lord Vaux did, however, have the foresight to set up an annuity of £20 a year for Anne, and this was on top of one she was already receiving after the death of her grandmother. This was almost certainly Elizabeth Beaumont, with whom Anne and Eleanor had spent much of their childhood. Henry Garnet, with whom she had a close bond, reported that Elizabeth Beaumont had tended to needs of priests, so she may well have provided a role model for the later work of Anne and Eleanor.

The sisters and Father Garnet continued to live in or near London (first London itself, then Uxbridge) after the arrest of Father Gerard for what seems to have been an untroubled couple of years. Little John was also with them, though such was the demand for his skill in making priest holes that he was probably often away. Anstruther, in *Vaux of Harrowden*, describes him as being habitually wrapped in a cloak 'of sad [i.e. muted] green cloth with sleeves, caped with tawny velvet and little gold stripes turning on the cape' which had been given to him by Sir William Wiseman (who had sheltered Father Gerard and Anne Line).

In June 1598, they and Garnet were living in a house owned by Robert Catesby called Morecrofts (or Moorcroft) in Colham Green, a hamlet near Uxbridge about 12 miles west of London, when they were visited by a priest recently arrived from the Jesuit college at Valladolid: Father Oswald Tesimond, who went by the name of Greenway when in England.

Tesimond had begun his journey with Fathers John Ruffet and Roger Filcock, whom he met in Bilbao. They endured an arduous passage to

Calais, crammed together in a cargo of chestnuts. Tesimond himself had embarked in such a hurry that he had neither food nor water of his own, and his only sustenance from the crew during the nine-day voyage (fearful of how long their supplies would last) was 'so little that I cannot venture to tell it lest I should not be believed'. As if that wasn't bad enough, his allocated resting place was right beside the vent from the vessel's galley, meaning that he was constantly choked by fumes, barely able to breathe or open his eyes. In Calais, Tesimond separated from his two companions. Filcock was captured within three years of landing in England and executed alongside Anne Line, while Ruffet was betrayed and executed the following year.

The timing of their arrival in Calais was unfortunate, since the Dutch were at that time blockading the port. Although they departed it under cover of darkness, the boat they took became becalmed and was fired on by the Dutch when daylight revealed their presence. All on board survived and Tesimond now landed in Brussels, where he acquired two new companions – Ralph Ashley, who would prove a valuable man to have around in the next few years, and another priest called Thomas Standish.

Finally, a lengthy, storm-tossed voyage aboard an English fishing smack took them to the mouth of the Thames, where they managed to talk their way past a guard ship, and they subsequently disembarked a couple of miles outside London. They made their way to a house which, unknown to them, had been raided only the previous night, and from there Tesimond was directed to Garnet, then at Morecrofts near Uxbridge.

Thanks to a proclamation issued following the eventual exposure of the Gunpowder Plot, we have a detailed description of Oswald Tesimond:

> 'Of a reasonable stature, black hair, a brown beard cut close on the cheeks and left broad on the chin, somewhat long-visaged, lean in the face but of a good red compaction, his nose somewhat sharp at the end, his hands slender and long fingers, his body slender, his legs of a good proportion, his feet somewhat long and slender.'

Tesimond had been with them a matter of days when news reached them that Morecrofts itself was compromised, and that a raid was imminent. Garnet sent Tesimond to a house in 'a village called Brentford', while he went to London to try to secure a place there. This resulted in a move to a house near Spitalfields, which was to be Tesimond's base for his remaining few years and which Anstruther believed to be the one in which Gerard had hidden after fleeing the Tower.

Even the new London base was not safe for long. Tesimond learned from Roger Filcock, the young man who had travelled part of the way to England with him, that a spy – someone known to them – had taken a room in a house directly opposite in order to carry out surveillance. From that point on, Tesimond only ever ventured out at night, and never left by the front door (luckily there were two other exits). He also stopped shaving, growing his beard 'so long as to change my appearance very much'. He encountered his nemesis on several occasions, but the latter, although he may have had his suspicions, couldn't be sure enough to make an arrest.

Tesimond was safe for now, but Gerard's escape heralded a period of even more intensive hunting for Catholic priests, and Anne Line had been caught just a year or two later in 1601. John Lilly was taken with her, and having been told by Waad that they knew about the Spitalfields house and planned to descend on it, he managed to smuggle a message out from the Tower to Garnet. They were forced to flee once more, but Tesimond, a novice in such situations, was impressed by Garnet's calmness and clarity of thought when the news arrived. 'Without being the least disturbed, he spoke to all with his usual modest cheerfulness,' observed the young priest, going on to describe how the unruffled Garnet calmly gave those present instructions to hide all traces of their presence and make preparations for their departure. Some of his party were, quite naturally, alarmed, but Tesimond says that Garnet remained perfectly calm, both now and 'on some ten other occasions in dangers greater than this', and 'consoled and strengthened them all by a few grave words'. The Jesuit Superior 'proved himself to be an old soldier and experienced captain, accustomed to such assaults', declared Tesimond.

* * *

We last saw Father John Gerard in the company of Anne Line at the home of the Wisemans. Even though he had avoided capture during the destructive search of their property, it had become clear to him that his presence was jeopardizing the family's safety and peace of mind. It was time to move on. He had previously received several invitations to visit a 'noble family' in Northamptonshire, but his itinerary had not given him the opportunity to do so. He decided that now was a good time. The matriarch of the 'noble family' was Eliza Vaux, née Roper, sister-in-law to Anne and Eleanor. She already had a priest with her, but he had proved unpopular with them. Father Gerard found him to be a 'learned man and a good preacher' who had been with them for a year, but some of the household were prejudiced against him. Unfortunately, we aren't told why.

Gerard's movements at this period have caused a certain amount of confusion, partly due to his own rather loose wording in his autobiography, but also because of later biographers getting into a slight muddle about a specific location.

It is often assumed that Eliza was living at Harrowden when Gerard joined her. This is perhaps because Harrowden is referred to by Gerard as the family's ancestral seat. Initially, however, Gerard clearly writes of 'the house in which she was actually living' when he arrived, and *then* goes on to say 'there was another and *larger* house … at a distance of about three miles, which had been the old family seat' (my italics; source: *During the Persecution*). Harrowden is 3 miles from Irthlingborough, and although the reverse obviously applies, the key point is that it was by far the larger of the two. Eliza was, then, at Irthlingborough. Anne had been baptized in Irthlingborough, and her father, William, Lord Vaux, had been buried there four years previously. As it turned out, however, neither of these places were deemed suitable for their purposes, so another house was sought, leading to a second area of confusion, which we shall come to in due course.

Like Eleanor Vaux, Eliza was a grieving widow, having lost her husband at around the same time that Lord Vaux died. Eliza was around 35 at this time, the daughter of John Roper, Baron Teynham, of Badmangore Manor, near Sittingbourne in Kent. She had married George Vaux, stepbrother of Anne and Eleanor, and the couple had taken over the Irthlingborough house. But their married life, which was a loving one – not always the case in those days of unions arranged for political and financial expediency – was short-lived. George's death came within weeks of that of his father, Lord Vaux. In his autobiography, Father Gerard describes Eliza as being 'pious and devout, but even now still overwhelmed with grief at the loss of her husband'. He noted that she had barely ever left her room for a year after her husband's death, and for three years after that could not bring herself to be in the part of the house where he had died. To add to her woes, Lord Vaux's interminable financial penalties for his recusancy had resulted in a reduction of his financial support for Eliza, and by now she could barely afford to run the house. But 'a wise woman', Gerard remarked, 'builds up her house and is proved in it'. His arrival lifted Eliza's spirits to such a degree that Anne and other family members begged him to act as chaplain to their stepsister-in-law and her children.

Gerard accepted, and saw it as his first mission to 'wean my hostess' mind from that excessive grief'. He counselled her and taught her Catholic meditation. Eliza, whom Gerard found to be a highly intelligent woman ('her mental powers were of a very high order'), soon began to benefit from his help. Gerard recalled:

'In the first place, therefore, she resolved to lead an unmarried life; secondly, to aim at poverty in this sense, that all her actual fortune, and all that she might ever have, should be devoted to the service of God and his ministers, while she herself should be but their servant to provide them with what was necessary.'

Gerard next turned his mind to finding a new base for them. He had applied to take on another priest to help him, and extra room to receive transient Jesuits and Catholic gentry, hold meetings and so on would be welcome. The Irthlingborough house he described as 'very poorly appointed ... not only old, but antiquated'. Harrowden Hall was, as we have seen, much bigger and only 3 miles away, but it too had suffered over the years and was 'in some part quite ruinous'. Eliza made it clear that she would go wherever Father Gerard felt she could be of the most use, whether that be 'the most remote part of the island' or the heart of London.

Gerard knew that the capital was too risky, especially as Eliza was the daughter of a well-known recusant. Eliza herself did some scouting in her part of the East Midlands, and Gerard accompanied her to view some of the properties on her shortlist. This is where the second area of confusion arises.

John Morris, who includes Gerard's autobiography in his *Condition of Catholics under James I*, concludes that the place they settled upon must be Stoke Poges ('Pogis') in Buckinghamshire. But this assumption appears to be based on Gerard's comment that the place they finally found had been 'built by the late Chancellor of England'. Morris took this to mean the manor house at Stoke Poges, quite reasonably so since it was indeed the former home of the man in question, Sir Christopher Hatton. But Gerard himself had been doubly wrong in his original assumption.

The house at Stoke Poges *was* owned at one time by Hatton, though not built by him. More to the point, Gerard was getting his Hattons mixed up – easily done, since there was another Christopher Hatton around at that time. He was an MP (though he never held the office of chancellor)[1] and he owned Kirby Hall in Northamptonshire. This was in Eliza's current locality (something Gerard said they were aiming for) and a much more likely venue for them to choose than Stoke Poges, over 60 miles to the south in a county with which neither was familiar.

This was worked out by Philip Caraman in his *Autobiography of a Haunted Priest* and Anstruther concurred with him, but Stoke Poges is still often associated with Gerard and Eliza Vaux.

Kirby Hall was a mansion about 20 miles north of Irthlingborough, and at that time less than thirty years old. It was a 'truly princely place', said Gerard, and remote enough for the comings and goings of priests and others not to attract attention. Unfortunately, the plan started to unravel even before they had a chance to move in.

Gerard arranged for Little John, along with an assistant called Hugh Sheldon, to go to Kirby ahead of them and work his magic there, creating hard-to-find hiding places. But something was nagging at Gerard.

Soon after arriving in Irthlingborough, there were increasing concerns about the make-up of the staff that Eliza had around her. Non-Catholic servants in such families were always a potential source of betrayal; some

---

1. https://www.historyofparliamentonline.org/volume/1604-1629/member/hatton-christopher-1605-1670.

of Eliza's were happy to convert to Catholicism, but through Gerard's influence Eliza dismissed most of them. This might seem harsh, but life and liberty depended on trusting those around them: servants tended to know who was visiting and of future travel plans, and were almost inevitably privy to many secrets. Gerard knew that there were those who were prepared to pay handsomely for such information.

As it turned out, the vetting procedure didn't go quite far enough. 'There was another … who brought great trouble upon us,' he reports ominously. This unnamed servant's loose tongue soon led to local gossip about the notorious Jesuit John Gerard joining the new tenant, the Dowager Lady Vaux, at Kirby Hall, and the efficiency and omnipresence of the Elizabethan spy network meant that this news quickly reached London. While Little John and Hugh Sheldon were busy at work inside the house, a raid took place.

Thanks to the sheer size of Kirby Hall, and the searchers not having enough men to completely surround the place, Little John was able to slip away unnoticed. Sheldon was caught and imprisoned, but gave nothing away and was released after about four years.

The pursuivants had been hoping to find at Kirby not Little John, whose presence locally they may not even have been aware of, but Eliza and Gerard. When they discovered their mistake, they made all haste to Irthlingborough. Oblivious to these events, Gerard was having lunch in his room with another priest and a layman when the gang arrived. Eliza had been feeling unwell and was resting in her own room, so when the raiders arrived there was no one to oppose or delay them in the way that someone like Anne Vaux would have, and they began to move through the house unimpeded.

Hearing the commotion and at last realizing what was happening, Gerard grabbed anything that might be incriminating and led the others in the direction of the priest hole. The route took them past a room already being searched, but it was the only way to get to safety, and luck was on their side as they swept past and reached the hiding place unnoticed. The search lasted until nightfall without turning up anything, and the uninvited visitors left with their tails between their legs.

It was during the discussions afterwards that it emerged that the manhunt had not been the result of treachery, but of mere idle talk.

Nevertheless, the culprit was dismissed, though 'without unkindness'. The move to Kirby, of course, had to be abandoned, leaving Eliza and Gerard back at square one.

Rather than trying to find yet another location, they decided that Eliza would divert her energies into making Harrowden Hall, the ancient residence of the Vaux family, fit for use. The main thrust of the project was the building of a new wing to the house solely for the use of Gerard and any visiting priests. This became not just a residence, but a Jesuit headquarters and a college for preparing boys for eventual entry into priesthood. Sir Everard Digby and Robert Catesby, future Gunpowder Plotters, were among the people Gerard ministered to at this time. Gerard also spent a lot of his time travelling, providing spiritual support to those who sought it and endeavouring to convert those who might be receptive.

The new wing at Harrowden offered Little John what may have been his first and only opportunity to create a whole building with a priest hole organically incorporated into its design, as opposed to having to adapt an existing structure. Needless to say, Owen did his work well; which was just as well, since there would come a time when the efficacy of his design was the only thing that stood between safety on the one hand and torture and execution on the other.

Chapter 11

These Wild Heads Had Something in Hand

Anne Vaux and The Gunpowder Plot

In the meantime, Anne, Eleanor and Garnet had moved to a house called White Webbs on Enfield Chase, another location which would come to play a significant role in the story of the Gunpowder Plot. Today, the area (the house itself no longer exists) is still fairly rural, but it is near a busy junction of the M25 and close to the towns of Enfield and Waltham Cross. In 1600, it was yet another relatively isolated spot surrounded by woodland. The house was a substantial one, owned by Dr Huicke (or 'Hewick'), physician to both Henry VIII and Elizabeth I. It was large enough to accommodate a number of priests at any one time, and had been leased by an intermediary employed by Anne Vaux, using her 'Mrs Perkins' pseudonym.

'Mrs Perkins' moved in first, probably with Eleanor, and three months later there arrived 'Mr Mese', 'an ancient, well sett gentleman, but playne in Aparell'.[1] This was Henry Garnet, who was actually only 45 in 1600. The sisters nursed him through a severe illness at around this time. For a few brief years, this little community was able to live in relative peace, and numerous priests were regularly able to come and go without attracting undue attention. Jessie Childs, in *God's Traitors*, discovered that in 1602 Anne and Eleanor took in two starving priests from Portugal who had been on the run, and kept them safe for several months. Then, on 24 March 1603, a visitor arrived whose name would within a couple of years become infamous throughout the land: Robert Catesby. He brought with him momentous news, the repercussions of which would soon be felt by them all: Queen Elizabeth had died, and King James VI of Scotland would soon be travelling south as James I of England.

---

1. Anstruther, *The Vaux of Harrowden*.

It's a well-known story, particularly among those with an interest in the Gunpowder Plot or this period in general, that there was an initial hope – expectation is not too strong a word – that James's reign would herald an era of toleration of Catholicism. Although a Protestant himself, James's mother was Mary, Queen of Scots, who had of course been a Catholic. Furthermore, his wife, Anna of Denmark, though ostensibly a Lutheran, certainly seems to have had strong Catholic sympathies, though whether she actually converted, as is often taken for granted, is still debated. James was even reported to have specifically assured Thomas Percy that he would deal fairly with Catholics, so spirits and hopes for the future soared.

But while James was more open-minded than Elizabeth and was known to welcome theological debate, as time passed by, any dreams of a more relaxed, tolerant climate withered and died. Indeed, the amount taken in fines for recusancy in 1605 was greater than any year during the long reign of Elizabeth,[2] and the rumblings of discontent began to grow. For the most part it was a mixture of frustration and grumblings. However, a hot-headed gentleman called Robert Catesby (the true leader of the plot which was to follow, not Guy Fawkes, who, though a vital cog, was essentially a hired hand) gathered around him a group of like-minded men, including the disillusioned Thomas Percy, who were prepared to take direct action.

My book *The Gunpowder Plot Deceit* explores the extent to which the plans were known about by Robert Cecil well in advance of the arrest of Guy Fawkes, and to what extent it may even have been encouraged by agent provocateurs in order to gain maximum anti-Catholic propaganda from the almost theatrically dramatic last-minute exposure. However, while I have no doubt that there are significant question marks over the official version of the events surrounding the plot, what the book does not do is go so far as some and claim that there never really was a plot, and that the plotters were mere patsies. There can be no doubt that Catesby, Fawkes and the rest believed in what they were doing and intended to go through with it.

---

2. Williamson, *The Gunpowder Plot*.

Before the chain of events reached this point, further anti-Catholic legislation ensued, some of it aimed specifically at the Jesuits. By 1605, Catesby was beginning to draw more men into his inner circle, and secret meetings were held in various places (including White Webbs) as the plan progressed. Most of the plotters were related in one way or another, and several had family ties with the Vaux.

With the planning and preparations for the plot moving inexorably forwards (but not because of it), Anne, Eleanor and Garnet were on the move again. They had reason to believe that White Webbs may have come under the beady eye of the authorities, and while they didn't yet think the place had been completely compromised, a decision was made around the Easter of 1605 to spend only short periods there and seek an alternative main base. The manor house at Erith, by the Thames but well out to the east of London, was settled upon. The arrangements for renting the house were made for them by Robert Catesby, and it was perhaps because of this and the probability that Cecil by now had at least some idea of the existence of the plot, or *a* plot, that the Erith house was also being watched only a few months after they had moved in.

Garnet and the Vaux sisters became aware of this. 'We find ourselves being betrayed in both places ... and are forced to wander up and down until we get a fit place,' Garnet reported at the time.

In June 1605, Catesby met Garnet at a lodging house where he was staying in Thames Street, London, and played a self-serving and unscrupulous trick on the priest which was to put him in mortal danger. The conversation had drifted (no doubt at Catesby's prompting) towards the seemingly never-ending wars in the Low Countries. Guy Fawkes had fought in this conflict, and it seemed that Catesby might lead a regiment abroad in the near future. It was to this background that Catesby asked Garnet about the Church's position on the likely deaths of innocent civilians caught up in the confusion and chaos during the storming of an enemy-held town. At this point, Garnet had no idea of what Catesby and his friends were planning in England and treated it as the theoretical question it appeared to be. Admitting that it was a theologically tricky area, he propounded that while it could never be acceptable to deliberately target non-combatants, during an attack as part of a 'just' war, what we would today call 'collateral damage' was inevitable and therefore would not leave one liable to condemnation.

But Catesby was being disingenuous at best and duplicitous at worst, because he had an ulterior motive for asking the question – one which had nothing to do with the wars in the Low Countries. It would later emerge that Catesby used the priest's 'sanction' as leverage when it came to persuading wavering fellow conspirators to follow their plan to its grim conclusion, thus duping both sides. Because of the justness of their cause, blowing up Parliament – Catholics, surrounding civilians and all – was morally and theologically acceptable according to the senior Jesuit in the land.

After some time passed and the conversation he had had with Catesby had had time to sink in, Garnet developed an uneasy feeling. The next time he saw Catesby, he warned him to 'look to what he did if he intended anything, that he must not have so little regard of innocents'.

Garnet's worst fears were confirmed the following month, July 1605. He, Anne and Eleanor were staying at Fremland, a Catholic house in Essex, and were visited by Robert Catesby, Francis Tresham and Tresham's brother-in-law, Lord Monteagle. They no doubt met Garnet primarily for spiritual reasons, but at some point the conversation turned to more worldly matters. Now wary of what the men might be up to, Garnet asked Monteagle about the possibilities of English Catholics rising up against James, something he was vehemently against, and which the Pope had only recently issued an edict against. Monteagle's reply must have concerned the priest: 'If ever they were, they are able now. The King is so odious to all sorts.'

Final confirmation of what was afoot came later that month. Robert Catesby, under seal of confession, told Father Tesimond about the Gunpowder Plot in detail, giving him permission to tell Garnet, his superior, also under seal of confession. An agitated Tesimond hurried to Garnet at Fremland and poured out what he knew. While this must have been a heavy burden to bear, it did, of course, put Garnet in an invidious position. Thomas Campbell (*The Jesuits 1534–1921*, Vol. 1, p.159) describes it as a 'foolish' thing to have done, saying he was 'bitterly reproved' for it, and ascribing Garnet's subsequent execution directly to this act by Tesimond. This seems harsh. The first point – whether Tesimond should have told Garnet – is debatable. The main point of confession is to admit to sin, and Tesimond hearing about Catesby's plan clearly was not a sin of his own. However, it was a matter which troubled him and which he knew was bound to have repercussions that would involve Garnet personally. This leads to the suggestion that Tesimond effectively signed Garnet's death warrant. There are two arguments against this. The first is that, as alluded to above, Garnet would conceivably have wanted to know about Catesby's plot – Garnet was part of Catesby's circle, and forewarned is forearmed. Additionally, later events would indicate that Cecil and the government didn't really *care* whether Garnet and the other Jesuits in England were directly involved in the plot; they were marked men anyway, and would have used the excuse of the plot against them – especially Garnet – regardless.

Later writers have criticized Garnet himself for not taking decisive action once he knew what was afoot. Both he and Tesimond expressed their condemnation of the plot, and Garnet commanded Tesimond to 'hinder it if he could'; the latter assured Garnet that he had strongly protested against the idea at the time and would do what he could to try to talk Catesby out of it.

Although Garnet was bound by the rules of confession and unable to tell anyone what he knew, least of all the authorities, he has been criticized for not attempting to pressure either Catesby or any of the others he knew to be involved to drop their foolhardy and murderous plan. The fact that he did not do so is sometimes interpreted as Garnet turning a blind eye to the venture, the implication being that while he may have condemned it, he wasn't exactly desperate to prevent it from going ahead.

This is unfair and unlikely. Everything we know about Garnet leads to a picture of a reasonable and compassionate man, but also a very shrewd and intelligent one. While he may have believed that Catesby and his co-conspirators might succeed in blowing up parliament, he would also have been aware that the next phase of the plan – the death of James sparking a general uprising, the overthrow of the Protestant government and the replacement of the king with a Catholic-supporting monarch – was a pipe dream. Garnet's lack of any further direct action was surely at least in part down to a desire to immediately distance himself from the plotters, judging that Cecil and others would be only too keen to jump on any pretext to associate him with any such plot. In this he was being very shrewd, as future events would show.

* * *

Uneasily leaving the plotters to do what they would, Garnet, Anne and Eleanor, and a large group of other Catholics – which included Eleanor's son, William, the limping Little John and several priests – embarked in August 1605 upon a trek of around 200 miles to St Winefride's Well in North Wales, which had been a destination for pilgrims for countless centuries. Sister-in-law Eliza and her priest and companion, Father Gerard, swelled the numbers when the group passed through Northamptonshire, and there were eventually more than thirty pilgrims plus probably at least as many servants.

They had all been through tough times and faced more of the same in the future, and one of the reasons Garnet gave for leading them to Wales was that of providing his growing flock with a spiritual boost, recharging their batteries as we might say now. Although he doesn't say so, it possibly also struck him that it wouldn't do him any harm to be out of London – England even – lest anything Catesby and his fellows were planning should come to fruition in the immediate future. Leaving the plot aside, in those days, everywhere Garnet tried to settle down soon became compromised. White Webbs (from where the pilgrimage set out) had become too risky a place to stay for more than a few days, and now the same fate had befallen the latest refuge in Essex. 'I have no reliable abode,' the priest wrote wistfully.

But even in trying to get away from it all, Garnet was to unwittingly establish further links between himself and the plot. Both on the way out and on the return journey, his party made overnight stops at various Catholic houses. This wouldn't have been considered surprising or suspicious, had it not been for the owners or occupants of those places.

There was Norbrook House in Fulbrook, Warwickshire, the home of John Grant; a house rented by Ambrose Rookwood, who took the opportunity to join them on the journey to Wales; Thomas Wintour's family's home, Huddington Court in Worcestershire; Rushton Hall in Northamptonshire, belonging to Francis Tresham, where Garnet, Anne and Eleanor stayed on the return journey; and Gayhurst, a house in Buckinghamshire owned by Sir Everard Digby.

Every single one of these men were, or would soon become, Catesby's co-conspirators.

None of the plotters explicitly gave anything away, but Anne Vaux was beginning to have her suspicions that something big – something shocking – was bubbling under the surface. At both Norbrook and Huddington, she noticed that far more horses were in the stables than one would normally expect. Bearing in mind that Anne was Garnet's close confidante and that she had probably already picked up on some of his anxiousness about what Catesby might be up to (even though he would never have told her any of the details he had learned during confession), she told Garnet that she 'feared these wild heads had something in hand' and begged him to have a word with Catesby after they had returned from St Winefride's Well. Catesby assured the priest that the gathering of an unusual number of horses was part of the preparations for his planned military expedition to Flanders, and although this never actually came about, it was at that time a genuine possibility which the pair had talked of before. Garnet accepted the explanation, but Anne, who had become aware of some sense of nervous apprehension among the womenfolk at some of the houses where she had stayed, was not satisfied. Indeed, after the discovery of the plot, a large cache of weapons and ammunition, for use in the optimistically expected uprising, was also found at Huddington.

Once the pilgrimage was over, Anne and the others found themselves in the same dilemma of needing a safe place to stay at a time of increasing scrutiny and persecution. It was now October 1605, and Garnet needed to find somewhere to host one of his twice-yearly gatherings of Jesuit priests. With no other options available, he decided that they must risk Harrowden Hall. They were accompanied by Digby and his wife; Catesby subsequently arrived, but it was a brief visit and the two men departed that night. We now know that it was during a discussion as they rode away that Digby was initiated into the Gunpowder Plot by Catesby.

Once the priestly gathering was over, Garnet, Anne and Eleanor were offered the use of Coughton Court near Stratford-upon-Avon by Digby, who was not the owner but currently had a lease on the place. It was a favour which, if they had had the benefit of foresight, they might well have declined. As it was, they, along with Little John, arrived at the end of October.

They had been there less than a week when, at 6.00 am on 6 November, they received shocking news. It was brought by a breathless and agitated Thomas Bates, servant to Robert Catesby. Anne's worst fears were confirmed: Bates's master had been exposed as one of the men behind a plot to blow up the king and the parliament buildings, and the attempt had been foiled during the previous night. Arrests had already been made, but most of those involved had fled London and a major manhunt was already underway. There could be no doubt that any known associates of the plotters would become prime targets of the authorities.

* * *

It's well known that the search for Guy Fawkes in the early hours of 5 November was ostensibly prompted by a letter received by Lord Monteagle a few days previously. There has been a great deal of discussion and controversy about this mysterious and cryptic letter; not just in modern times, but almost from the moment its existence first came to light, and with good reason. (I explored the idea – I would go so far as to say likelihood – in *The Gunpowder Plot Deceit* that the letter itself did not mark the first time the government became aware of the plot.) The identity of the writer of the letter is the main area of interest and fascination, and despite there being a long list of candidates, a definitive answer has never been settled upon. For us, the relevance is that one of the names on the list is that of Anne Vaux.

Despite his position in the royal court, Lord Monteagle was himself from a Catholic family and it is almost certain that he subscribed to that faith himself. If he did subscribe to the Catholic faith, he did so discreetly. However, during the reign of Elizabeth he had been linked with those who supported the Spanish invasion and along with several future Gunpowder Plotters had even taken part in the disastrous Essex rebellion: against the queen, but more specifically designed to bring down his enemy, Robert Cecil. (It actually had the opposite effect on Cecil's position.) Monteagle not only survived the fallout of all this with just a fine and short term of imprisonment, but went on to conveniently and successfully reinvent himself as a loyal subject in time for the accession of James I.

Monteagle was intimately connected with some of the plotters, if not the plot itself, and it should be noted that the letter managed to reach him at his Hoxton home on the very day, just over a week before 5 November, that he had unexpectedly decided to leave the city and dine there for the first time in some weeks. Thomas Wintour was working for Monteagle in some sort of secretarial role at the very time of the Gunpowder Plot, using this role to assess the mood around Westminster when his companions were worried that a previous cancellation of the opening of parliament might mean they had been discovered. Monteagle knew Catesby and Percy well, and was married to a daughter of Lord Vaux's ally, Sir Thomas Tresham, making him the brother-in-law of plotter Francis Tresham. It was Tresham who had unsuccessfully pressed his fellow plotters to save Monteagle's life by warning him to miss the rescheduled opening of parliament, thereby making him in the eyes of many the prime suspect as the sender of the letter. The plotters themselves suspected it, and the theory persists to this day.

We are really only interested in the letter in respect of whether Anne was involved, but for what it's worth, the view that it was manufactured by Cecil as a means of bringing his propaganda coup to a dramatic conclusion must be near to the top of the list of possibilities.

* * *

Anne Vaux came into the picture as a possible author of the 'Monteagle letter' partly because of her close connections with leading plotters, and especially her prior knowledge, or at least suspicions, that 'something' was about to happen. This may, quite understandably, have nagged at her conscience until she felt compelled to do something. Additionally, a correspondent to the *Gentleman's Magazine* during the 1830s asserted that the handwriting of the Monteagle letter bore strong similarities to one written by her which is held in the National Archives, although this has since been strongly disputed.

One of the arguments against Anne having been the author of the letter – and this also applies to another suspect, Mary Habington (see below) – is that Monteagle, because of their family connections, would probably have recognized Anne's undisguised handwriting. If he had, she would certainly have been cited by the authorities as an accomplice of the plotters. However, this overlooks Monteagle's unique position of having a foot in both camps, and it's not at all unlikely that he would have wanted to protect her, keeping quiet about recognizing the hand.

All that aside, ultimately, I don't believe Anne – a shrewd, intelligent woman with plenty of dealings with 'the enemy' – would have taken such a risk, at least not in that way. If she *had* been behind the letter, she would surely have either disguised her handwriting or dictated her message to a trusted third party.

Another reason against her having written the Monteagle letter is to do with her spelling. In a still-existing letter she wrote to Garnet when he was in prison, Anne, despite her eccentric spelling, uses the word 'you' numerous times and consistently spells it in the 'correct' (i.e. modern) way on every occasion. The writer of the Monteagle letter starts by using that spelling, but then strays into 'yowe', which he or she uses five times. Next, the writer of the Monteagle letter spells the word 'your' inconsistently – 'youere', 'youre' and 'your' – whereas Anne uses 'your' and 'yor'. The Monteagle writer writes 'frends', while Anne writes 'frendes'; and the Monteagle writer says 'as soon as yowe have *burnt* the letter', but Anne refers to having '*burned* a letter'.

Of course, if it had been Anne, this could have been a deliberate ploy; but to alter the spelling of the odd word yet make no attempt to disguise one's handwriting would make little sense. Anne, we know, was a sensible woman.

Anne probably didn't know quite enough about the Gunpowder Plot to have written the letter anyway. The Monteagle letter includes the passage 'they shall receive a terrible blow this parliament and yet they shall not seie who hurts them'; 'they shall not seie who hurts them' implies that the writer knew the 'terrible blow' involved gunpowder (just about the only means of a remote attack available then), as opposed to, say, an armed raid on the parliament building. Although Anne had probably guessed that some sort of uprising was afoot, it's unlikely that she knew what form it would take, nor – equally importantly – when.

There was a suggestion in a letter to *The Times* on 30 November 1839, repeated by Thomas Lathbury (*Guy Fawkes: or the Gunpowder Treason*) the following year, that Mary Habington, Monteagle's sister and wife of the owner of Hindlip Hall, dictated the Monteagle letter to Anne in order to save her brother. Her husband, Thomas, was sentenced to death after the plot for sheltering Garnet and Oldcorne, but was not only reprieved but released thanks to Monteagle's intervention. It would seem odd, however, to dictate such an important message not only to such a well-known recusant, but to someone so short-sighted that her writing was sometimes virtually unreadable.

Could it even be that the conscience of either Garnet or Tesimond got the better of him, and one or the other dictated or gave the gist of it to Anne to commit to paper? Again, this is unlikely, and the above objection still applies. Conspiracy theories are fun, but more often than not the most obvious answer is the correct one and Francis Tresham, described as the least committed of the plotters, is still, whether he physically wrote the letter or dedicated it, the best bet.

* * *

After the Spanish Armada, Garnet wrote that 'far more than any other priest in the country I am suspect [*sic*] of stirring sedition and raising the Catholics to support the King of Spain'. He must now have been experiencing a sense of deja vu. Knowing that Coughton Court would be high on the list of places to be targeted by the authorities, Anne, Eleanor and Garnet fled. Inevitably, of course, their very flight only added to the appearance of guilt, and this was heightened by their association with some of the plotters and the places to which they now headed.

Flying from London, Thomas Wintour rode to Norbrook and then on to Huddington Court, both places where the Vaux sisters and Garnet had stayed during their recent pilgrimage. Catesby foolishly went to White Webbs, not only staying there but drawing so much attention to himself that even Garnet heard of his presence while he was still at Coughton. Needless to say, White Webbs was raided, though Catesby had fortunately moved on before it happened and the searchers had to content themselves with a haul of 'Romish relics'. It also emerged that one of the servants looking after the place was in the employment of 'Mrs Perkins, widow', and another worked for 'Mr Meaze'. Cecil probably wasn't aware at the time, but 'Mrs Perkins' was the pseudonym of Anne Vaux, while 'Mr Meaze' (sometimes 'Mese') was in fact Henry Garnet. Catesby had also rushed to Huddington.

The bulk of the escaping plotters then rendezvoused at Holbeche House, which at that time fell within the county of Staffordshire, where the hunters finally caught up with them. A number, including Catesby, were shot in what is sometimes described as a gun battle, whereas in fact although the weary plotters didn't give themselves up, neither did they offer any armed resistance. The four who survived the attack were taken to London for interrogation. Others who had not gone to Holbeche were arrested closer to London.

Garnet's own movements during this period, in the company of Anne and Eleanor, were of necessity so shrouded in secrecy, and often almost certainly involving only very brief stays, that retracing their steps is impossible. Nonetheless, this must have been an extremely distressing not to mention terrifying time for them all. The one location we do know of comes from a report from an informant's report received by Cecil:

> 'On Saturday last I entreated a Berkshire gentleman going then home, to enquire of Mrs Perkins's abode. This evening I received a letter from him ... that about a fortnight or three weeks before that she was at Hartley Court in Berkshire, the house of one Mr Speake, but what is for the present become of her he cannot yet learn. It seems she is not to stay there, for that Hartley Court is since on the sudden sold ... He writes further that, at the very time of the late mischievous practice, there was great resort of dangerous persons to and from that house.'[3]

Hartley Court was around 80 miles south-east of Coughton Court, and 'Mrs Perkins' was, of course, Anne Vaux.

We have already heard about White Webbs, and although the Erith house where the Vaux sisters and Garnet had recently stayed did not

---

3. Cecil Papers Vol 17, British History Online.

immediately come under suspicion, because it had been rented by Catesby the servants left behind to manage it took flight as soon as they heard of the smashing of the plot and subsequent manhunt.

The plotters had all very quickly either been rounded up or killed, but Anne, Eleanor and Father Garnet remained at large; for now.

Chapter 12

Why Then, Lady, You Must Die

The Arrest of Eliza Vaux

Eliza, the Dowager Lady Vaux, heard of the arrest of Fawkes and, like Anne, was well aware of the likely repercussions.

News of the plot and its unravelling seemed to spread throughout the country almost as fast as it would in the modern electronic age. Father Gerard and others had been staying with Eliza at Harrowden, and as soon as they heard about what had happened in London, they sent a young man called Henry Huddlestone and a servant called Batty to warn Father Garnet and the Vaux sisters at Coughton Court, unaware that they themselves had already been visited by Catesby's servant with news of the dramatic developments.

What made things even more awkward for Eliza at this time was that the potentially awkward contents of a letter she had written some months previously had recently been brought to light by someone with a grudge.

Eliza had been hoping to get her son, Edward, who was now the fourth Lord Vaux and soon to turn 17, married into the family of the Earl of Suffolk. This would have been a prestigious match, but the negotiations were dragging on and at one point a frustrated Eliza unburdened herself in a letter to her friend Agnes, Lady Wenman. She told Lady Wenman she suspected the delays were at least in part to do with the Vaux being 'obstinate Papists'. Worse still, Eliza also tossed in the phrase that it felt like 'Tottenham would turn French' before anything happened.

Unfortunately for Eliza, when the letter was delivered it first came into the hands of Lady Wenman's mother-in-law, Lady Tasborough, who promptly opened and read it, then attempted to cover her tracks by resealing it. Her efforts didn't fool Lady Wenman, and despite Lady Tasborough's feeble claim that the letter had been only 'lightly sealed', Agnes made her displeasure known.

The sneaky opening of the letter almost certainly came about as a result of an already existing animosity between the two women. Lady Tasborough later admitted to 'some dryness or mislike' between herself and Lady Wenman, and this may have extended to Eliza, by association or otherwise.

So it was that immediately the Gunpowder Plot became public knowledge, in what seems to have been a deliberate act of spite, Lady Tasborough remembered the letter and informed Cecil of its content, hinting that it showed Eliza had advance knowledge of the plot yet had done nothing to alert the authorities. Worse still, Eliza tried to get the letter back, but this only served to raise further suspicions against her.

Cecil would have already known perfectly well that Eliza and her family were 'obstinate Papists', so there was no great revelation there. And although the line about nothing changing until Tottenham turned French might seem to have a sinister connotation, especially so soon after the exposure of the plot and with France being a Catholic country, Cecil was again unlikely to have had many concerns. Anstruther explains that it was an old saying which meant that 'something extraordinary was going to happen'. It almost certainly alluded to the problems over arranging the significant marriage. However, other sources give a more likely explanation for the use of the phrase in this particular context. In 1536 (so almost contemporary with Eliza), the Duke of Norfolk was warned that he might be sent to the Tower for annoying Henry VIII. Upon hearing the rumour, Norfolk responded: 'When I shall deserve to be there, Totynham shall turn French' (*Letters and Papers Foreign and Domestic, Henry VIII*). In this context, it was being used in a similar way to the modern 'pigs might fly' and meant it was either highly unlikely or would never happen (correctly, as events proved), which fits in with Eliza's increasing frustration and pessimism about the marriage possibility.

The main point here is that unlike the Spanish Armada, there was no likelihood of a French invasion of Tottenham or anywhere else in England. Furthermore, Father Tesimond didn't hear that something was afoot until taking Catesby's confession in July 1605, and it was the following month when Anne Vaux noticed the unusual number of horses at various Catholic homes. Eliza wrote her letter in May, so couldn't possibly have had an inkling of what was being planned at that point.

Perhaps if she had said that Tottenham would soon turn *Spanish*, Cecil might have justifiably wondered what was behind it. Nevertheless, it was decided that an explanation was required.

As if she didn't already have enough enemies, the Westminster rumour mill was, naturally enough, working overtime and Eliza's own father, Sir John Roper, got to hear of the letter. He immediately wrote to Eliza, and although the letter has been lost to history, we can safely assume when we look at her reply that he was taken in by the stories which were circulating about his daughter (both regarding her involvement in the plot and the reasons for the delay in Edward's potential marriage to a daughter of the Earl of Suffolk):

'Sir I can not but mervayle att your straynge & unlooked for letters. I wissh your self & all others showld know I ame as innocent & free from the euer knowinge of that plotte as who so euer is most free, & doe as much abhore the intention, tor anye letters of myne I wissh that maye be shewed & the uttermost made agaynst me, so confident ame I of euer writinge anye thinge, which it was impossible I should [have erased] neuere knowinge nor imagininge as god doth best know & as it is playne enough to freends heare, howe easy so euer your self to be beleeve the worst uppon I know not what reporte.

'I did receue your former letters wherin you did much blame me for refussing the match & offer of my La: of Suffolke; by that I see you heare straynge things & untrewe, but tyme will lett you see & know better howe I haue proceeded in that matter, & I sentt you a letter of my Lo: of Northampton that maye make it playne unto you that nowe wee wer to expect answer from him of the sertaynty of that match & to that end my sone had a perpos to haue come upp to London himself one thorsday or friday last if by chance Sir George Farmore & his La: had not come to supere to us one wedensday nyght & towld us the first newes of this pitefull & tragecall intendment & then I thought nott beste to send him …

'Your obediend daughter

'Eliza Vaux'

Unfortunately for Eliza, the whole country was on high alert in the immediate aftermath of the discovery of the Gunpowder Plot, and both the messenger carrying this letter to London and the two men Eliza sent to warn Anne and Eleanor of the alarming news from the capital were detained. The most direct route would take the servants through Warwick, about three-quarters of the way to their destination, but before they got there they heard it was swarming with searchers and they diverted northwards towards Kenilworth. It made no difference; they were intercepted in that town.

The High Sheriff of Warwickshire, Sir Richard Veney, gleaned some interesting information from them. Huddlestone admitted that by chance on 5 November itself his mistress's party had encountered four of the plotters on their travels: Wright, Catesby, Percy and one of the Wintour brothers, Thomas. Huddlestone, Batty and others who were rounded up were taken to the Tower for further questioning, where they provided more information but remained consistent in their defence of the priests. 'Most of the prisoners have wilfully forsworn that the priests knew anything in particular, and obstinately refuse to be accusers of them, yea, what torture soever they be put to,' Cecil admitted in a letter.

Still, there was enough circumstantial evidence to bring Eliza Vaux and Harrowden Hall under suspicion, and an order was given for a search to be conducted there for John Gerard.

Over a hundred armed pursuivants duly descended on the house, and unlike some such searches this was to be a thorough, ruthless and professional job. The party included several knights of the realm, and the operation was conducted with so much secrecy that even these men didn't know why they had been summoned until they arrived at the house of William Tate, a justice of the peace and former High Sheriff of Northamptonshire, who was to head the raid.

They and their men arrived at Harrowden just after midday on 12 November 1605. Before making their presence known, they surreptitiously posted sentries at all exits. By chance, Eliza's son, Edward, returned from a visit to town just as the pursuivants were readying themselves to strike, so they simply accompanied him into the house.

They were taken straight to Eliza's room. Here they announced themselves, and Tate demanded that all keys be handed over – not just internal and external doors, but those for boxes, cupboards, chests and the like. Eliza conducted herself calmly and respectfully, complying promptly with their requests without resorting to any of the common delaying tactics in such situations. Her composed demeanour might be viewed as a testament to her faith in the skills of Little John. Someone was left to keep watch on Eliza while the investigation commenced.

An initial complete search of the house revealed nothing, so Eliza and Edward were pressed on what they knew about the plot. They both not only denied any involvement, but categorically condemned it. Nevertheless, the searchers remained at Harrowden for three days, even examining clothes chests and Eliza's letters and papers for some clue as to the presence of Gerard or any other priest.

When the news was passed to Tate that Batty had spoken of a barrel of gunpowder being left at Harrowden by Eliza's servant, Francis, the search was resumed in earnest. On the evening of 14 November, the third day of the search, Tate, for reasons he doesn't explain, felt that he was in a part of the house where 'this hidden serpent should seem to lurk'; his instincts were right. Before taking drastic action, he gave one of Eliza's servants who was in the room with him the opportunity to reveal the whereabouts of any hidden entrance. Presumably thinking that the priest hole was about to be discovered anyway, and to save his mistress's walls and floors from being torn up, the servant opened the secret compartment.

Tate declared it 'the most secret place that ever I saw, and so contrived that it was without all possibility to be discovered'. But to his disappointment, inside he found not Father Gerard or any other priests, just 'many popish books and other things incident to their superstitious religion'. It was enough for Cecil to command Tate to bring Eliza to London.

What Tate did not realize was that this wasn't the only priest hole at Harrowden. Gerard was in another, so cramped that he could not stand upright during a search which went on for several days, but secure nevertheless. As time passed and the watchfulness of the raiders was gradually relaxed, the servants even felt it was safe enough to get Gerard out from his hiding place and warm him by the fire. Little John had proved his worth once again; in the words of Godfrey Anstruther, 'The lame little lay-brother had outwitted a hundred men.'

Eliza arrived in London on 18 November, but when asked about Father Gerard she said that that 'she knoweth him not' (Anstruther, p.318). She did concede to what she probably was aware the authorities knew anyway – that Catesby and Digby had visited her. There was also a visitor called Mr Darcey: what she didn't reveal was that this was in fact Father Garnet. Similarly, she confessed that Huddlestone had passed on to her news of his accidental meeting with Catesby, and that Percy and others had joined them and 'whispered to Catesby', after which they took to their horses and departed. Catesby's last words to Huddlestone had been 'haste thou home'.

When asked about the letter she had written to Lady Wenman, Eliza said she couldn't remember everything that was in it; she conceded that she had written something about Tottenham turning French, but doesn't appear to have been pressed further on the matter, confirming that it was not only an innocent remark but a well-known saying with no sinister undertone.

Nevertheless, the Privy Council decided that both Eliza and the seven plotters' wives who had been brought in must remain in captivity, though under house-arrest with selected aldermen, since 'it was not thought fit to commit [them] to prisons'. Edward, the young Lord Vaux, was questioned by Cecil himself and his answers were sufficient for him to be dismissed on the condition that he remained in London. Eliza had to appear before the full Privy Council, but while proudly declaring herself a 'firm Catholic', she condemned the plot unequivocally and assured them that she had been backed in this by 'those that had care of her soul'. But when pressed about her relationship with Father Gerard, she both denied it and reminded them that asking her to admit to it was tantamount to asking her to incriminate herself, which was contrary to English law. It was put to her that because he was a traitor and a 'chief plotter', she must tell them of her dealings with him. Eliza, of course, could honestly say that she was completely sure that he was neither of those things.

Their final ploy was to remind her that she was now 'in the king's mercy to live or die', but that if she told them where Gerard was she would both avoid execution and not have any of her estates taken from her by the Crown. She defiantly told them that she did not know where he was, but that if she did she still would not tell them.

'Why then, Lady, you must die,' they told her. Eliza merely replied: 'Why then, I will die, my lords – for I will never do the other.'

As she was leaving, one council member who had been a personal friend escorted her to the door and made a last attempt to make her change her mind to avoid certain death. 'Then, my lord, I will die,' she persisted calmly. This final exchange took place as he was opening the door for her. Some of Eliza's servants were waiting for her outside and overheard it, and were overcome with tears of anxiety and anticipated grief.

Eliza's courage and strength of spirit can't be doubted; but although we can be sure she meant what she said, the members of the Privy Council did not. It was one of the usual crude stratagems – empty threats, designed to make people talk – but she was made of sterner stuff. Far from being executed, Eliza wasn't even committed to prison, but returned to house arrest. Similar threats were made to her weeping servants, but they also stood firm. Because of their lowly status, they were sent to prison until a decision was made about what to do with them.

Back at Harrowden, the pursuivants, while not actively searching any more, kept a watch on the house both inside and out for around ten days. A kind of cordon was set up, and any traveller passing within 3 miles of Eliza's home was liable to be stopped and questioned.

By this time, it was assumed that if Gerard was hiding somewhere in Harrowden, he would either have had to give himself up or have stubbornly starved to death. In fact, despite the close attentions of the guards, servants were managing to secretly supply Gerard with food during the night.

When the last of the pursuivants had finally gone, Gerard slipped away to another safe house. Once there, news of what had happened to Eliza and the things that were being said about him and other Jesuits reached Gerard's ears, and it prompted him to write what we would now call an open letter, protesting his innocence in anything relating to the plot. It was a worthy but futile gesture. Whether or not the Privy Council believed him and his fellow Jesuits to be the masterminds behind the Gunpowder treason, they were certainly determined to cling to and disseminate that view, and their propaganda campaign did a good job of carrying the general Protestant populace along with them.

Eliza was eventually freed from house arrest. She still had to remain in London, but in quarters of her own choosing. Father Gerard himself boldly entered the capital and rented a house towards the end of November, and Eliza helped him furnish it and remained in constant touch with him by letter.

Just before Christmas, Eliza's cousin, Francis Tresham, became the first of the arrested plotters to die. He wasn't executed, however, and was to be the only plotter to die a 'natural' death. The cause was supposedly a serious urinary tract infection, which seems to have been a long-term condition. In keeping with everything surrounding the Gunpowder Plot, however, there were rumours that all was not as it seemed. There were rumours that Tresham had either been poisoned or even spirited into exile. This latter scenario would have been a difficult piece of subterfuge to pull off, however, since his (or someone's) head was removed and sent to Northamptonshire, where it was affixed to a pole alongside those of Catesby and Percy. This was Tresham's home county, so it would have been a foolishly risky strategy to put someone else's head on public display there. The headless body was 'tumbled into a hole, without so much ceremony as the formality of a grave', in the words of a government agent.

Chapter 13

Where is Mrs Ann?

Anne Vaux and the Arrest of Father Garnet

The Vaux sisters, Father Garnet and Little John had moved from Coughton Court and made the 16-mile journey eastwards to Hindlip Hall, across the Warwickshire border into Worcestershire. Little John would have known this place inside out, since it was a big house and he had already built several priest holes there in the past. But the little group of allies were destined not to find peace anywhere during this period, and within weeks the Privy Council in London had issued orders for a large-scale raid at Hindlip, similar to that which had taken place at Harrowden.

The man chosen to lead the operation was Sir Henry Bromley, a justice of the peace who had played a leading role in tracking down those Gunpowder Plotters who had fled to the Midlands.

Bromley and his posse approached Hindlip at dawn on 20 January 1606, but didn't immediately enter. This may have been due to the fact that the actual owner, the staunchly Catholic Thomas Habington (often referred to as 'Abingdon' in contemporary accounts), was not at home but was expected back. It was evening by the time he did arrive, and, despite being shown the warrant for the search, he refused Bromley entry, swearing that he would 'die at his gate' rather than let them in. Habington was no stranger to brushes with the authorities. He and his brother, Edward, had been involved in the Babington Plot. Edward, the more heavily involved, had been executed, while Thomas served a six-year prison sentence. But his defiance against Bromley was sheer bluster and bravado, of course, and it wasn't long before every corner of Hindlip Hall was being intensely probed.

Habington's stalling had given Garnet and other priests then at Hindlip ample time to secrete themselves and remove all traces of their presence.

But the pursuivants, the most experienced of whom were now more knowledgeable as to what sort of thing to look for and where, worked diligently, and during the course of an intensive three-day search actually uncovered numerous hiding places. As at Harrowden, the skill with which they had been thought out and created astonished the searchers. We are lucky enough to have an eyewitness account of the events, which tells us that two of the priest holes were 'so ingenious framed, and with such art, as it cost much labour ere they could be found'. Three more were discovered in or around chimney breasts, 'so strangely formed, having the entrances to them so curiously covered with brick, mortared and made fast to planks of wood, and coloured black like the other parts of the chimney, that very diligent inquisition might well have passed by without throwing the least suspicion upon these unsuspicious places'.[1]

Yet astonishingly, despite the uncovering of no fewer than eleven hiding places, nothing more than books and 'popish trumpery' was found during the three days. Hindlip was a veritable rabbit warren; other priest holes remained undiscovered – and these were the ones sheltering the priests. Once again, Little John's ingenuity had won the battle; but tragically for him this time, not the war.

The priest hole in which Little John and Ralph Ashley (who had accompanied Father Tesimond to England) had been hiding was not exposed by the searchers, but on the fourth day the two dusty and dishevelled men emerged voluntarily in circumstances which have remained a matter of debate to this day.

Their hiding place was in a 'long and fair gallery', and it's said that the two men, hearing the voices and footsteps entering and leaving the room, realized that there was a pattern to the comings and goings of the patrolling guards. They duly timed their emergence to the moment when they believed the sentries were furthest off, and headed for the door. But they either made a mistake with their calculations or the watchers changed their habits, because on their return journey they encountered Little John and Ashley and challenged them.

The pair claimed to be part of the household staff, and rather optimistically told the pursuivants they would be 'content to depart, if it pleased them'. It did not please them.

---

1. Anstruther, *The Vaux of Harrowden*.

Why did they leave the security of their hiding place so relatively soon? The pair themselves cited hunger, but there has long been a theory that Little John, fearing his master, Father Gerard, would either be found or soon succumb to hunger himself, deliberately sacrificed himself in the hope of making the searchers assume they had done their job and bring the raid to a premature end. Garnet and Gerard themselves both speculated that this was the case. It certainly fits with the Little John we know, but not really with the facts, since the escape plan he and Ashley devised shows that they were intent on giving the searchers the slip rather than giving themselves up.

Little John, who perhaps surprisingly gave his real name of Nicholas Owen, was clutching a single apple when he was caught, which they said was the only food they had during the three days. Yet that begs the question of if they really were starving, why had they given themselves up without even eating it?

Sir Henry Bromley believed he had captured two priests: 'Hall' (Father Oldcorne) and 'Greenway', the name Father Tesimond went under. But even if this had been the case, Gerard and Garnet were the big prizes, and Bromley was growing tired and impatient. 'I never did hear so impudent liars as I find here,' he complained in a letter to Cecil. 'All recusants, and all resolved to confess nothing.' Cecil perhaps read that with a smile on his face. He employed people who knew how to deal with 'impudent liars'.

Bromley resolved to stay on longer in the hope of finding more hidden priests. His persistence paid off, albeit indirectly, after the search had been going on for eight days, when Garnet and Oldcorne finally gave themselves up. This was probably the longest and most extensive such raid ever carried out. Philip Caraman, in *Henry Garnet 1555–1606 and the Gunpowder Plot*, suggests that the unusual length and persistence of the search points to a betrayal by someone, presumably a servant – Bromley didn't just hope, but *knew* that Father Garnet was present.

Upon seeing the dusty couple appearing 'like two ghosts' apparently out of nowhere, the first pursuivant they encountered fled in fear, calling for reinforcements. When he returned with his back-up, Garnet calmly 'bade them be quiet' and told them they would come peacefully.

There is some confusion, even conflict, over the conditions in the priest hole and, as with Little John and Ashley, exactly why the two men surrendered themselves. Some food was found in the hole, but a closer examination of the hiding place revealed that this chimney backed on to 'a gentlewoman's chamber', and in that room they found that a hollow reed had been inserted through a small gap, allowing 'cawdles [thickened drinks], broths and warm drinks' to be poured through for the sustenance of the men. This helped explain how they had been able to survive so long in confinement, and it seems very likely that this 'gentlewoman' was Anne Vaux, who was certainly present and whose bond with Garnet was strong.

The official account claimed that Garnet and Oldcorne had no means of disposing of their bodily wastes, and that they had reached a point where they could bear the overpowering stench no longer. However, this is at odds with Garnet's own version in a letter written to Anne Vaux on 4 March, when he said that they had 'meanes to do *servitii piccoli* [urinate]' and, 'having with us a cloase-stool [commode] we could have abidden a quarter of a year'. This last phrase could actually be interpreted in two ways: either they *had* a commode and therefore they could have lasted longer, or *if only* they had the use of a commode they could have lasted longer. Garnet also states that 'neither of us went to the stool all the while' and that the first thing he requested after emerging was to be assisted (he could barely walk) to a 'house of office', i.e. a toilet. If this is true, there could hardly have been an unbearable smell. It would seem very odd for Little John, who know very well what it was like to hide in one of his creations, to make provision for one bodily function but not the other. The most likely scenario is thus that the official account was wrong: there was no stench, because the two men chose not to (or even were unable to physically bring themselves to, in such a confined space) make use of the commode.

In summary, it would appear that the decision by Garnet and Oldcorne to give themselves up was forced upon them by a combination of the swelling and pain in their legs, their inability to defecate (which in itself must have been painful after so many days) and, as Garnet described it, hearing the search getting closer to their hiding place, leading them to believe they were about to be caught anyway.

Sadly, if Little John really did give himself up to save Garnet, his plan may have had the opposite effect. The Jesuit himself believed that far from causing the search to end sooner, Little John's capture made the pursuivants even more curious about other hiding places.

The two priests, Little John and Ashley, along with Habington, Hindlip's owner, were transported to the home of the man in charge of the operation, Sir Henry Bromley. Bromley had no personal animosity towards Garnet or any of the others, and treated them well. After about a week (but with Garnet still far from recovered from his swollen legs), the journey to London began. Anne Vaux, in the company of Dorothy Habington, made her own way to London, but the connection between Anne and Garnet was well known to the authorities, so once there she couldn't risk visiting him in prison for fear of being arrested herself.

The Gunpowder Plotters who had been imprisoned in the Tower could have cleared Garnet of any involvement in the plot. Unfortunately for him, they were now all dead – and their executions may well have been brought forward for that very reason. Shortly after Garnet's arrest at Hindlip, at the end of January 1606, Digby, Grant, Bates, Rookwood, Keyes, Fawkes and the Wintour brothers were executed over a two-day period, and it is now generally believed that the unexpected haste with which the trials and hangings were carried out was as a direct result of Garnet's capture. Cecil, knowing that to a man the plotters would testify to the priest playing no part in their scheme, wanted them out of the way before the Jesuit himself could be tried.

Garnet was surprisingly well treated in the Tower itself, and seems to have been kept in or near the same Cradle Tower that had housed Father Gerard before his escape – though visits to friends in the Salt Tower were no doubt out of the question. As usual, he managed to smuggle out letters, in one of which he spoke of being kept in a 'very fine chamber' and allowed claret with his meals. Father Oldcorne was in the neighbouring room, and Garnet's gaoler even pointed out a hole through which they might secretly communicate. Garnet being housed next to Oldcorne and the two men having a means of speaking to each other was all very convenient – too convenient. Garnet has been accused, with some justification, of naivety in not realizing that this had all been arranged so that private conversations between the two priests could be listened to by strategically posted men.

Garnet's mention of becoming aware that Anne Vaux was in London and that he hoped to get a message to her was one of the things they picked up. Garnet was using the old trick of adding secret notes in orange or lemon juice to seemingly innocuous letters, but Cecil's men were by now wise to the trick too.

They had discovered that messages written using lemon juice could be made visible by wetting the paper; as soon as the paper dried, the secret writing would disappear again and the recipient would be unaware that it had been intercepted. Orange juice messages could only be read by having heat applied to them, after which the interference was impossible to conceal. Nevertheless, Cecil employed master forgers capable of creating authentic-looking copies of letters, complete with hidden orange juice additions, which could be passed on to the intended recipient.

In one such message, Garnet referred to his visits to White Webbs in the company of 'the 2 sisters', i.e. Anne Vaux and Eleanor Brooksby, née Vaux. 'Where is Mrs Ann?' he asked. 'Mrs Ann' did in fact send him a message in invisible ink, which was written on the paper in which some 'biscuit bread' she sent to him was wrapped, but he did not get the opportunity to privately reveal the secret ink and felt obliged to burn it unread. She was, however, successful in getting another letter to him on the back of a piece of paper in which she had wrapped his spectacles. It's a rare opportunity to hear Anne's voice', and so is reproduced here with her own spelling preserved:

> 'on Saturday at supper the aturne sead that when you yeare in excamening you fened your self sike to goe to yeay camber and coming and coming [*sic*] thether you seme to take sume marmelate which even then was sent you and burned a letter which yor kepper seing did tel, and you being excamened sead that it yas a leter that a frend had sent you and fering that ther meight be anething of danger to the partey you burned it and that you had akmoleged that you knew of the powther action but not a practeser in it. The paper sent you with the Box was concerning my self, if this cum safe to you I will wryte and so will more frendes who wolde be glad to haue derection. Who should supply you roume for myselfe. I am forced to seeke new frendes my olde are mos carles of me. I beseihe you for

god sake aduies me what cours to take, so long as I ma here from you I [go] not out of Lunon. My hope is that you will contenu your care of me and commende to sum that will for your sake helpe mee. To leve with out you is not life but deathe now I see my los. I am and euer will be yours and so I humbly beseihe you to acounte me. O that I meight see you.'

Anne wrote in large capital letters, almost certainly because of her extreme short-sightedness. This made writing in orange juice, which even with the best of eyesight was difficult to see on the page as one wrote, particularly difficult for her, and some of her surviving letters are impossible to decipher. In one of his replies to a secret message Anne had sent him, Garnet wrote: 'Your last letter I could not read. Your pen did not cast ink.'

Although Garnet was being treated well for now, those arrested with him, including Father Oldcorne, were enduring regular torture, despite it resulting in little coming to light that was incriminating or which Cecil didn't already know. Little John was on the end of some particularly cruel treatment.

Gerard was also in London and discovered, presumably from some inside informant, that the master priest-hole maker had been hung from the manacles for up to seven hours, sometimes even with weights attached to his feet, on a number of occasions. This would be bad enough, but as we have heard, Little John happened to suffer from an abdominal hernia. (In view of subsequent events, it was probably an abdominal not an inguinal hernia, as it is sometimes described.) Not only would hanging from the manacles have been even more agonizing than for others, but it caused the rupture to open up further. A metal plate was strapped to his middle to keep his guts in while the torture continued, but this may have only made matters worse. His intestines did eventually spill out, leading to his lingering and unimaginably painful death.

The Tower authorities claimed that rather than face further torture, Owen committed suicide by stabbing himself with a knife given to him for eating his meals. This is almost certainly a lie. For one thing, Little John is hardly likely to have been given a sharp knife (and it has been described as having no point to it). Secondly, if he had wanted to commit suicide and did have a knife sharp enough to kill himself with, he would surely have targeted his throat or neck in order to cause a *relatively* quick and *relatively* painless end. Thirdly, Father Gerard, who had undergone very similar torture, pointed out that anyone who had spent so many hours hanging from manacles would have grotesquely swollen hands and wrists and simply would not be capable of handling a knife.

My own view, as espoused in *The Gunpowder Plot Deceit,* is that if the sheer forces of the combined manacles and weight did not cause the final catastrophic and fatal injury to his abdominal wall, then the edge of metal plate that was designed to protect him may have actually pierced his flesh, allowing the bowels to emerge.

The brave and loyal little man who had saved the lives of countless priests and others, and whose masterly handiwork can still be seen today in a few surviving country houses, was no more.

Chapter 14

The Jesuit Has Not Had Fair Play

Anne's Arrest and the Execution of Garnet

Although Anne Vaux had stayed away from the Tower, it may be that she planned to risk a visit, since Garnet advised her to 'come not hither except with good guides, and when Waad [the Lieutenant Governor of the Tower] is abroad, for he is often with me or in the gallery hard by. You may see me, but not talk.' But in another invisible message, he warned that the authorities not only knew about 'Mrs Perkins', but added ominously that 'they name her sister also, and will have her'.

At some point, Garnet, fully aware of the fate that lay ahead of him whatever the truth and whatever his defence, wrote a touching note to Anne releasing her from her vow of obedience to him and advising her to find a replacement, suggesting 'your sister and nephew to look out for themselves till the bruit be passed'.

Anne's reply was, unfortunately, just as hard to decipher as her other letters. Godfrey Anstruther attempted to piece together the muddled lines and overwritten words, which is again presented here with her own spelling, and with Anstruther's guesses in square brackets where there is any uncertainty:

'Good father I have receued you spectakels and thouth it be the greatest cumfort [I have had in the?] world to here from you, yet this is the greatest greife ecap [except ?] your takeing that I euer hade for that it semeth you leaue me [unto my?] selfe, and that is so great a [grief?] as nothing in the [whole?] world can be more, hou ma I euse my wou of pouerty and what is your will absolutely for my going or steing.

'I will cum to be [aquainted?] with you I will be your sister [ever?] if I can, [and if you please?] to geue me leave ... god and you know my unworthenes. I beseich you healpe me with your prayers, thus in most dewtyful maner I commende my selfe to you.'

Reading this is pretty hard work. I append here a tidied-up version with modernized spelling and Anstruther's guesses incorporated, which makes the poignancy of the note even clearer:

'Good father, I have received your spectacles, and though it be the greatest comfort I have had in the world to hear from you, yet this is the greatest grief except your taking that I ever had, for that it seemeth you leave me unto myself, and that is so great a grief as nothing in the whole world can be more. How may I use my vow of poverty, and what is your will absolutely for my going or staying?

'I will come to be acquainted with you. I will be your sister ever if I can, and if you please to give me leave ... God and you know my unworthiness. I beseech you help me with your prayers. Thus in most dutiful manner I commend myself to you.'

To underline Anne's utter devotion to Garnet, she did decide to enter the lion's den, even though fully aware that she would only be able to gaze on him from a distance and no conversation would be possible. Garnet, or someone on his behalf, made an arrangement with his gaoler for Anne to arrive at an appointed time, when she would be conveyed to a place where Garnet could be seen at his window. On the day, though, Anne, her senses on full alert, picked up signs that she was being led into a trap. She aborted the mission before catching a glimpse of Garnet, but unfortunately, in doing so, she was walking into a different sort of snare. As we now know, Anne and Garnet's messages were being intercepted, and the authorities knew all about the planned rendezvous. Their plan had never been to arrest Anne there and then (so, ironically, she *would* have been allowed to see Garnet from afar), but to have her followed when she left, leading them to the house where she was staying and hopefully catch others – preferably Jesuit priests.

The wily Anne soon realized she was being tailed, however, and changed course away from her house and towards Newgate Prison, ostensibly to visit Catholic prisoners. When the men following her realized what was happening, they lost patience and swooped anyway. They 'stayed her', Gerard later reported, 'and with some rough usage carried her back to the Tower ... and there committed her prisoner, which is a very unwonted place for a woman to be committed in'.

Anne was questioned on the same day. She admitted that she ran White Webbs, that she had been at Coughton and also at Hindlip before travelling to London with Dorothy Habington. At first she had stayed at Dorothy's lodgings on Fetter Lane, but had since made short stays in various places. These she refused to name, so they were presumably Catholic family homes.

Anne was also open about the pilgrimage to St Winefride's Well and the fact that Catesby, Thomas Wintour and Tresham visited her home 'divers times'. In answer to further questions, she told of her worries about the number of horses she had noticed when visiting the homes of Wintour and Grant upon the return from the pilgrimage, and that she had told Garnet 'she feared these wild heads had something in hand, and prayed him for God's sake to talk with Mr Catesby and to hinder anything that possibly he might, for if they should attempt any foolish thing it would rebound to his discredit'. Anne told her interrogators that Garnet had indeed spoken to Catesby, who had reassured him, as we heard earlier, that the horses were for his military expedition to the Low Countries. As for Garnet's involvement in the plot, Anne wrote a statement the next day, stating:

> 'I am sore to here that Father Garnet should be ane yease pryve to this most wicked actions as him selfe euer called it. For that hee made to me maney greate prostertations to the contrari diversetimes since.'

She was then pressed further about meetings with Tresham and Catesby in particular, and again stressed that Garnet had more than once done his best to dissuade them from doing anything rash, at one meeting saying: 'Good gentlemen, be quiet. God will do all for the best. We must get it by prayer at God's hands, in whose hands are the hearts of princes.'[1]

* * *

---

1. *Ibid.*

Henry Garnet was subjected to over twenty interrogations sessions during his time in the Tower, but, perhaps surprisingly, seems to have only been taken to the torture chamber once. He even seems to have been able to talk himself out of a second session in the manacles: 'I pleaded I was hardly dealt with, having told all I could ... What if I confessed nothing in my next torture – must I be tortured again?' They argued the point with him, but in the end the torture was 'deferred till another time', and in fact doesn't seem to have taken place.

Garnet's day-long trial took place at the Guildhall on 28 March 1606, and was observed by a concealed James I. The charges had nothing to do with his religion or place in the Jesuit order, but largely related to conspiring with Catesby to bring about a regime change by blowing up the House of Lords and assassinating King James. He was innocent of all of these things – the worst he could be accused of was not revealing what had been told to him under the seal of confession – but of course there was never going to be any other verdict but 'guilty'.

While he waited for the day of his execution, Garnet wrote to Anne advising her on what to do after his death. In case she needed to flee Britain, he gave her the name of a contact in Saint-Omer, France, but he hoped that she would be able to stay and carry on as before under a new priest. He ended the letter, which was written in normal ink, by telling her: 'You may assure yourself your innocency is such that I doubt not but if you die by reason of your imprisonment, you shall die a martyr. Farewell ever most beloved to me in Christ and pray for me.'

Even though the trial was concluded and the verdict settled, Cecil and Waad were conscious that it had been based on 'evidence' (including blatantly doctored witness statements) that would never have stood up in any trial conducted in normal times. King James himself remarked that, 'The Jesuit has not had fair play',[2] and as an interesting aside, Garnet had been one of the Catholics praised by the king for helping expose the Bye Plot against him just over two years earlier. Rather than leaving Garnet to compose himself and prepare for his death, they made one last sly attempt to give the court's decision a veneer of credibility which would suit their propaganda purposes. The priest had learned of the

---

2. Morris, *The Life of Gerard*.

Gunpowder Plot not directly, but from Gerard, who in turn had heard it during a confession taken by Tesimond. They now told Garnet that 'Greenway' (Father Gerard) had been caught, and had admitted that the details of the plot had *not* been given to him under the seal of confession. Garnet believed them, and they were thus able to twist his subsequent statements to make it seem as if he had been lying all along.

In his final letter to Anne Vaux, the weary priest began: 'It pleaseth God to multiply my crosses.' He refers to the 'taking of Mr Greenwell' (Garnet's own variation on Gerard's pseudonym), but although Anne would almost certainly have known this to be untrue, she had no way of letting him know. Indeed, unaware of the machinations then going on behind the scenes, this statement probably puzzled her. Garnet ended his letter: 'Yours in eternity, as I hope, H.G.'

Garnet had reason to believe that the Spanish ambassador in London had tried to intercede on his behalf in an audience with King James. Whether or not this meeting did take place, James did at least direct that at the execution, Garnet should not be cut down until he was dead before the usual butchery commenced.

As well as writing to Anne, the priest drew up his own account of his involvement with the plotters and others. It countered some of the accusations made against him, but it was also designed to protect some of the other peripheral characters who, like him, had been tainted by association with Catesby and his co-conspirators: 'I have thought it my part to set down as briefly as I can the whole state of my cause, thereby to satisfy my friends, and to take away all occasion of scandal.' When he wrote of 'scandal', he would have had several matters on his mind, but probably foremost was the repeated accusation that he and Anne Vaux had been in a relationship that was of a sexual or romantic nature. Even though there was no substance to the stories, it's true to say that for an unmarried woman to have such a close relationship with a man outside of marriage was then, and for centuries afterwards, considered disreputable behaviour at best, scandalous at worst; when that man was a celibate priest, tongues wagged all the more, even among Catholics who might be expected to understand the situation. One man plaintively asked his priest: 'I pray you ask Father Walley [one of the pseudonyms used by

Garnet] ... with what case he can carry a gentlewoman up and down the country with him, and thereby give such a bad example to his subjects.'

The stories continued to haunt Garnet to the end of his days. 'I never had discourteous word of the Commissioners but only once,' he said of his trial. He was referring to a letter he had received from Anne. She had signed it off 'from your loving sister, A.G.', and Cecil had jumped on the use of the initial 'G' (rather than 'V'), saying: 'What, you are married to Mrs. Vaux? She calls herself Garnett.' Anne would have been using his initial to indicate her sisterly feelings, and Cecil would have known this and probably never really believed there was anything improper about their relationship. In fact, Cecil's outburst seems to have pricked his conscience, since the next time he met the priest, Garnet says Cecil 'asked for forgiveness, and said he spoke in jest, and held his arm long on my shoulders'.

On the morning of 3 May, Father Henry Garnet was led from his place of confinement, across a courtyard to the hurdle on which he was to be bound and dragged away in the traditional manner to meet his end. Friendly words were exchanged as he passed through a group of sympathetic onlookers. One of the servants who used to bring Garnet his meals said, 'Farewell, good sir', to which Garnet smiled and replied: 'Farewell, good friend Tom. This day I will save thee a labour to prepare my dinner.' Next, Mrs Waad, wife of the Lieutenant of the Tower, said: 'God be with you and comfort you, good Mr Garnet. I will pray for you.' 'I thank you, good madam,' Garnet replied. 'And for your prayers, you may keep them at this time; and if it pleaseth God to give me the perseverance, I will not forget you in my prayers.'

Then, for a brief moment, Garnet caught a glimpse of Anne Vaux thrusting herself forward from behind a guard. There was no time for any farewells, as she was quickly grabbed and whisked away, but she had at least gained her final sighting of the man who had been at the centre of her life for two decades. It transpired that she had been given permission to watch Garnet leave for the last time from a vantage point inside the Tower, but, either owing to Anne's persuasive powers (and it's not impossible that money changed hands) or a simple misinterpretation of his instructions, the gaoler had allowed her to join the throng in the courtyard.

With Anne looking on, Garnet, wearing a hat and long black cloak, was strapped to the hurdle and drawn away by three horses towards St Paul's Cathedral, in the grounds of which a scaffold had been built. As he was thus dragged along, he closed his eyes and held his hands to his chest in prayer.

A great multitude had assembled at St Paul's (on the site of the current cathedral). People perched on walls and crowded at windows in surrounding buildings, and in the cathedral yard temporary stands had even been erected to give those who could afford it a better view.

As often happened at the executions of Catholics, futile attempts were made to get Garnet to convert, and in his case also extract a last-minute confession, all of which, needless to say, the priest deflected courteously but firmly.

Once he had mounted the scaffold, yet another go was made at persuading him to confess to treason, and despite his emphatic denial of the charges, the Recorder, the officer behind the attempt, cried to the crowd: 'Do you hear, gentlemen? He asketh forgiveness for the Powder Treason!'

'You do me wrong,' countered Garnet. 'For I have no cause to ask forgiveness for that whereof I was never guilty.'

Still, the Recorder wouldn't let it lie, and there followed some bickering as Garnet gamely defended himself. He was allowed a final address to the gathered throng, during which he stated his spiritual case as well as his innocence in temporal matters, but even now the dignity of the moment was shattered by interruptions, with one bystander accusing him of having married Anne Vaux. Garnet responded:

> 'That honourable gentlewoman hath great wrong by such false reports. And for my own part, as I have always been free from such crimes, so I may protest for her upon my conscience that I think her to be a perfect pure virgin ... She is a virtuous good gentlewoman, and therefore, to impute any such thing unto her cannot proceed but of malice.'

Garnet was then allowed to kneel in prayer for a short time, after which he removed his cloak and was led to the ladder. After mounting it, he paused to make the sign of the cross. Even now, attempts were made to get him to admit his guilt or convert, all of which he confidently dismissed.

Garnet prayed out loud for the king and royal family, even the State. Finally, he made the sign of the cross once more, prayed briefly in Latin, then crossed his hands across his chest and told the hangman he was ready. The ladder was whipped away, and if the report provided by Gerard is accurate, Father Henry Garnet dangled from the rope without a struggle and with his hands still across his chest until the moment of death. His demeanour certainly made an impression on the crowd, because when the hangman made to cut Garnet down before he appeared to be quite dead, there was such a clamour against it that he held off. Eventually, someone rushed forward and pulled on the priest's legs to hasten his end.

The final acts of violation were the ritual disembowelment, the throwing of Garnet's intestines into a fire and the removal of his heart, which was held aloft to the customary cry: 'Behold the heart of a traitor!' Even this didn't seem to elicit the usual response. Gerard, one of the few leading English Jesuits of this era to escape with his life, tells us that the crowd's utterances scorned the idea that Garnet was a traitor, 'and generally, the people went away much satisfied of his innocency and sanctity'. A Catholic priest mingling among the mob was one of several people to dart forwards to collect some drops of Garnet's blood, and Garnet's shirt was acquired for 'a person of great account'.

Chapter 15

Never Had a Priest Been Taken Under her Roof

The Last Days of the Sisters of Mercy and their Priests

Regardless of the positive impression made by Garnet's demeanour at his execution, Cecil's propaganda machine milked the Gunpowder Plot for all it was worth and stoked the antipathy towards Catholics in general to levels previously unknown – the effects of which were to persist for centuries. Gerard and Tesimond (the latter of whom had narrowly escaped with his life when someone tried to make a citizen's arrest on him as he was walking down the street) realized that the prevailing conditions in England meant that their continued presence and survival there were no longer tenable. They had no choice but to escape the country. This was brought home to Tesimond forcefully when he spotted a copy of the proclamation bearing his description posted on a London street. Pausing briefly to read it, he became aware of a man who had sidled up beside him and was now gazing back and forth between the poster and his face. Finally, the stranger, in the tradition of those pre-police force days, grasped Tesimond's arm and declared him under arrest in the name of the law. The street was crowded, so Tesimond allowed himself to be meekly led away without creating a scene – but he had a plan. The man was much smaller than himself, and as soon as they turned into a quiet side street, Tesimond tore himself free, pushed his captor over and ran off.

He left London for Suffolk, then fled England as he had arrived: hidden among a boat's cargo. On his inward journey it had been chestnuts, and this time it was slaughtered pigs. It was worth it, though, because he escaped the government's clutches and went on to hold teaching and other posts in a variety of French and Italian cities.

Remaining in England, Gerard was forced to continue moving from place to place like a stalked animal. We have no details of the people who helped him or houses he stayed in during this period, but it's unlikely that he would have risked staying with Anne Vaux. Her stepsister-in-law, Eliza Roper, played her part though, providing him with a thousand florins to make him comfortable during his final weeks in England and upon his arrival on the Continent. Whether by chance or design, Gerard slipped away into exile dressed as a servant of Spain's ambassador to London on the day that Garnet was hanged, 3 May, with Rome being his ultimate destination.

Cecil's tentacles spread a long way, however, and in 1609 while in Louvain, in what is now Belgium, the British ambassador in Brussels found out about Gerard's presence and pressured Archduke Albert to expel both him and two other priests. Gerard hastily departed, then promptly returned under the name of Thompson. Rome remained his base, though he worked with various English colleges and devoted some of his time to writing both an account of the Gunpowder Plot and his own life story.

* * *

It wasn't just priests who decided it was too dangerous to remain. Eliza's sister, one of her daughters and son Edward (now Lord Vaux), along with several close relatives of the plotters themselves, all fled abroad. Some went through the proper channels and were granted official permission to leave, the government's attitude no doubt being 'the more, the merrier'.

Eliza managed to persuade Cecil to release her from being restricted to living in London, and she returned to Harrowden. With her family scattered, she had only her youngest daughter, Catherine, for comfort, though she did also take on a priest to replace Gerard.

Prior to this, Eleanor (but strangely, not Anne) pops up in recusant records in the East Midlands. From Jessie Childs (*God's Traitors*) we learn that in 1588, 'Mrs Helline Brookesbye, widow' and her six servants avoided the clutches of the Sheriff of Leicestershire. (Helen was for a long time a variation on Eleanor. Was she known to Anne and her family as 'Helen'?) She may well have headed for a bolthole in Tamworth, for that is where we seem to find her four years later when 'Mrs Elizabeth Brooksbye alias Edwards ... a most wilful and seditious recusant' came to the attention of the magistrates. Elizabeth was the name of Eleanor's mother and sister, and Jessie Childs adds that her false name of 'Edwards' (which the authorities has clearly seen through) was a tribute to her late husband, Edward. Eleanor avoided having to appear at the county assizes by scurrying back to Leicestershire.

Anne Vaux was still a prisoner in the Tower when her beloved Father Garnet was taken away to meet his fate, as was her servant, James Johnson. There was a report that someone tried to let White Webbs but was turned down because it was suspected that he was acting on behalf of 'Mrs Perkins'. This was probably paranoia, since it would have been an oddly imprudent move on her part to contemplate a return to such a completely compromised and tainted location. Sister Eleanor had been lying low, and there is no record of the place or places she was staying during this traumatic post-plot time.

Johnson the servant was granted his freedom at the beginning of August, but as so often with anything involving the government and Catholics during this period, the motive behind it wasn't as altruistic as it might have seemed. He was to unwittingly act as live bait, being followed upon leaving the Tower and leading the agents to a house occupied by a Lady Grey. That was of particular interest to Cecil, since there had already been reports of suspicious activity connected to this place. But Anne Vaux, whose restrictions were lifted a few weeks later, had no links with this house. She must have got in touch with Father Garnet's acting replacement as Jesuit Superior, because he reported that Anne was 'much discontented that she is not with Mr Ducket' (another of Garnet's false names), but that he had 'put her in good hands again'.

Anne either remained in London or returned a few months later, because she was named in a report which had been doing the rounds about a 'miraculous' relic of Garnet's execution. When Garnet's (fortunately extinct) corpse was being butchered, a bloodstained ear of straw 'did strangely leap' from the basket into which his limbs and head were being tossed and was caught by a Catholic onlooker. He kept it as a memento, and someone to whom he later showed it pointed out that the ear appeared to bear the image of a face – which was inevitably interpreted as being a likeness of Garnet. The report continued that it had been shown to Anne Vaux, who borrowed it for a time. This was in November, the first anniversary of the Gunpowder Plot, the event which had turned all their lives upside down. From another person who was allowed to look at the straw while it was temporarily in Anne's possession, we learn that she was then living in Clerkenwell. News of this wondrous relic rapidly spread far and wide, and it was even shown to Cecil and others in the Privy Council. It had by then been set in crystal to preserve it, and equally predictably it wasn't long before it was claimed to have cured and converted numerous people. It found its way to the Jesuit college at Liège, but went missing sometime during the French Revolution.

* * *

Eliza Vaux returned to Harrowden, which in 1611 was subjected to another raid; this time in search of Father Gerard, thanks to erroneous reports that he had secretly re-entered England. It was preceded by none of the usual courtesies and was a particularly violent raid. An eyewitness later commented: 'The Lord Vaux's house was almost pulled down by the mob.' Needless to say, the priest wasn't found, but two other priests were and Eliza was once again carted off to London, questioned by the Privy Council and then committed to the Fleet Prison. Cecil is said to have seen the prisoners arrive from his window and complained: 'These are not the ones I sought for.'[1] By now, Cecil was not a well man. He made the lengthy journey to Bath to take the waters there, but that nemesis of Catholics, highly astute and devious in equal measure, died in 1612.

Eliza, meanwhile, was tried and made to forfeit all of her lands and properties. Her son, the young Lord Vaux, had acted quickly and arranged for ownership of most of the estates to be transferred to a number of trustees, but Eliza was ordered to be imprisoned 'during the good pleasure of the said Lord King'. Edward himself, just 23, was arrested when he returned to England after hearing of his mother's situation, and was subjected to the same order of forfeiture.

The young Lord Vaux was released from prison and placed under house arrest in October 1613, and towards the end of the following year was allowed to spend a few months at Harrowden. The date when he was finally granted his freedom is not known.

---

1. Anstruther, *The Vaux of Harrowden*.

His mother did not fare so well, Eliza remaining a prisoner, either in Newgate itself or in a house nearby. Despite petitions to have her released, especially during the two hot summers she spent incarcerated – when plague and other disease tended to be rife – she doesn't seem to have gained her freedom until 1615 or 1616. When she was finally allowed out, she did not return to Harrowden. Perhaps the damage caused by the latest raid was considered too great to warrant repairs, but it wouldn't be surprising if the place simply contained too many ghosts. She settled instead at Boughton Manor near Northampton, a house which had been owned by the family since the days of Anne and Eleanor's grandfather, Nicholas, the first Baron Vaux of Harrowden. After this, Eliza begins to fade from view as far as written records go.

She is listed in 1616 as a recusant in Boughton. If the list itself is anything to go by, she was living with her son, William (who must have been in his mid-20s by then), and a footman of the same name. Her eldest son, Edward, the fourth Lord Vaux, is not among the names recorded.

Three years later, Eliza is referred to not in English records but in a document drawn up in Brussels. In a list of benefactors to a newly founded church for Benedictine nuns, we learn that Eliza donated an image of St Benedict. Father Gerard made a donation under an assumed name, as did Lady Digby, widow of the plotter Sir Everard, who had now withdrawn from secular life and joined the community of nuns there.

In 1621, Eliza's name crops up in *New Shreds of the Old Snare*, a blatantly anti-Catholic polemic written by John Gee. He writes of one Mary Boucherm, who was taken into service in the house of someone only referred to as 'Lady A'. Mary was a Protestant, and Lady A generously promised not to 'pervert' her if she joined her household. But before long, according to Gee, the vultures began to circle: a group of Jesuits, including Father Percy, who had lived with Eliza Vaux, and eventually Eliza herself, 'concocted a devilish plan' to convert her during the course of numerous visits. The story even features appearances by Dickensian-style apparitions on the same mission: but our doughty heroine resists them all.

Our penultimate glimpse of Eliza dates to when she was about 60 years of age. Edward, Lord Vaux, had – like a number of young Catholic men – chosen to fight abroad for Catholic forces rather than endure the Protestant tyranny at home. But the government became uneasy about the weapons and other military equipment such men brought back and stored in England, either when their service was over or in between campaigns. Edward came to the attention of the authorities in Northamptonshire for that reason in 1625. A deputation was sent to Boughton to look for arms, and during the search a justice of the peace, Mr Knightly, was subjected to 'several oaths and uncivil misdemeanours' by Lord Vaux. Knightly reported the matter to the nobleman's mother, Eliza, and although we don't know what her response was, it clearly did nothing to placate Edward, who subsequently struck Knightly in the face several times and hit one of his assistants on the head with a cudgel, drawing blood. The visitors made a strategic withdrawal and referred the matter to London, resulting in the issuing of a warrant for Edward's arrest. His violent behaviour led to a period of incarceration in the Fleet Prison.

This unseemly story is hardly a fitting way for Eliza Vaux to bow out, so fortunately we have something a little more uplifting to conclude her story. In the same year as the above altercation, her friend Mary, Lady Fermor (who had been peripherally involved in the 'turning Tottenham French' debacle which had got Eliza arrested), left Eliza two silver boxes. They were engraved with elephants' heads and were intended for keeping 'metridate' (probably 'mithridate', a supposed antidote to poison) and treacle.

This will was proved in 1627, and is the last known mention of Eliza's name in any document. Like others featured in this story, as an excommunicated 'outsider', she could not be buried in the local churchyard, nor could her name and date of death be entered into the parish records. We must thus allow her to fade away, but not before noting that she left her mark in other ways.

Her son, Edward, dogged by recusancy fines in the manner of so many of his kind, had two-thirds of his estates sequestered and then found himself in the Upper Bench Prison having run up debts of £10,000. Upon the Restoration of the monarchy, Edward successfully petitioned King Charles II in 1660 to have his sequestrations suspended until the merits of his case could be investigated, but he died the following year, aged 73.

* * *

The year 1665 is the one we mostly associate with plague in London, but while that was undoubtedly the worst of its kind (the Black Death aside), serious outbreaks of plague weren't unknown at other times, and there was a series of them towards the end of the first decade of the seventeenth century. One of these was in 1607. Hundreds died, and one place badly hit was the White Lion Prison in Southwark, where most of the inmates and staff succumbed. One of the few prisoners to remain healthy was a man called William Wright, and when he had done his bit nursing the sick and burying the dead, he took advantage of the breakdown of discipline and organization to abscond. From London, Wright headed to Leicestershire. This was perhaps the result of advice from contacts, because it was there that he joined Anne and Eleanor Vaux, for William Wright was a Jesuit priest and he became Father Garnet's permanent successor.

Father Wright was 45, the same age as Anne, when he entered the lives of the Vaux sisters. He was born in York but had spent most of the last twenty years teaching philosophy abroad. His English mission began not long after the Gunpowder Plot, and got off to an inauspicious start. His first base was Hengrave Hall, Suffolk, but he was captured within a few months, hence his presence in the White Lion Prison.

At around the time he came to Leicestershire, Eleanor's son, William, died and she inherited from him the house originally owned by her late husband. This was in Shoby, and it is where the priest and the two sisters set up home. The anti-Catholic frenzy that had followed the Gunpowder Plot had by now died down. All of the plotters were dead, as was their supposed spiritual leader and mastermind, Henry Garnet. The persecution of recusants continued, but as far as we know, there were no further dawn raids of the kind the Vaux sisters and others were regularly subjected to. The story of Anne and Eleanor and their part in the Catholic Resistance is drawing to a close.

Their names don't appear in the records for another five years following the arrival of Father Wright, and this time it was they who were the hunters rather than the hunted.

We heard how, in 1594, Anne pursued Sir Thomas Tresham for the £500 her father had earmarked for her. Both men were now dead: Lord Vaux the year following Anne's chancery case, and Tresham (who was a major landowner but also massively in debt) in 1605, the same year as his son, the Gunpowder Plotter Francis, but the money had never been paid.

In 1612, Anne and Eleanor sued Thomas Tresham's widow, Lady Meriel Tresham. Lady Tresham did not dispute that the money owing was outstanding, but he had been wiped out financially and she pleaded that her money and the goods she owned now had no connection with her late husband. The court found in favour of the Vaux sisters.

This move seems somewhat churlish on their part. Even if she was legally responsible, morally – as far as we know – she played no part in withholding the money owed, and she must have been as badly hit by her husband's fines and penalties as was he. It's impossible to know to what extent the legal action was motivated by lingering enmity between the two families, financial hardship on the part of the Vaux sisters or a simple determination to see that justice was done.

It was long thought that there was a gap of around ten years before Anne and Eleanor appeared in written records again, but in 2017, Kathryn Summerwill, a researcher at the University of Nottingham, revealed a couple of tantalizing possible mentions from the archives in that county. In 1612, a Mistress Smith of Broadholme, a small village close to Lincoln but then within the county of Nottinghamshire, incurred the wrath of the churchwardens, who labelled her 'an obstinate recusant'. The following year, when she appears again, they seem to have uncovered her real name: Mistress Vawse, a 'papist'.

In 1612, Anne Vaux was busy suing Lady Tresham, making it somewhat less likely that the Nottinghamshire recusant is our Sister of Mercy. On the other hand, it is probable that Anne would have left this action in the hands of a legal representative, so may not even have needed to be present when the case was heard. Then, in 1614, the same person pops up yet again:

> 'There is a recusant, commonly called Mrs Smith, but as we do of late understand, her name is Mrs Anne Vaus; she has been excommunicate almost ever since her coming here; her family also are all recusants; there are usually three menservants and four or five women servants, besides "comers and goers" of we know not how many. One of the menservants is about 40 years of age and

he is called John, but we do not know his other name; the other menservants are called William, one of them is above 60 years of age and the other about 40; we do not know the women's names, but one of them is about 60 and the others about 24 or 26.'
(University of Nottingham Manuscripts & Special Collections AN/PB 295/5/35.) https://blogs.nottingham.ac.uk/manuscripts/2017/11/01/anne-vaux-recusant/Kathryn Summerwill)

Anne Vaux was about 52 at this time, and it's interesting to note that one of the 'servants', William, is adjudged to be the same age as 'Anne Vaus' – as indeed was Father William Wright. This very much does all have a Vaux ring to it, especially a lament by churchwardens who arrived to get the names of all those living with her, only to find 'they would not let us in … We could not find any of their names.'

If this is our Anne, the reason for her being in such a remote part of Nottinghamshire is hard to fathom. The most obvious conclusion would be that she had been hounded out of Shoby, in a neighbouring county, in the way that she had been forced to leave so many other places, but we know that she had not deserted it completely because the very last traces of her take us back to that place.

Anne appears in the recusancy records in 1623, now in Shoby, and again in 1625 with Eleanor, when their address was listed as Leicester Castle. They both owed a great deal of money in fines, but they appear to have neither paid nor been imprisoned for non-payment.

At around this time, we do know from A.C.F. Beales (*Education Under Penalty*, 1963, p.209) that Eleanor adopted her grandson, Edward Thimbleby (she was by now living in Derbyshire – see below), and put him under Wright's tutelage. He was there for four years, but Eleanor was probably no longer alive by the time his schooling came to an end.

According to her grandson, Eleanor died not long after the imposition of the fine mentioned above. She would have been about 65. Nature had finally achieved what the authorities had failed to do, and broken the earthly connection between what Anstruther describes as 'the two inseparable sisters'.

* * *

Anne's final appearance in the Leicestershire records is in the following year, 1626, but by then she may have already moved on since we know that by the end of 1625, she had already secured a new base of operations in Derbyshire, demonstrated by the fact that she is named in a letter by a government minister located in that county. She and Father Wright moved from Shoby to Stanley Grange, a few miles north-east of Derby, which is said to have been a monastic house until being sold off during the Reformation (though Anstruther disputes the veracity of this). Whatever its history, it was here that Anne and her priest set up a clandestine Jesuit school, with Anne passing herself off as a tenant farmer. Researcher Simon Hollingworth was told by a present-day owner that there was a chapel and classroom in a cellar or underground room beneath the barn, and even that there were escape tunnels leading off it.[2]

Eleanor was probably still alive then, since the minister, Sir Francis Coke, wrote:

> 'At Stanley Grange, a house standing alone in Appletree Hundred, the doors were at first shut against us, but after a little while opened, where we found only two women in the house, who gave us to understand that the Grange belonged to one Mrs Vaux, a farmer thereof to Mrs Powdrell of West Hallam ... both the one and the other being notorious recusants. Upon search of the said house we found so many rooms and chambers as I have never seen in so small a content of ground, and amongst others there were two chapels, one opening into the other, and in either of them a table set to the upper end for an altar, and stools and cushions laid as though they had been lately at Mass. Over the altars there were crucifixes set, and other pictures about. There were beds and furniture for them in that little house to lodge forty or fifty persons at the least.'[3]

So, if there was an underground area, it either hadn't been constructed or put to use yet, or the modern owners were mistaken. Anne doesn't appear to have faced any action after these finds, and continued her work with

---

2. http://freepages.rootsweb.com/~alanbloor/genealogy/Grangehistory.htm.
3. Anstruther, *The Vaux of Harrowden*.

Wright uninterrupted for several years. However, Eleanor certainly died soon after the move to Stanley. Eleanor, who would have been around 65 when she died, has been a slightly shadowy figure in our story when compared to sister Anne and others. Her apparent chronic fragility of mind and body meant that she was never able to play as prominent a part as the other Sisters of Mercy, but she was always there by Anne's side and the latter no doubt valued her sister's companionship.

In 1635, by which time Anne was in her early 70s, there was another visitation by the authorities, and, almost as if the original report had been forgotten about, the Archbishop of Canterbury received news of a Catholic school where 'most of the gentlemen's sons' were to be found, numbering ten or eleven. A warrant was issued by the Privy Council and an agent by the name of Lumley was sent to

> 'apprehend any Jesuits, and bring them to be examined, with all such children as he shall find there ... to inform himself whose sons they were ... as also to seize upon all books and papers and massing stuff, and locking them up in a chest cause them also to be sent up.'

The school was in session when Lumley made his appearance, and the Jesuit *Annual Letters* state that Wright and his pupils were 'roughly handled' and despatched to London. There is no mention of Anne being taken away, no doubt her age being taken into account in that regard. Wright ended up in prison, but the boys were returned home. Father Wright died in 1639.

* * *

The 1635 raid was almost certainly the last time Anne Vaux ever had to face up to the omnipresent pursuivants who had dogged her throughout her adult life. The last recording of her name is an indirect one. In February 1637, a Thomas Higgins, '*servus dominae Faux*' ('servant of the lady Faux'), was buried in the churchyard at nearby West Hallam.

The spring of that same year saw the death of Frances (now Sister Frances) Burrows, who more than five decades previously had, as a little girl, bravely defied the pursuivants during a raid on the Vaux property in Ashby. Like both her adoptive mother Eleanor and Eleanor's sister, Anne, she seems to have suffered constant ill health. Father Tesimond reported that she had been 'sickly all her life long, and weak'.

Much of what Tesimond was able to pass on about Frances probably came from the woman herself in later years. She claimed that while still a child, she was alone in the garden at an unnamed Catholic house when there was a knock at the door (so presumably a walled garden). When she opened it, she found herself face-to-face with a man dressed in white robes of a kind she had never seen before, even though she was very used to the company of priests. He tried speaking to her but she couldn't understand him, but by using hand gestures he made her understand he would like something to eat. The stranger ate the modest meal Frances brought him from the kitchen, blessed her and departed.

When she told the men of the house what had happened, they went out in search of the mystery visitor in white, but there was no sign of him and neither had any neighbour seen him. Three years later, when she was in Louvain to get a flavour of what it might be like to join a religious order, she encountered Augustinian friars and said she now recognized the habit of the strange man she had once encountered. The interesting thing about Frances's story is that even if her visitor had been genuine, he would surely never have openly roamed the countryside wearing the distinctive white habit of that or any other Catholic order.

This helped Frances in her decision to commit herself to a convent, which she did with the aid of Father Garnet when she was approximately 19. Admirable although her defiance in the face of an armed, hostile raid on Ashby Manor was, during which she had been personally threatened with death, it may have been a sign of a certain general tendency towards feistiness. Indeed, Tesimond speaks of how she suffered 'much contempt in the community because she had some little defects, which though she laboured hard to subdue, she could not wholly overcome them but that sometimes hasty or rash word come from her'. She would have been about 57 when she died at St Monica's, Louvain.

* * *

For a final word on Anne Vaux, it would be hard to better Godfrey Anstruther's assessment of her legacy:

> 'Never had a priest been taken under her roof, and it was only when they were without a house of their own that Garnet fell into the hands of his enemies. Even then she did not desert him, and no risk was too great for her to run.'

A true Sister of Mercy.

Appendix I

Brief Overview of Catholicism in England After the Vaux Sisters

The reign of James I was a false dawn and led to the Gunpowder Plot, but this was followed by his son, Charles I, marrying the French Catholic Henrietta Maria. This might have seemed like a good sign, but Henrietta Maria's religion made her unpopular and she wasn't allowed a coronation. The marriage was one of the things that led to Charles's eventual overthrow during the Civil War. Nevertheless, even during Anne Vaux's lifetime, a Catholic bishop was appointed to England (the appropriately named William Bishop), and although he made sure to keep a low profile, he was not persecuted or hunted in the way that Garnet and his like were.

When the monarchy was restored with the return of Charles II, also married to a Catholic, there was more cause for optimism. Charles's brother, James, Duke of York, converted to Catholicism and Charles himself did so on his deathbed. But anti-Catholic sentiment was still widespread and strong, and it proved to be another false dawn. Charles's Catholic brother, now James II, was forced from the throne as a result of the Glorious Revolution in 1688, replaced by the staunchly Protestant William of Orange.

Nevertheless, even by the time of William, things had still moved on a great deal since the days of paranoia, torture and execution. Many restrictions were placed on Catholics, especially the gentry and upper classes, who were barred from office, for example. Fines could still theoretically be imposed for refusing the oaths of allegiance and supremacy, but they were not vigorously pursued in the way they had been under Elizabeth I and James I.

Progress was real but slow, and along the way there always seemed to be a new scare which was falsely laid at the door of Catholics, setting back their cause for more freedoms. These included the wholly phoney Popish Plot to supposedly assassinate Charles II, along with the Great Fire of London, the cause of which was attributed to various groups or individuals, including Catholics.

There was, however, a gradual and growing softening of attitudes, and acceptance that Catholics were here to stay and part of the fabric of English life, however irritating it might be to some. Two Relief Acts in the second half of the eighteenth century removed many of the barriers which had prevented Catholics from playing a full part in society, including allowing them to openly practise their religion. The second Relief Act, in 1791 – over 150 years after the death of Anne Vaux – finally abolished the offence of recusancy.

One of the final major changes came with the Catholic Emancipation Act of 1829, which allowed Catholics to sit in Parliament. This Act was so hotly contested that Wellington, then prime minister and a supporter of the measure, became embodied in a running argument with the Earl Of Winchilsea which grew so acrimonious that it led to a sensational duel. Thankfully, both men saw sense and deliberately aimed wide.

To this day, though, no Catholic may become the king or queen of Britain and Northern Ireland.

Appendix II

The Featured Priests and Associates

Edmund Campion

Campion was born in London in January 1540, the son of a bookseller. By all accounts he was recognized as an outstanding scholar, thinker and speaker, one whose talents caught the eye of Elizabeth I when she heard him give a talk in Oxford during her first royal visit to the university in 1566. He had ordained as an Anglican deacon only a year or two previously, but found himself increasingly drawn towards Catholicism. In 1570, he was taken on by Lord Vaux to teach his son, Henry, and possibly other of the Vaux children. But when he returned to Oxford, his refusal to preach what Anstruther describes as 'no popery' sermons led him to abandon a 'brilliant career' just four years after Elizabeth had been so impressed by him.

Campion left England and for a few years led something of an itinerant, though spiritually profitable, life. He went first to Ireland, and among his other temporary homes were the Douai seminary in the Low Countries; Rome, to which he made a pilgrimage on foot and joined the Jesuits; and Prague, by which time he was ordained in the Jesuit order (which had been in existence for only six years) and was a professor of rhetoric and philosophy. He returned to England in 1580 as part of the first wave of Jesuits sent to supply the spiritual wants/needs of Catholics in the country of his birth.

We have seen how he arrived that summer on the same boat as Robert Persons disguised as a jewel merchant, managed to bluff his way out of arrest when the authorities believed him to be another man they were looking for, and was shepherded away by Catholic friends including Henry Vaux, Lord Vaux's son (who may have been the 'good angel' he wrote of).

Campion's mission took him all over the country, but we have seen how his inability to turn down requests to preach led to a risky and ultimately fateful visit to Berkshire and betrayal by a spy among his congregation.

Campion was one of the 'Forty Martyrs' canonized in 1970, a list which also featured Margaret Clitherow, Henry Garnet, Anne Line, Nicholas Owen ('Little John'), Robert Southwell and Margaret Ward.

Roger Filcock

Born in Sandwich, Kent, in 1570, Filcock studied in Rheims and Valladolid, but when he tried to join the Jesuits was advised to spend some time gaining experience in England and then reapply. He sailed to England (landing on the coast of his home county) in company with Oswald Tesimond in 1598, when he was 28.

Under the pseudonym of Arthur Naylor, he found his way to Father Garnet, who accepted him into the Society of Jesuits in 1600. He was due to return to Valladolid to commence his period as a novice, but before he could depart he was betrayed by a former fellow student at that place. Filcock was arrested and sent to Newgate, and after a trial which, typical of the time, was almost devoid of evidence against him, he was found guilty of high treason. On 27 February 1601, Filcock was dragged to Tyburn on a hurdle, arriving shortly after the execution of Anne Line, whom he had known and whose confession he had taken. Her lifeless body was still hanging by its neck when he was led to the gallows, and Filcock kissed the hem of her skirt before he himself was hanged, drawn and quartered.

Henry Garnet

For most of the time when the events in this story took place, Garnet was the senior Jesuit priest, the Jesuit Superior, in England. He was known for his calmness and assuredness in the face of adversity and danger – of which there was plenty. But every man has his limits of endurance, and there are signs that he eventually fell into what we would now call a depression as priest after priest was caught, tortured and executed. Indeed, his own fall was never more than one minor lapse in vigilance, one unforeseen betrayal away. Even this, though, did not deter him from continuing his work.

Henry Garnet was born in Derbyshire near its border with Nottingham, and went to school in that town before continuing his education at Catholic-oriented Winchester School. He was an outstanding scholar but turned down the chance to go to Oxford, with its anti-Catholic disposition, preferring instead to work as an apprentice for a leading London legal publisher.

After a few years of this, at the age of around 20, Garnet could no longer ignore a spiritual urge which must have been developing for some time, travelling to Rome to join the Society of Jesus and commencing studies to become a priest at a time when there were as yet no Jesuit priests in England. During his ten years in Rome, a Jesuit presence was established in England, but the priests had been continually hounded by the authorities until only one, Father Weston, remained at large, and it was decided that their numbers needed to be bolstered.

He was initially based in London, but travelled widely before settling with Eleanor Vaux at Shoby in Leicestershire. It was there that he experienced his first pursuivant raid – the one foiled by the brave young Frances Burroughs.

Garnet's arrival in England coincided with the turmoil following the Babington Plot, and within a couple of years the Spanish Armada added to the woes of English Catholics. It was a time of harrying and persecution, arrests and executions. Garnet, though desperately wanted by the government, managed to remain in the shadows during all this time. But the next major crisis put him personally in the spotlight as never before: the Gunpowder Plot.

For all the trickery and machinations of the government, there were at least circumstantial reasons for linking Garnet to the plot because of his association with several of the main players, Catesby in particular. Garnet was as good as tricked into giving his tacit blessing for actions such as those intended by the conspirators when he replied to a hypothetical case disingenuously posited by Catesby.

Garnet was further implicated when Catesby divulged the full details of what was planned during confession with Father Greenway, and then gave him permission to pass the information on to his superior.

Garnet was one of those accompanying the Vaux sisters to St Winefride's Well a couple of months before Guy Fawkes was captured, a peregrination which entailed meetings with several plotters during stopovers. When news of the arrest of Fawkes and others reached him at Coughton Court, where he was staying with Anne and Eleanor Vaux, they all left as quickly as possible and went to earth. Garnet managed to remain at large for nearly three months before the searchers caught up with him and Father Oldcorne at Hindlip Hall in Warwickshire.

Henry Garnet had worked diligently and effectively among the English Catholic communities and avoided arrest for twenty years – an incredible achievement for any Jesuit in those troubled times, but even more so bearing in mind that his senior position made him a prime target. After months of interrogation and possibly torture, and a trial whose outcome was a foregone conclusion, Father Garnet was hanged, drawn and quartered in the precincts of St Paul's Cathedral on 3 May 1606.

John Gerard

From a Lancashire family but probably born in Etwall, Derbyshire, in 1564, Gerard's father had been one of those rounded up for his involvement in the plot to spring Mary, Queen of Scots, from the captivity imposed upon her by Elizabeth I. His biographer, John Morris, believed he was likely born at Bryn, Lancashire, where his family had properties, but most modern accounts give his birthplace as Etwall, another place with family connections.

He attended Oxford at the age of 15, studying under a Catholic tutor, but because he refused to attend Protestant services the young Gerard was obliged to return home after less than a year. Fortunately, his education continued as his tutor had accompanied him home. He then spent three years at Douai in Flanders, where he was befriended by a young Jesuit and began to develop an interest in that sect. He moved on to the Clermont Jesuit college in Paris in order to study Jesuit philosophy in more depth, and then in Rouen he sought out Father Persons and told him of his desire to commit himself to the Society of Jesus.

First, though, he wanted to return to England to sort out more worldly affairs. In 1583, Gerard crossed the Channel, and although he was not yet a priest he had not obtained the necessary travel documents and was arrested by port officials. He was eventually committed to the Marshalsea Prison, but friends arranged for his release on bond. He returned to Rome and was ordained in the year of the Armada, 1588, and entered the Jesuit order. He had not been in the best of health, and in the same year, believing that the English climate would suit him better than the heat of Rome, he gained permission to make the hazardous trip.

Gerard was accompanied in the boat by Father Oldcorne, but after landing at night the pair embarked on the long, hazardous and exhausting journey towards London separately before finding their way to rendezvous with Father Garnet.

Gerard began his mission in the county where he had landed – Norfolk – in the guise of a 'gentleman of moderate means'. He later accepted an invitation to spend time in Suffolk, and after two years was summoned back to London by Garnet, but though based there, Gerard made frequent visits to northern counties.

John Gerard was perhaps the most fortunate of all the Jesuits operating in England at this time. As we have seen, during a gathering of Jesuits priests at Baddesley Clinton, he experienced his first pursuivant raid but was saved – along with Garnet, Southwell, Oldcorne and others – by Little John's subterranean priest hole. A treacherous servant brought about a raid at Braddocks, but again Little John saved the day with his false fireplace. Pursuivants swooped on his house in London, but he happened to be visiting Garnet when it happened. He was finally captured in the same year as this last close shave, but despite being tortured was able to escape the dreaded Tower of London in almost Hollywood fashion.

Gerard accepted an offer to join Eliza Vaux, widow of George, at Harrowden and was able to help lift her out of the depression she had fallen into since the death of her husband. A planned move to Irthlingborough was scuppered when Gerard was once again put into danger by a servant (albeit this time an inveterate gossip rather than a traitor), and he once again avoided capture at the hands of pursuivants by a whisker (thanks in no small part to the courage and quick-thinking of those around him). He remained at Harrowden with Eliza and a period of relative peace ensued, allowing Gerard to continue his work until the disastrous smashing of the Gunpowder Plot put all leading Catholics, and especially priests, in the spotlight as never before. Gerard's association with several leading conspirators meant that his name was high up on the list of the most sought-after of all.

Gerard endured a nine-day search of Harrowden before the raiders finally admitted defeat. Knowing it would only be a matter of time before they were back, he made for London and a place 'known to no one'. Although he felt he could have stayed there indefinitely and continued his mission, he decided it was time to get out of England, where, he explained, 'I might renew my spirit and recover strength for future labours'. However, Gerard was never to return to his native shores.

When the opportunity to leave the country presented itself, Gerard took it. The arrest and torture of Father Garnet prompted the Spanish ambassador to persuade Gerard to join his party when it made a trip back to the Continent, even providing him with the livery of his own servants to wear so that he would blend in. They sailed on 3 May 1606 – the day of Garnet's execution.

'All went well,' Gerard wrote later, 'and I do not doubt that I owed it to Father Garnet's prayers.'

Still a relatively young man, he continued his work in Europe for over thirty more years, dying in Rome in 1637.

John Mush

The priest who would give us such a precious insight into the life and death of Margaret Clitherow was born in 1551 or 1552 in the same county as her, Yorkshire, and possibly even in the same city, or at least within a few miles of that place.

There is a story, unsubstantiated by any reliable primary source, that as a youth or young man he was allied to the household of the Vavasours. Be that as it may, his spiritual blossoming led him to travel to Douai in March 1576, and in October of the same year he was sent to Rome as one of first to enrol at the newly founded English College there. Following his ordination, he was dispatched back to England in 1582 or 1583, where he became chaplain to Margaret Clitherow. Margaret Munro, in her biography of Clitherow, speculates that Mush may have known Margaret from before he became a priest.

Within three or four years of his arrival, Father Mush was one of two priests whom Margaret was arrested for sheltering. As we know, she met a terrible end, and Mush himself was caught in the autumn of 1586 at the home of one Richard Langley and condemned to death. In the event, Langley was executed but Mush managed to escape before his sentence could be carried out.

He managed to resume his work in York, as well as writing his *True Report of Life and Death of Mistress Margaret Clitheroe* (sic). His mission often took him south; in 1587, a spy reported back to his masters that he had been spotted in Mitcham, Surrey, and the following year he was sighted in London.

Mush is the only priest in this list who was not a Jesuit. After a trip to Rome in 1593, Father Garnet was upset to hear that Mush had complained to the Pope of a certain lack of hospitality towards him by the Jesuits in London. Mush's attitude appears to have softened soon afterwards, and he was one of the priests sent to try to smooth the waters in a dispute between secular folk and Jesuit priests locked up in Wisbech Castle, Ely, Cambridgeshire (although Godfrey Anstruther in his *Seminary Priests* writes that Mush's 'fluent pen was often invoked on behalf of the anti-Jesuit party').

John Mush's later years seem to have been blighted by poor health. His final move was to Wing, near Leighton Buzzard in Buckinghamshire, where at the time of his death in 1612 he is believed to have been chaplain to a Lady Dormer.

Edward Oldcorne

Oldcorne's father was a Protestant, but his mother was a Catholic and one of the York women who spent time in prison for recusancy. He was related to Alice Oldcorne, who was arrested with Dorothy Vavasour when the latter's house was raided, but the specific connection isn't clear. Among Edward's York schoolmates were three boys who would go on to feature in the Gunpowder Plot: the two Wright brothers and Guy Fawkes.

After initially studying to be a doctor, Oldcorne changed tack, training in the priesthood in Rheims and receiving ordination in Rome, being accepted into the Society of Jesus. The need for priests in his home country meant that he was despatched alongside Father Gerard without having undergone the probationary period that was normal for a novitiate.

Once in England, the Jesuit Superior, Father Garnet, sent Oldcorne to the West Midlands, where, in the words of Father Gerard, he spent 'eighteen years of toil and labour in the Lord's vineyard, and watered it, at length, with his blood'. Oldcorne went to Coughton Court before settling at Baddesley Clinton. He also spent time at Hindlip Hall, whose owner, Sir Thomas Habington (or Abington/Abingdon), was a staunch Catholic who had narrowly escaped execution for his alleged involvement in the Babington Plot. Also living there was Habington's sister, Dorothy, and the problem – or, as far as Oldcorne was concerned, the challenge – was that she was an ardent Protestant. While there was no fear that she would betray her own family or their new priest, Oldcorne could simply not rest while there was a soul in such close and constant proximity in need of 'salvation'. To his credit, after experiencing very strong initial resistance as he endeavoured to 'reclaim her from her errors', the day came when Dorothy Habington 'flung herself at his feet, bathed in her tears, and desired to be received into the catholic church'.

Father Gerard revealed in his autobiography that Oldcorne 'treated his own body 'with great harshness'. He regularly fasted, wore hairshirts and 'had many ways of macerating his flesh'. This was almost too much even for Gerard, who hints that Oldcorne went to such extremes that it threatened to hamper his mission. He was often ill, and on one occasion caused a blood vessel to rupture which led to him vomiting blood 'in quantities', though Gerard doesn't record which particular form of self-torture brought this about.

Gerard puts the onset of Oldcorne's 'mouth cancer' down to his general tendency to abuse his body as a way of atoning for his sins. A doctor wanted to remove 'decayed' bone from Oldcorne's jaw, but the priest refused lest it hindered his ability to preach.

He was one of those who joined Anne and Eleanor on the pilgrimage to St Winefride's Well, and had more reason than most to be grateful for deciding to join the party, since after being given waters from the sacred place he was cured of his 'cancer' (Richard Challoner, in *Memoirs of Missionary Priests*, describes it as a 'cancerous ulcer in the mouth'). More accurately, the cure was brought about by his repeatedly licking a stone taken from the holy waters and offered to him before he actually arrived at the well. 'St Winifred was beforehand with him,' says Gerard wryly. Believers would be justified in claiming this as a genuine and incontrovertible miracle, while sceptics might wonder whether the 'cancer' was an abscess or something similar that his own immune system somehow managed to deal with.

Gerard was caught with Garnet in the manhunt which followed the Gunpowder Plot. After being tortured in the Tower, he was sent to Worcester for trial and eventual execution on 6 April 1606.

Nicholas Owen ('Little John')

Owen deserves to be included here as, while not a priest, he was a man whose story is woven into that of the English Jesuit mission, without whose courage and technical ingenuity the movement would probably have collapsed through wholesale arrests before it really got off the ground.

Unlike Robin Hood's ironically nicknamed giant sidekick, the Little John of our story actually was very short in stature. This attribute can only have benefited him in his endless hours toiling in confined spaces during the many years he spent both literally and metaphorically carving out a reputation as the supreme priest-hole builder of the era.

Little John had trained in carpentry, but could clearly turn his hand to any kind of building work. To call his hiding places 'holes' does not do them justice, since he not only put a lot of thought into concealing their whereabouts and entrances, but wherever space allowed he added little touches for the comfort (relatively speaking) and convenience of those who would be confined in them, such as means of supplying food and drink, toilet arrangements etc. We have seen how at Hindlip Hall a hole was drilled, small enough not to attract attention, but large enough to admit a quill through which liquid could be fed.

The layout of a house meant that this was by no means always possible, but temporary safe refuge from pursuivants was by far the paramount goal, and his designs proved themselves time and time again.

Owen was born into a recusant family in Oxford in the mid-1550s, being trained in his craft by his carpenter father before going on to serve an apprenticeship with a joiner in his home town. Edmund Campion arrived in Oxfordshire while he was still serving his apprenticeship, and it's quite possible that Owen was in attendance when the priest secretly preached to locals in the house of a Catholic gentleman. If so, he would have had a taste of things to come and may even have been inspired as to the future course of his life, since in what would come to be a familiar pattern, a spy alerted the authorities, who raided the house. Campion took refuge in a priest hole, but the hiding place succumbed to the persistent and violent efforts of the searchers. Campion was caught and subsequently executed. It is often stated that Little John actually worked for Campion, but biographer Tony Reynolds (*St Nicholas Owen: Priest-Hole Maker*, 2014) convincingly argues that this idea stems back to a case of mistaken identity by an early writer.

Something else which may have had a strong effect on the path Little John subsequently chose was that two of his brothers became Catholic priests, one of whom was arrested and narrowly escaped death. Reynolds speculates that Owen may have become drawn into the Catholic resistance movement as the result of meeting Father Garnet, who was preaching to prisoners in the Marshalsea at the time when his own brother was there. What we can be fairly sure of is that Owen's active involvement began in around 1588, when he became servant to Garnet.

Priest holes were already common before Little John came onto the scene, but tended to be crude and relatively easily detected by determined searchers, as illustrated by Campion's capture. Nicholas Owen was to change the game, weighting it more in favour of the hunted. His time with Garnet coincided with the priest basing himself near London but just outside the city walls, in Finsbury Fields, close to one of the gates into the capital. Finding a secure headquarters was always a delicate balancing act. The city itself was so populous that one might blend in more easily than anywhere else in the country, yet the place was teaming with spies, and although populous, was geographically not particularly extensive. On the other hand, although houses in rural areas like Finsbury and also Enfield (where White Webbs was) were more remote and secluded, newcomers and visitors stood out and were more likely to attract attention. At the house to which Owen followed Garnet, no visitors were allowed during the day nor any fire lit, even in the coldest of weather, and it was a rule to speak in low voices at all times. The priest would spend a lot of his time travelling around the country, and his aim was to give the house the appearance of being unoccupied. Owen performed the usual tasks of a man-servant, but probably built his first ever priest hole in this property, down in the cellar. This was used by a servant to hide Catholic paraphernalia when the house was later raided. Luckily, Garnet was away, but he had to let the Finsbury property go.

Within a few months of taking up his position, Owen travelled with Garnet and Oldcorne to Hindlip Hall in Worcestershire, where Garnet was to take up residence, and there can be little doubt that Owen occupied his time creating safe spaces here, and subsequently at various other large houses in this area and further afield. One of these was Baddesley Clinton, where Owen created several priest holes, including converting the tunnel which had originally been a kind of sewer where the house's waste was discharged into the moat. Owen diverted the sewage outlet to leave one section clear. It was narrow and cramped, but long enough to admit several people. Perhaps the most uncomfortable part for anyone using it as a hiding place was that its floor was perpetually ankle-deep in water from the adjacent moat.

This was the priest hole which proved its worth when Baddesley Clinton was raided during one of the twice-yearly gatherings of priests, while Eleanor Brooskby was able to make use of another place built by Owen in the main body of the house. Her sister, Anne Vaux, was able to pay the searchers off after a lengthy and violent ransacking.

At around this time, Father John Gerard was being sheltered by the Wiseman family at Braddocks (or Broad Oaks) in Essex, and Nicholas Owen was once again sent to do his thing, one of the two priest holes he made surviving to this day. Gerard and others were present when pursuivants descended on the house and made the most thorough search imaginable, but Owen's craftiness defeated them.

Garnet, with Little John by his side, now spent a great deal of his time travelling the country ministering to Catholics and meeting regional priests. But it was on a trip to London, where he had been charged with finding a new house for Gerard now that Braddocks had been compromised, that the pair were betrayed by a servant and captured. Little John was taken to the Counter (or Poultry Compter) Prison, while Gerard was initially put under house arrest with one of his captors.

We saw how Owen was suspended from manacles for hours at a time (it's surely feasible that this first torture session led to his hernia, rather than it having been a pre-existing condition, as assumed by many) but provided his tormentors with no incriminating information. He was finally released when a wealthy Catholic, perhaps alerted by Garnet – who would certainly have got to know what had happened through the grapevine – paid off his gaoler. Owen rejoined Garnet at a time, towards the end of the sixteenth century, when things were looking bad for the Jesuit mission, which had been decimated by a series of arrests and executions.

After Gerard's spectacular flight from the Tower, Owen was among those waiting for him at Garnet's latest house in Spitalfields, and he it was who had horses ready for the priest and his fellow escapee to get further away from the capital. It has been speculated that Nicholas Owen himself was the brain, or one of the brains, behind the practicalities of the escape, though while he was clearly in on the plot and it is certainly the kind of thing we could imagine him concocting, there is no evidence for this.

Owen's next task was to begin work on priest holes at Kirby Hall, where Gerard had joined Eliza Vaux. We have seen that he narrowly escaped when it was subjected to a surprise raid, and when Eliza and Gerard abandoned Kirby for Harrowden, Owen is likely to have begun work there too, still on loan from Father Garnet. After that he joined Garnet and the Vaux sisters when they moved to White Webbs, endeavouring to make it as secure as possible, and went on to do the same thing at Gerard's new house just off the Strand. It was during this period, the early years of the seventeenth century, that the already partially disabled Owen suffered another serious leg injury. He was loading a horse with goods to be transported to Gerard's house when the animal shied and fell on him, fracturing his leg. Worse still, while he was recuperating at an inn, it was realized that the broken bone wasn't setting properly, and he was forced to endure the agony of having it broken again and properly aligned. Biographer Tony Reynolds believes the hernia also happened at around this time.

In the build-up to the Gunpowder Plot, Owen is thought to have created the secret hiding place at Irnham Hall near Grantham, after which he joined the large party on the pilgrimage to St Winefride's Well. He was arrested at Hindlip House during the manhunt which followed the arrest of Guy Fawkes, possibly passing himself off as Father Garnet in order to try to save that priest's own neck (his captors certainly believed him to be a priest). His fate has been described in detail in the main narrative: the horrendous torture he was subjected to over many hours for several days in the Tower, how it led to the catastrophic worsening of his hernia and consequent eruption of his bowels, followed by a slow and agonizing death which the sheepish authorities tried to pass off as suicide. Nicholas Owen would have been approximately 55 when he gave his life for the cause he had done so much to serve.

Robert Persons

Persons was born in Somerset in 1546, and, like Campion, attended Oxford. He arrived in England with Campion, according to *The Jesuits 1534–1921* (Campbell, 1921, p.139), in the guise of a naval officer – although other accounts say a captain in the army – apparently putting on a very convincing display of military swagger which enabled him to breeze past the watchful eyes at the port. Things didn't go quite so smoothly for Campion, as we have seen elsewhere.

He took the same route that Campion later would, being met by supporters and guided to London and taken in by Edward Brooksby, husband of Eleanor Vaux. Besides touring Gloucestershire, Herefordshire, Worcestershire, Warwickshire and Derbyshire, Persons set up an underground Catholic printing press. However, his English mission proved a very short one.

After the capture of first Campion and then Stephen Brinkley, the man who had run his secret printing press, Persons fled England. He continued his work in France, Spain and finally Rome, where he died at the age of 63.

Robert Southwell

Southwell was probably born in 1561, to a Norfolk family. He must have displayed religious inclinations from an early age, as he later wrote that his father 'in merimente' sometimes called him 'Father Robert' (this despite the father, who was attached to the royal court, not himself being a Catholic, although he did eventually convert).

Southwell became an author and poet in addition to his priestly duties. In his mid-20s, he travelled, like many of his kind, to Douai and was admitted to a Jesuit school while boarding at the English College there. He also then followed the well-trodden path to Rome, where he not only joined the Society of Jesus but began to make his mark as a writer on spiritual matters. In May 1586, he set off for England with Henry Garnet. They landed near Folkestone and made their separate ways to London.

After Father Weston's arrest, Southwell was allocated to replace him in London. He endured four hours of hiding behind panelling when Lord Vaux's house in Hackney was subjected to a search in 1586.

Just as others were aided by the Vaux sisters, Southwell came under the patronage of Anne Howard, Countess of Arundel and Surrey, whose husband was locked up in the Tower. He probably based himself in her house in Spitalfields, where he set up a printing press to promulgate his own writings and those of other members of the Catholic Underground.

Worked tirelessly, he didn't just attend to the spiritual needs of existing Catholics but 'laboured with great fruit in the conversion of many souls, and amongst them several persons of distinction', according to Richard Challenor's *Memoirs of Missionary Priests*.

In 1591, he was one of those with Father Garnet who barely escaped capture at Baddesley Clinton, and time ran out for him when he was betrayed the following year by an acquaintance of Richard Topcliffe. After a period of imprisonment and torture, Southwell, still only in his early 30s, was subjected to a protracted execution by hanging at Tyburn in 1595.

Oswald Tesimond

Tesimond, who would go under the alias 'Greenway', was born in the north of England in 1563. He went to school in York, supposedly with Guy Fawkes, though the latter was seven years older. He joined the English College in Rome when he was just 17 and was accepted as a Jesuit four years later.

In 1597, aged 34 and by now a Jesuit priest, he left the English College at Valladolid on the first leg of a journey to England, but in Bilbao met up with two other priests on the same mission, one being

Roger Filcock. He later teamed up with Ralph Ashley (who would later be arrested with Little John at Hindlip Hall), the pair arriving in London in March 1598.

He was another of those who made the pilgrimage to St Winefride's holy well. It was shortly after this that Catesby revealed the details of the Gunpowder Plot to Tesimond during confession, which information he passed on to Father Garnet, also under seal of confession, from which point on the whole of the Jesuit priesthood found itself in even graver danger than it had been hitherto.

After escaping from an attempted citizen's arrest, Tesimond was smuggled out of the country in a cargo boat and settled in Europe. He died in Naples in 1636, at the age of 73.

William Wright

Yet another product of York's covert Catholic community, Wright, whose father was a local apothecary and recusant, was born in 1562, the year before Oswald Tesimond, but he embarked on his Catholic studies much later, when he was edging towards his mid-20s. He became a Jesuit priest in Rome in 1581 and went on to hold theology professorships in Austria for over twenty years, but was one of the brave souls who felt driven to fill the void left in England by the arrests and executions which followed the Gunpowder Plot.

He arrived towards the end of 1606 and became chaplain to the Gage family at Hengrave Hall in Suffolk. However, his arrival fitted into a depressingly familiar pattern: he had been there only a matter of months when he was betrayed by an informant, arrested and thrown into the Tower. After several days of interrogation, when it became clear he had been out of England when the plot had taken place, he was sent to the White Lion Prison. After three months in that place, a plague that had spread through the whole of London ravaged the prison itself; some prisoners were released in an effort to limit the spread of infection, but others, including Wright, escaped during the general chaos.

He joined Anne and Eleanor Vaux at Shoby in Leicestershire, establishing a mission in the area. When Eleanor died, he remained with Anne when she moved to Stanley Grange, near West Hallam, Derbyshire.

William Wright was a chronic asthma sufferer, sometimes experiencing life-threatening attacks, and towards the end of his life he had to endure the agonies of 'the stone' (probably a bladder stone).

One day in January 1639, while in London, he performed his priestly duties in the usual way, after which he turned to a fellow priest and said: 'Remember me at the altar …' Wright then fell into a 'fainting fit' from which he never recovered. He was 79, and had devoted fifty-eight of those years to the Jesuit cause.

Appendix III

Locations Mentioned in the Book

Ashby Magna Manor House

Near Lutterworth, Leicestershire
Eleanor Brooksby inherited this house upon the death of her husband, Edward, in 1581. She and Anne moved here from **Grace Dieu** soon afterwards. While here, she adopted the plucky Frances Burroughs, who was to stand up to the bullying of recusants during a raid. Father Garnet joined them here five years after they moved in. They moved to **Baddesley Clinton** in 1588, probably because of the need for a larger house to host the twice-yearly Jesuit meetings.

The manor house no longer exists.

Ashby Magna is sometimes referred to as 'Great Ashby', but in fact, although 'Great' is the correct translation of the Latin word 'Magna', you won't find Great Ashby on any map. The parish is, and seems to always have been, Ashby Magna.

Ashby St Ledgers

Near Northampton
Father Gerard visited Robert Catesby here before the Gunpowder Plot, which is said to have been conceived and developed in a room over the gate house

At this time, it was owned by Catesby's widowed mother. It has since been enlarged by Sir Edward Lutyens; it still stands, and is in private ownership.

Baddesley Clinton

Near Kenilworth, Warwickshire
Father Henry Garnet is said to have earmarked this moated house as an ideal base for his operations after initially living with Anne and Eleanor

at **Grace Dieu**. It was rented from its owner, Henry Ferrers, in 1588, and Little John was soon set to work creating a number of hiding places, including a 6ft-square chamber, and a secret underground passage that ran around two sides of the house. Three years after they moved in, the house was subjected to a raid but Little John's handiwork defeated the searchers.

It is now owned by the National Trust, and a priest hole can be viewed in the kitchen.

Braddocks

Near Saffron Walden, Essex
The home of William Wiseman, Braddocks was built in about 1560. Eleanor's son, William Brooksby, married William's daughter, also called Eleanor.

Little John's clever priest hole beneath one of the fireplaces is where Father Gerard had a narrow escape, when two pursuivants decided to light a fire to warm themselves up during a break from their labours.

Anne Line was also here during Father Gerard's time, the priest helping her out after the death of her husband. She subsequently moved to a house he procured in London.

The house is sometimes called 'Broadoaks', 'Broad Oaks' and even 'Braddox' in old documents, and to add to the confusion was built by Edward Bradoack.

Braddocks remains in private hands. Parts of the original building still exist, including the priest hole beneath the false hearth where Gerard hid, and the garret which served as a secret chapel. The priest hole was rediscovered in the 1930s when author Granville Squiers, touring the country to write a book about such places (*Secret Hiding Places*, 1933), persuaded the then owners to poke about in the unused fireplace, thus exposing for the first time in centuries the place where Father Gerard had such a close shave.

Boughton Manor House

Near Northampton, Northamptonshire
Very little is known of the long-demolished place where Eliza Vaux spent her last years. In *A History of the County of Northampton*, Vol. 4 (1937), it

is described as 'a gabled building enclosing three sides of a quadrangle', set in a 'park and adjacent grounds ... well wooded and interspersed with temples, triumphal arches, and artificial ruins'. This description originated in about 1820, when the house was almost totally demolished. By the time the county history was published, nothing at all was left of Eliza's final home.

The ancient house – not to be confused with the historic mansion Boughton House in the same county – was demolished about 100 years ago, and the new one has no associations with the Vaux family.

Coughton Court

Near Stratford-upon-Avon, Warwickshire
This had been the home of Sir George Throckmorton, who married Catherine Vaux, the great-granddaughter of Anne and Eleanor. Plotters Robert Catesby and Francis Tresham both had Throckmorton mothers, and both knew the place well.

It was still owned by that family when Anne, Eleanor and Garnet arrived here from **Gayhurst House** in late October 1605, and it was while they were here that they got news from London of the exposure of the Gunpowder Plot, forcing them to take flight.

Today, Coughton Court is owned by the National Trust, and a priest hole can still be seen in the Tower Room. It is, in fact, a double priest hole: if pursuivants found the opening, there remained a concealed second hideout beneath the first, which they would hopefully not think to search for after their initial success. It was almost certainly constructed by Little John, and it is a testament to his work that after the extremes of the Catholic persecutions faded from memory, the main priest hole remained hidden for over 200 years, unknown to successive generations of new occupants, and the second one was not uncovered until the early twentieth century. When it was opened, a small portable altar was found inside.

Erith Manor House

Near Dartford, Kent

This house was on the southern bank of the Thames in Kent, in the vicinity of Erith's modern High Street.

Anne, Eleanor and Garnet rented this place after getting wind that **White Webbs** was coming under scrutiny. But the arrangements were made by Robert Catesby in his own name, and Francis Tresham was one of their visitors at some point. It wasn't long before Erith, too, was being watched.

Because of the Catesby connection, in the immediate flap after the downfall of the Gunpowder Plot, the servants left in charge of the house after its Catholic occupants fled, decided, not unreasonably, to swiftly abandon their posts. The sole person left behind to keep an eye on things was 'but a Littell gerle, who upon the fear of these sudden departures was so frighted therewith as that the neighbours in commiseration of her sent a poor woman of the town to stay there with her'. To the best of our knowledge, both the kindly local woman and the 'Littell gerle' were left unmolested by the authorities.

Gayhurst House

Near Milton Keynes, Buckinghamshire

This place is sometimes referred to as 'Gothurst' in historical accounts, presumably deriving from an original Old English name of Goats Wood (*Gat Hyrst*) (Survey of English Place Names: http://epns.nottingham.ac.uk/browse/id/53282ee4b47fc407e3000360).

Gayhurst House was an Elizabethan house built on the site of a Roman villa, and its name derived from the village of the same name. It was the home of plotter Sir Everard Digby, and it was here, on the return journey from **St Winefride's Well**, that Anne's suspicions were aroused by the number of fine-looking horses Digby had stabled.

Allan Fea, in his *Secret Chambers and Hiding-Places*, described it as 'one of the finest late Tudor homes in the country'. Like **Coughton Court**, it had a double priest hole, one beneath the other. It was accessed via a pivoting floorboard through which one dropped into a secret passage, leading to the hiding place.

The building still exists, but this noble house was ignominiously converted to flats in the 1970s.

Grace Dieu

Near Loughborough, Leicestershire
Originally a priory housing a small number of nuns, it was sold after the Dissolution and came into the hands of John Beaumont, who turned it into a manor house. Anne and Eleanor were the offspring of his daughter, Elizabeth, after her marriage to William Vaux. After their mother died and William remarried, the children were sent to live at Grace Dieu with their maternal grandmother.

It was sold towards the end of the seventeenth century and partially demolished by the new owner, with the remainder left as a ruin, in which state it exists today. It has something of a reputation as a haunted location – perhaps the ghosts of Anne and Eleanor?!

Green Street

East Ham
'Green Street', in the period we are interested in, can refer to the actual street of that name, but also an estate or hamlet which grew up around it.

Edward Brooksby, Eleanor's husband, owned a house here and allowed it to be used as the base for an underground Catholic printing press. This was probably Green Street House, which survived into the twentieth century and, appropriately enough, served as a Catholic school in the Victorian era.

Hackney

East London
The Vaux family owned a house in Hackney, then a pastoral area away from the bustle of London, popular with the gentry. The property in question was Brooke House, a brick-built structure previously in the possession of the Percy family, and used by Henry VIII for a private meeting with his estranged daughter, Mary, at which they were able to patch up their

relationship. It was sketched by Hollar in 1642 and visited by John Evelyn and Samuel Pepys in 1654 and 1666, respectively. Hollar's drawing shows an attractive-looking place with turrets, but although Evelyn and Pepys admired its garden, which grew oranges and 'a great variety of exoticque plants' (Pepys), they were in agreement that the house itself was less impressive in the flesh.

Nevertheless, it did have its own double priest hole, with a second hiding place concealed behind the first. Allan Fea tells that, unusually, the entrance was high up in one wall, leading to a hideout in the roof space.

It stood on what is now Upper Clapton Road, near its junction with Kenninghall Road.

After the Vaux era, Brooke House was for a long time a 'private madhouse' – in fact, from 1759 right up until the Second World War, by which time it was the oldest building in the district. Like much of East London, though, it suffered severe bomb damage during the war, and was eventually demolished in 1955.

The local authorities had the foresight to commission a survey of the ancient place during demolition. This revealed parts of a ceiling that Anne Vaux would have seen, which included the coat of arms of Lord Hunsdon, a previous owner.

Harrowden Hall

Near Wellingborough, Northamptonshire
This was the Vaux ancestral home, but no trace of it remain and little is known of the building. Anne and Eleanor were born here, but when still quite young they were sent away to live with their grandmother in Leicestershire after their father's second marriage. Later, their grandmother, Eliza Roper, took over the place and turned it into a secret Jesuit training school, and Father Gerard spent a lot of time here.

The present Harrowden Hall, although impressive and Grade I listed, is not the original building. The house Anne would have known was pulled down and built over towards the end of the seventeenth century or into the early eighteenth century. It is currently the home of a golf club, but it can be hired for events; one nice touch is that this includes use of the 'Vaux Room'.

Hartley Court

Near Reading, Berkshire

This manor house was owned at the time by 'one Mr Speake'. Anne Vaux was reported as having stayed here for a time very soon after fleeing **Coughton Court** in the wake of the discovery of the Gunpowder Plot. This would almost certainly mean that Eleanor and Father Garnet were with her. The manor house may have been a known Catholic centre, because it was abruptly sold soon after their (probably very brief) visit.

Hartley Court has been much altered, but is still standing and is a Grade II listed building.

Hindlip Hall

Near Worcester, Worcestershire

Often called 'Henlip' during Anne's time, the exact year it was built isn't known. But it must have been before 1575, since Elizabeth I was entertained there in that year.

It was the home of the Habington family, and described by Father Gerard, who lived there on and off throughout the 1590s, as being 'so large and fair a house that it might be seen over a great part of the country'.

It was raided on at least two occasions, one of them resulting in the arrests and eventual deaths of Fathers Garnet and Oldcorne, along with Little John and Ralph Ashley. Allan Fea provides a report compiled by a pursuivant after their capture:

> '[There were] two cunning and very artificial conveyances in the main brick-wall, so ingeniously framed, and with such art, as it cost much labour ere they could be found. Three other secret places, contrived by no less skill and industry, were found in and about the chimneys, in one whereof two of the traitors were close concealed. These chimney-conveyances being so strangely formed, having the entrances into them so curiously covered over with brick, mortared and made fast to planks of wood, and coloured black, like the other parts of the chimney, that very diligent inquisition might well have passed by, without throwing the least suspicion upon such

unsuspicious places. And whereas divers funnels are usually made to chimneys according as they are combined together, and serve for necessary use in several rooms, so here were some that exceeded common expectation, seeming outwardly fit for carrying forth smoke; but being further examined and seen into, their service was to no such purpose but only to lend air and light downward into the concealments, where such as were concealed in them, at any time should be hidden. Eleven secret corners and conveyances were found in the said house, all of them having books ... upon the fourth day, in the morning, from behind the wainscot in the galleries, came forth two men of their own voluntary accord.'

The existing Hindlip Hall is of a later date. The original was severely fire-damaged in the early 1800s and demolished soon afterwards.

Huddington Court

Near Worcester, Worcestershire
This ancient moated house, with its two priest holes, only plays a small part in the story of the Sisters of Mercy, but a more significant one relating to the Gunpowder Plot, in which the Vaux sisters became unwittingly embroiled.

It was the home of plotter Thomas Wintour and made a handy stopping-off point on the journey to and from **St Winefride's Well**. As at some of the other watering holes, Anne noted the number of stabled horses and other troubling signs here.

Huddington is one of the places where planning meetings were held prior to the Gunpowder Plot. A number of the fleeing plotters came here from London after Fawkes's arrest before moving on to Holbeche House, where they made their 'last stand'.

The house was subsequently confiscated by the government, but quietly returned to the family a year or two later. It is still in private hands and has Grade I listed status.

Irthlingborough

Northamptonshire

The modestly sized manor house here was the Vaux family home. Anne and her siblings were born here, and Little John performed his usual engineering feats in the house. When they had flown the nest, Lord Vaux's son from his second marriage, George, took over the property with his new wife, Eliza (Roper). After George's death and the arrival of Father Gerard, Eliza abandoned Irthlingborough for larger premises: **Kirby Hall**.

Kirby Hall

Near Corby, Northamptonshire

A palatial Elizabethan country house leased and sub-leased to various people including, in 1598, one Thomas Mulsho, who was probably acting for Eliza Vaux. She lived here for a time along with Father Gerard, and Father Garnet sent Little John along to undertake his usual work. A former servant, quoted in Anstruther's story of the Vaux family, said of Kirby Hall: 'It was truly a princely place, large and well-built, surrounded by gardens and orchards, and so far removed from other houses that no one could notice our coming in or going out.'

Nevertheless, pursuivants did descend upon the house in 1599, not long after Eliza took up residence. Luckily, Eliza was away at the time, and although Little John was at home, he managed to slip away.

It was badly damaged by fire in the nineteenth century, but was restored and is now owned by English Heritage.

Morecrofts/Moorcroft

Near Uxbridge, Middlesex

This house in Colham Green near Uxbridge was Garnet's final base before his capture and execution. It was owned by Gunpowder Plotter Robert Catesby; some accounts say that he sold it to Garnet, but the priest, who regularly had to move on when the place he was staying at became compromised, usually rented houses and this is more likely the case with Morecrofts. It's also the place where Father Tesimond met

Garnet after his clandestine arrival in the country, and to which Father Gerard fled after his escape from the Tower of London.

There is a house in the same location which, according to some local historians, is a much-altered version of the same building, but Anstruther (*The Vaux of Harrowden*), writing in 1953, says that the original Morecrofts has 'long disappeared'.

Norbrook House

Near Stratford-upon-Avon, Warwickshire
Another property associated with the pilgrimage to **St Winifrede's Well** and the Gunpowder Plot, Norbrook was owned by plotter John Grant and was a known shelter for priests.

Grant laid up arms and ammunition at this house when the plot was being planned, and he and some fellow conspirators hastened here to make use of this cache after Fawkes's apprehension – still vainly hoping to lead an uprising.

The centuries-old Norbrook House that Grant knew didn't last long after his arrest at Holbeche House and subsequent execution, and a different building now stands in its place.

Rushton Hall

Near Kettering, Northamptonshire
This was owned by Lord Vaux's friend, Sir Thomas Tresham, and was inherited by his son, the plotter Francis – the only plotter to die of natural causes (albeit prematurely, and while still under arrest). Yet again, it is a place that Anne and the entourage visited on their Welsh pilgrimage.

Little John was at work here for a time, with at least one priest hole created in a chimney. It was put to use by Father Oldcorne, but later forgotten about and not rediscovered until 1832. Little John is said by some to have excavated an escape tunnel leading away from the house, but there are doubts about the veracity of the story and he was not known as a tunneler.

A very grand but much-altered Rushton Hall is currently in use as a hotel, and is a Grade I listed building.

St Winifrede's Well

Flintshire, Wales

The origins of this holy spot that Anne, Leanor, Father Garnet and others were so keen to visit are shrouded in myth and mystery. Its name comes from the daughter (there are several variations on the spelling of Winifrede) of a local prince who was decapitated but brought back to life, his head restored to its rightful place, by a local saint. It gained a reputation as a place of both pilgrimage and healing, and quickly began to attract many visitors.

By the time Anne and co. visited, a shrine and chapel had been built on the site, along with a bathing pool fed by a spring. They arrived as part of a thirty-strong group, which included Little John and Father Oldcorne. Oldcorne believed he had cancer of the mouth and had set out in the hope of a miraculous cure. He actually was cured – but not quite in the way he expected.

As he related it to Father Gerard, they stopped at the home of 'two maiden sisters, poor indeed in their way of life, but rich in the fear of God'. These sisters possessed a stone taken from the holy spring; Oldcorne placed it in his mouth for a time – no doubt praying as he did so – and half an hour later pronounced himself pain-free, strength restored and cured of the cancer. His subsequent visit to the well became, therefore, an opportunity to give thanks.

Pilgrims have continued to flock to St Winefride's Well, and it has gained Grade I listed status.

Salt Tower and Cradle Tower

Tower of London

Father John Gerard eventually found himself in the Salt Tower after his capture in London. This then almost 400-year-old structure is in the south-eastern corner of the site, and was frequently used to house Jesuit prisoners. Religious graffiti carved into its internal walls from that period, including Jesuit symbols, can still be seen today. Gerard was taken for torture in the Salt Tower's basement dungeon.

Fifty yards away was the Cradle Tower, thought to be where Anne Vaux's spiritual guide, Father Garnet, was kept before his execution. By a combination of persuasion and bribery, Gerard was able to visit a fellow Catholic prisoner. The view from this tower on the outer wall of the Tower gave him the idea for his daring and successful escape.

Shoby Manor House

Near Melton Mowbray, Leicestershire
Sometimes referred to as Shoby Priory, although it was an ecclesiastical house it doesn't appear to have been a priory itself. Eleanor inherited it upon the death of her Brooksby father-in-law in 1615, and she and Anne crop up in recusancy records in 1623. When Eleanor died about 1625, Anne, along with a Father William Wright, moved on to **Stanley Grange** in Derbyshire.

Dating back to the early sixteenth century, it exists in a partly rebuilt form today as Priory Farm and is a Grade II listed building.

Stanley Grange

Near Derby, Derbyshire
This place was where the nomadic Anne Vaux lived after the death of her sister and companion, Eleanor, in 1625. She must have stayed here for quite some time, since it was raided during her occupancy in 1635, and the last reference to Anne in any records in relation to this place is 1637.

The building she knew no longer exists.

Thame Park

Near Oxford, Oxfordshire
This was the home of Sir Richard Wenman and his wife, Agnes. It was Agnes's interception of Eliza Vaux's 'Tottenham turning French' letter to Lady Tasborough which landed Eliza in deep trouble.

White Webbs

Near Enfield, Essex
A large house on Enfield Chase and bordering on the Royal Forest, often used by Anne and Eleanor, and having strong associations with the Gunpowder Plot.

When Anne took it on, she sent servant James Johnson (coincidentally or otherwise, when Guy Fawkes was caught he gave the name 'John Johnson') to prepare it for her use. She arrived in her 'Mrs Perkins' guise, and had with her Eleanor and 'Mr Mese' – Father Garnet. After the discovery of the plot, a witness described White Webbs, in relation to Father Garnet's occupation, as 'a spacious house fit to receive so great a company that should resort to him thither, there being two beds placed in a chamber' (i.e. two beds in each chamber).

Robert Catesby rashly came here when he was on the run after hearing of the Monteagle letter, despite knowing that the authorities were fully aware that it was being used by the Catholic underground movement. Garnet and Anne had already stopped using it for that reason, and although Catesby moved on before being caught, for Catesby to come at all was a decision that Anstruther describes as 'unaccountable lunacy that characterises the actions of most of the conspirators at this time'.

The Whitewebbs (the modern spelling) building of today is neither the original one nor does it stand where the old one did. According to Allan Fea, the original White Webbs was 'full of trapdoors and secret passages', and the still existing King and Tinker pub was one of its outbuildings.

York

Margaret Clitherow and Dorothy Vavasour locations
Thanks to York having preserved its history far better than many cities one might mention, there are several places associated with Margaret Clitherow which can not only be visited today, but which in some cases wouldn't look so very different to 'The Pearl Of York' if she was somehow able to revisit them.

Davygate, where she was born, has changed beyond recognition and the house no longer exists. But her marriage to John Clitherow took Margaret to the famous Shambles, which is one of York's best preserved and most famous thoroughfares. A medieval house, originally believed to have been where Margaret lived, was turned into a shrine and opened to the public. However, it was later realized that the door numbering had changed and that the actual Clitherow residence, the ground floor of which was a butcher's shop, was across the street.

Another surviving building (albeit with alterations) with links to Margaret Clitherow is The Black Swan on Peasholme Green in the city centre. Margaret is said to have arranged for priests to lodge here, although this is an oral tradition with no contemporary written corroboration.

Pilgrims wishing to pay homage to Margaret Clitherow can move on from the shrine in the Shambles to Bar Convent, Micklegate Bar. It was not established until well after her death and has been completely rebuilt anyway, but it does house a Clitherow relic – her mummified hand, inside a glass display case.

Finally, on Ouse Bridge where Margaret was pressed to death there is a plaque marking the spot. The inscription says she was 'martyred for her Christian Faith', but as we have seen, this is not strictly true.

The Vavasours appear to have been living near the 'Common School House' on Ogleforth, a narrow street where, ironically, a Catholic boys' school would be established 200 years after Dorothy died for her loyalty to that faith. Much later, but equally appropriately, a maternity hospital was set up on the street. Today, few if any of the buildings in the narrow thoroughfare date back as far as the Vavasour's time.

By 1576 – perhaps never feeling comfortable on Ogleforth after the emotional *and* physical damage caused by the 1574 raid – Dorothy and Thomas had relocated to a house on the east side of King's Square. There is a report by R.H. Skaife, quoted in Longley, to the effect that this new residence had a frontage of 59ft, and extended for 116ft down St Andrewgate. That would make it a fairly substantial building – a number of shops and other properties now occupy the same footprint. It may have been known as King's Court at the time of the Vavasours' residency, although at some point in or before 1627, forty years after Dorothy's death, the building's name was changed to Duke Gill Hall.

Bibliography

Anstruther, Godfrey, *The Seminary Priests: a Dictionary of the Secular Clergy of England and Wales, 1558–1850* (Vol. 1), (St. Edmund's College, Ware, Ushaw College, Durham, 1969) (Internet Archive)

Anstruther, Godfrey, *Vaux of Harrowden, a Recusant Family* (R.H. Johns, Newport, Wales, 1953) (Internet Archive)

Beales, A.C.F., *Education Under Penalty: English Catholic Education from the Reformation to the Fall of James II, 1547–1689* (Athlone Press, London, 1963) (Internet Archive)

Campbell, Fr Thomas, *The Jesuits 1534–1921*, Vol. 1 (Encyclopedia Press, New York, 1921) (Jesuit Library Online)

Caraman, Philip, *Henry Garnet 1555–1606 and the Gunpowder Plot* (Farrar, Straus, New York, 1964) (Internet Archive)

Caraman, Philip, *The Other Face: Catholic Life Under Elizabeth I* (Shed & Ward, New York, 1960) (Internet Archive)

Chaloner, Bishop V.A.L., *Memoirs of Missionary Priests* (Manchester, 1803) (Internet Archive)

Childs, Jessie, *God's Traitors: Terror & Faith in Elizabethan England* (Vintage, London, 2015)

Claridge, Mary, *Margaret Clitherow (1556? –1586)* (Fordham University Press, New York, 1966) (Internet Archive)

Devlin, Christopher, *The Life of Robert Southwell, Poet and Martyr* (Farrar, Straus and Cudahy, USA, 1956) (Internet Archive)

Dodwell, Martin, *Anne Line: Shakespeare's Tragic Muse* (Book Guild Publishing, London, 2013)

Fitzalan-Howard, Henry Granville (14th Duke of Norfolk, ed.), *The Lives of Philip Howard, Earl of Arundel, and of Anne Dacres, his Wife* (Hurst and Blackett, London, 1857)

Fraser, Antonia, *The Gunpowder Plot: Terror & Faith in 1605* (Random House, London, 1999)

Gardiner, Samuel Rawson, *What Gunpowder Plot Was* (Longman's Green & Co, London, 1897) (Internet Archive)

Gerard, Father John, *The Autobiography of a Hunted Priest* (Pellegrini & Cudahy, New York, 1952) (Internet Archive)

Gerard, Father John, *During the Persecution* (Burns and Oates, London, 1885) (Internet Archive)

Guiney, Louise Imogen, *Blessed Edmund Campion* (R.T. Washbourne Ltd, London, 1914) (Project Gutenberg)

Hamilton, Dom Adam (ed.), *The Chronicle of the English Augustinian Canonesses Regular of the Lateran, at St Monica's in Louvain* (Sands & Co, London, 1906) (Internet Archive)

Hogge, Alice, *God's Secret Agents* (Harpercollins, 2005)

Holland, Nick, *The Real Guy Fawkes* (Pen & Sword, Barnsley, 2017)

Jardine, David, *A Narrative of the Gunpowder Plot* (John Murray, London, 1857) (Internet Archive)

Lake, Peter and Quester, Michael, *The Trials of Margaret Clitherow* (Continuum, London, 2011)

Bibliography

Lathbury, Rev Thomas, *Guy Fawkes; or, the Gunpowder Treason* (John W. Parker, London, 1840) (Google Books)
Law, Thomas Graves (ed.), *The Archpriest Controversy* (Camden Society, London, 1896) (Google Books)
Lessius, Leonardus, *The Treasure of Vowed Chastity in Secular Persons* (Scolar Press, Ilkley, 1974) (Internet Archive)
Longueville, Thomas, *The Life of a Conspirator, Being a Biography of Sir Everard Digby by One of His Descendants* (Kegan Paul, Trench, Trubner & Co, London, 1895) (Project Gutenberg)
Monro, Margaret T., *Blessed Margaret Clitherow* (Longmans, Green & Co, New York, 1947) (Internet Archive)
Morgan, Tony, *Power, Treason and Plot in Tudor England: Margaret Clitherow, an Elizabethan Saint* (Pen & Sword, Barnsley, 2022)
Morris, John (ed.), *The Catholics of York Under Elizabeth* (Burns and Oates, London, 1891) (Internet Archive)
Morris, John (ed.), *The Life of Father John Gerard* (Burns and Oates, London, 1881) (Internet Archive)
Morris, John (ed.), *The Troubles of our Catholic Forefathers Related by Themselves* (First Series) (Burns and Oates, London, 1872) (Internet Archive)
Morris, John (ed.), *The Troubles of our Catholic Forefathers Related by Themselves* (Second Series) (Burns and Oates, London, 1875) (Internet Archive)
Morris, John (ed.), *The Troubles of our Catholic Forefathers Related by Themselves* (Third Series) (Burns and Oates, London, 1877) (Internet Archive)
Prior, Mary (ed.), *Women in English Society 1500–1800* (Methuen, London, 1985) (Internet Archive)
Reynolds, Tony, *St Nicholas Owen, Priest-Hole Maker* (Gracewing, Leominster, 2014)
Squiers, Granville, *Secret Hiding Places – The Origins, Histories And Descriptions Of English Secret Hiding Places Used By Priests, Cavaliers, Jacobites & Smugglers* (Cope Press, 2013) (originally published by S. Paul, London, 1934)
Weinreb, Ben, Hibbert, Christopher, Keay, Julia, and Keay, John, *The London Encyclopaedia* (Third Edition) (Macmillan, London, 2010)
Williamson, Hugh Ross, *The Gunpowder Plot* (Faber & Faber, London, 1951) (Internet Archive)
De Yepes, Diego, *Historia Particular de la Persecucion de Inglaterra* (Madrid, 1599)

PDFs

Hart, A.M., *Francis Clark: A Man of his Time*, Fitzroy History Society, https://fitzroyhistorysociety.org.au/wp-content/uploads/2022/03/francis-clark-amhart-2015-2022-1.pdf
Longley, Katharine M., *The 'Trial' of Margaret Clitherow*, http://www.monlib.org.uk/papers/aj/aj75p335-364-longley-k-clitheroe.pdf

Articles

Wadham, Juliana, *Saint Margaret Clitherow: Her 'Trial' on Trial*, Ampleforth Journal, 1971, Volume 76

Thesis

Hickerson, Megan Lora, *Female Recusancy in Elizabethan England*, Graduate Faculty of Texas Tech University, August 1991, https://ttu-ir.tdl.org/bitstream/handle/2346/59865/31295006962954.pdf?...1

Websites
British History Online – The Cecil Papers (https://www.british-history.ac.uk)
British Jesuit Archives (https://www.jesuit.org.uk/history/archives)
History of York (http://www.historyofyork.org.uk/themes/catholic-resistance)
Oxford Dictionary of National Biography (https://www.oxforddnb.com/)
Tudor Times (https://tudortimes.co.uk/guest-articles/the-woman-who-kept-catholicism-alive)
University of Nottingham Manuscripts & Special Collections AN/PB 295/5/35 (https://blogs.nottingham.ac.uk/manuscripts/2017/11/01/anne-vaux-recusant/ Kathryn Summerwill)

Dear Reader,

We hope you have enjoyed this book, but why not share your views on social media? You can also follow our pages to see more about our other products: facebook.com/penandswordbooks or follow us on X @penswordbooks

You can also view our products at www.pen-and-sword.co.uk (UK and ROW) or www.penandswordbooks.com (North America).

To keep up to date with our latest releases and online catalogues, please sign up to our newsletter at: www.pen-and-sword.co.uk/newsletter

If you would like a printed catalogue with our latest books, then please email: enquiries@pen-and-sword.co.uk or telephone: 01226 734555 (UK and ROW) or email: uspen-and-sword@casematepublishers.com or telephone: (610) 853-9131 (North America).

We respect your privacy and we will only use personal information to send you information about our products.

Thank you!